G000270655

THE PEOPLE'S WAR
Malta: 1940/43

Laurence Mizzi

Translated by
Joseph M. Falzon

Printed and Published

by

Progress Press Co. Ltd.,

Valletta, Malta

1998

© Laurence Mizzi 1998

ISBN 99909-3-055-4

Cover picture:
Inside the shelter; water colour by Alfred Gerada (1895/1968).
Albert Ganado collection.

All rights reserved. No part of this book may be reproduced, stored in a retrieval system,
or transmitted in any form or by any means, electronic, electrostatic,
magnetic tape, mechanical, photo-copying, recording or otherwise,
without permission in writing from the publishers.

CONTENTS

About the Author

Laurence Mizzi is the author of a number of books, among them several on the war in Malta.
These include: *Dhahen tal-Gwerra, Ghall-Holma ta' Hajtu, Meta Faqqghet il-Gwerra, Maltin fil-Gwerra* and *Mixlija b'Kongura u Tradiment.*

FOREWORD

The crucial role which Malta, "the unsinkable aircraft carrier", as inston Churchill described her, played during World War II is well corded. An impressive number of books and other documentary evince has been produced over the years chronicling events during that omentous period in our history.

Many of these works particularly by former members of the British rmed Forces who served here during the war focus on the vital role ayed by the Three Services in the defence of these Islands. The efforts f those valiant men and women however would have been in vain had ιey not had the fullest support and most loyal co-operation of the civil-ιn population.

When Italy declared war on Britain and France in June 1940 the Maltese, almost without exception, put aside their political, ideological nd other differences and formed one common united front with the British. For almost three years men, women and children suffered with eroic doggedness first the savage air bombardments which often left a rail of death and destruction and then the pain of hunger and near starva-ion which almost forced the British to surrender in the summer of 1942.

The *People's War* is a collection of wartime reminiscences which I btained through personal interviews with some of the survivors of the Siege and which appeared in book form under the title *Maltin fil-Gwerra* 1992). Housewives and children, Dockyard workers, lawyers and doc-ors, teachers, priests and religious, servicemen and others - a hundred of hem - have come forward to relate their personal experiences which, more than half a century later, are still remembered vividly. Taken as a whole, theirs is the hitherto unwritten history of the Maltese people whose courage and endurance during the War were universally acknowledged and officially recognised by the award of the George Cross in April 1942.

I would like to register my thanks and appreciation to my lifelong friend, Prof. Joe Falzon, for enthusiastically undertaking the none too easy task of translating the text from the Maltese. My sincere thanks go also to Mr Ronnie Agius, Managing Director of Progress Press Co Ltd whose co-operation and advice have been invaluable.

I am particularly indebted to Chev Dr Albert Ganado for his permis-sion to reproduce three of the water colours from his collection of works by wartime artist Alfred Gerada.

15 April 1998   Laurence Mizzi

"The story of Malta from 1940 to 1944 is one of the great dramas of history ... undying honour is due to the Maltese themselves, men, women and children, who never lost faith in the darkest hours of blitz and starvation."

Lord Tedder
Marshal of the Royal Air Force

I. Children

PAWLU AQUILINA

On the morning of the first day of the war, I was walking in one of the streets of Siġġiewi with Father Anton Vella. Suddenly, I heard the sound of gunfire and saw puffs of white smoke dotting the sky. I turned to Father Anton and asked him what was going on. "Military manoeuvres," he said in a calm voice. As I soon found out, his calm manner was simply an attempt to avoid alarming us children. In fact, of course, what we heard and saw were the opening shots of a war in which we were all, in one way or another, to be involved.

In a few days the village square was crowded with refugees, carrying bundles, who had left their Cottonera homes to find refuge in Siġġiewi. I remember the square packed with green buses (green being then the standard colour for Cospicua buses), horse-drawn carts, vans and trucks of all shapes and sizes all loaded with articles of furniture, pots, pans and basins.

The war years have left me with several memories. The most vivid and dramatic was the witnessing of a mercy killing, a term which I was then too young to be familiar with. When the news went round that an RAF plane had crashed in the Handaq valley, several boys with myself among them, ran towards the site. The plane was blazing away furiously and soldiers were standing around looking helplessly at the wreck, unable to move closer. In the cockpit I could just make out the pilot's head; to me the pilot seemed to be still alive. The soldiers moved us away. Then as I looked back from a distance at the burning wreckage, I saw one of the soldiers raising his rifle, taking careful aim at the cockpit and pulling the trigger.

I remember another scene which was intensely macabre. Two German *JU 88*'s crashed on the rocky plateau at Ta' Zuta and as was our wont we hurried to the place in the hope of getting some useful bits from the wreckage - ball bearings for our scooters were the most sought after - and on reaching the remains we saw a man with a couple of hounds. The hounds were rummaging among the bits and pieces lying around and at one point began to gnaw at some flesh. A bystander could not stand this and asked the man to pull away his dogs. I can still hear the man's curt reply! "Let them eat to their hearts' content!" he said.

The food shortages did not hit us too hard at Siġġiewi and I believe the same can be said for the refugees who spent the war years in the village. When one lived in the countryside, one could usually find something to eat although staple foods like flour, spaghetti and sugar were very scarce. Although there were no smokers in the family, we regularly claimed our ration of cigarettes - the *Flag* brand, I remember - so that we could exchange them for flour and sugar with those who could not do without smoking.

AGNES AZZOPARDI

I was in my second year of primary schooling, aged seven, when the war broke out. The primary school at Luqa, where I lived, was soon requisitioned by the military and converted into barracks for servicemen. The schoolchildren were allocated to houses which had a shelter attached or which had a shelter in the immediate vicinity.

Minutes after entering the classroom one day, an air raid warning sounded. With the teacher and the only two pupils present at the time, I scurried down into the shelter and seconds later bombs began to rain down. One bomb landed right on the house, reducing it to a pile of rubble and blocking the entrance to the shelter in which we were taking cover. We were trapped inside until help arrived in the shape of men who cleared the entrance. In the meantime the teacher and the owner of the house did their best to keep us calm. The air raid had started at around half past one in the afternoon but we did not manage to get back home before sunset. I remember my father's first reaction was to take me in his arms and exclaim, "Dear daughter, if we are destined to be killed, let us all die together; as from to-morrow you will not be going to school until conditions improve." At first I did not get the trend of his words, but sure enough, much as I loved going to school, I was kept at home the following day, which made me very cross.

Among the many memories of the war years, the one which stands out most vividly is the tragedy which struck the village on the 9th of April 1942. I do not recall which day of the week it was, but I remember that all the family were at home on that day.

The site where the bomb fell on 9 April 1942.

The time was about half past one in the afternoon and my mother was busy laying the food on the table (soup, I remember) when the air-raid siren went. My mother proceeded to share out the food and all of us then went down into the shelter clutching our plates. We had barely tasted the food when explosion after explosion made the shelter shudder as if it would cave in. There was no doubt that the bombs could not have landed more than a few metres away. Silence returned abruptly and seconds later we heard a man's voice screaming that "everyone was dead". The voice was that of a man who lived a few doors away and who usually took cover in one of the shelters in the neighbourhood. Sobbing and with great difficulty he explained that a bomb had pierced a shelter and all the occupants had been killed. Men sud-

The 9 April 1942 memorial at Luqa.

(Photo N. Genovese)

4

denly seemed to spring up from nowhere and rushed to the scene of the tragedy to render assistance. In the meantime bombs began to rain down again and those of us who stayed behind in the shelter feared that the people who went to help, my father among them, would be killed too. None of the men seemed to care about the great risks they were taking as they struggled to save possible survivors. In fact, there were a few survivors but thirty-two perished on that unforgettably tragic day.

Two images come to mind when recalling that episode: one that of stretchers piled high with parts of human bodies recovered from the debris, the second that of the distraught father who had just lost eight of his nine children. The eldest of the nine, a soldier, had returned home only a few hours before after a long spell of duty and had gone down to the shelter to get some undisturbed sleep. The father had been brought to our house, or rather the only room that was still standing, in a state of shock; sitting slumped in a chair, he repeatedly counted on his fingers his nine children saying, over and over again, "I haven't got anyone left now". (One of his children, a girl, survived). To me, that day, the 9th of April 1942 epitomises the cruelty and destruction of the war.

Mgr LAWRENZ CACHIA

I was eight years of age when the war broke out, one of ten children; the eldest, a teacher, was twenty and the youngest, a baby born a few months before. My father was a police sergeant posted at Żebbuġ, where we lived. One of my earliest memories of the war is that of Government officials inspecting houses to prepare accommodation for refugees; after that I remember shelters being excavated in the streets, one of these being practically on our doorstep.

By the time the shelter was ready for occupation, the frequency of air attacks had increased sharply and we spent long hours cooped up in that shelter. Many prayers were said during those hours, the most popular being the rosary. One of the people who patronised this particular shelter was one Svagevitch, a refugee who was a tinsmith by trade, and also an artist of sorts. One day, this Svagevitch brought along his colours, his brush and some plaster and produced a wonderful effigy of Christ which was hung in the shelter.

Until a sizeable shelter became available in the school, pupils were taught in several premises in different parts of the village. I was taught in the old sacristy in one of two rooms which had been improvised into classrooms. When the school shelter was finished we were taken back to the normal school.

When air-attacks became less and less frequent we began to go for long walks in the country every Sunday. In ways which I could not understand, some of the children got hold of cordite and made small explosive devices which they would set off during the walks. The scolding which they would then get never seemed to have the desired effect at all.

Few bombs landed on the village but those that did caused considerable damage. One parachute mine landed near the chapel of Our Lady of Light but luckily failed to explode; later the bomb disposal squad exploded the device after evacuating the neighbourhood.

My family got through the war without any major mishap although like most of the population we suffered the pangs of hunger. The two members of the family who ran serious risks were my father and eldest brother. As a sergeant major in the Police Force, my father's duties included spells at the Price Control Office which was based at the Customs House in Valletta, and was therefore dangerously close to routine bombing targets. He was on duty during the *Illustrious* blitz. My brother had also joined the Police Force and occasionally had to do guard duties at fuel storage sites.

My mother, a very religious woman, made a vow that if all members of the family got through the war unscathed, she would not touch a fruit for the remaining years of her life. She stuck to that vow.

DORIS CAMILLERI

At the first sign of an air-raid warning my father would take up the two youngest children, wrap them up in a heavy coat and rush down to the nearby public shelter in which we had a cubicle which he had dug out himself. My mother, then expecting her seventh child, was always complaining that the three steps leading down into our cubicle were too steep for a woman in her condition. When air-raids became heavier and more and more frequent, we began to spend the night in the shelter instead of in the relative comfort of our home; beds of course were out of the question in the confined space of the cubicle and we slept on bunks fixed, like so many shelves, to the wall. Charlie, the eldest, was twelve; Guzi, at ten, was the apple of my mother's eye; then there was myself, aged nine, followed by the three youngest. We lived in a house in Gafa` Street, Mosta.

Of the entire war, the day that stands out most clearly in my memory is the 21st of March 1942. On that day, the siren sounded more strident and urgent than usual and as people trooped towards the shelter I heard some say, "We're in for something out of the ordinary to-day". Air-raid warnings followed one another in quick succession and people did not bother to get out of the shelter whenever the all-clear sounded. It was Saturday and I was wearing my cap, ready to go to church for confession. My mother was brewing some tea in our cubicle and I heard her ask one of the neighbours, a certain Vitor, to come in for a cup of tea; Vitor, however, declined out of prudence and remained standing in the passageway, holding her baby. I overheard my mother describing to Vitor a dream she had had during the previous night and which, as she said, had left her deeply disturbed. She dreamt that she saw stretching away before her an ink-black sea, with lots of human heads bobbing on the surface and rising in the distance, the Star of the Sea, that is the Virgin Mary. The events which followed on that day will remain imprinted in my memory for as long as I live.

Most people were taking cover but all of a sudden my father decided to go out; he told my mother that he had made an appointment with a businessman to finalise some deal. Seconds later I heard my brother Charlie call my mother to go up with him to see the German bombers. My mother was quick to warn him

Charlie Vella *(first, right)* with his two friends. The photo was taken the day before they were killed.
(Courtesy D. Camilleri)

to stay where he was but he disappeared. My other brother, Guzi, made as if he was about to follow Charlie, but as my mother grabbed him by the jumper, he leapt away leaving my mother holding shreds from his jumper. I was observing all this when my brother Guzi halted and stayed by Vitor's side in the passageway. The next instant a deafening explosion plunged the whole place into darkness and sent us reeling against the walls of the cubicle. In the ensuing panic I began to grope around and felt the heads of the three young ones. The straw mattresses on the bunks caught fire and burst into flames as I heard my mother mutter, "This is Vitor!" Vitor had been hurled into the cubicle by the blast and her body was now lifeless. We saw her baby crawl out from under the body, miraculously still alive. As the confusion grew, my mother lit up a match and could see that one of the two Englishwomen who regularly took cover in the shelter was badly injured. My mother immediately tore a strip from her clothes and stopped the bleeding with it. As mother and I walked through the passageway my eyes fell on the lifeless body of my brother Guzi, with his clothes in tatters and his body shrunk by the blast. My mother, her eyes blinded by the flaring match, did not see him; instead she stared at a leg wearing a heavy Army boot. "This is your father's," she exclaimed and burst into hysterical laughter. Although I was only nine I could realise that my mother's peals of laughter were not normal, and something inside me made me say, "That is not his foot, I've seen father go out; he is probably looking for us." A man suddenly appeared as if from nowhere, groaning with pain and looking as if he had just come back from the dead. When, hesitatingly, my mother asked, "Are you my husband?" he replied haltingly, "Yes......no". Silence reigned, the silence of death. As our eyes got accustomed to the dim light we saw dead bodies piled on top of each other. A number of RAF men appeared at the shelter entrance and picking their way through the piles of corpses grabbed us and took us outside. We walked in a state of shock towards our house and saw carts carrying bodies. We recognised that of Milda's mother, a refugee from Vittoriosa, horribly mutilated. The walls of Gafa` Street were black with the blast of the explosion. We learned later that three torpedoes had landed and exploded simultaneously at the entrance and the emergency exit of the shelter. That accounted for the tremendous havoc. For some reason or other fire broke out in the shelter too.

Our three youngest were taken to hospital and for two days we did not know their whereabouts. My father was dead as was my eldest brother, the latter's body almost beyond recognition from the effects of the blast. For three days we kept the truth hidden from my mother, partly because of some difficulties arising during the identification of the bodies and partly because she was pregnant. When finally she got to know, she wept for three whole days. After a few months my mother gave birth to a healthy girl, her seventh child.

While my mother was in hospital for the delivery, the parish priest called at our home and took all the children except myself to an orphanage. I went to live with my aunt and as soon as I was old enough, I brought my brothers and sisters back from the orphanage.

JOSEPH J CAMILLERI

As children we did not know the meaning of war, and certainly no idea of the death and destruction which wars bring about. We were very excited when we were given gas masks and when street lights were put out but no thought of the impending tragedies and havoc entered our young, immature minds.

The war certainly interrupted our education. As from the 7th of January 1941 students of my age began to attend lessons at the Lyceum between eight in the morning to half past twelve in the afternoon, first in the Lija primary school premises and then in a private house at Attard. Public transport was unpredictable and students had to find their own means for getting to school. One of the students in my class, a certain Mifsud, was in the habit of carrying in his satchel small explosive devices which he used to pick up from the fields. His idea of having a bit of fun was to terrify us by rolling one of these devices down the stairs as we were going down and laughing loudly as he saw us scurry down. One day we heard that he had been killed when one of these devices exploded as he was tampering with it. The same fate befell three other fellow students from Mosta: Edwin Gatt and the brothers Francis and Albino

Bezzina. Another classmate of mine perished when he was buried under the rubble of his home during the night.

During the first months of the war we had no proper bomb-proof shelters. Some Government workers came to our house one day and put up blankets over doors and windows as a protection from gas attacks; the roof of one room was reinforced by scant-lings and planks. We often slept in the crypt underlying the church; it was said that as many as five hundred people were spending the night there. When my grandmother fell sick, we used to spend the night with her and in the event of an air-raid warning we used to huddle under a large solid table on top of which were piled a few mattresses. We felt perfectly safe! We then dug our own shelter attached to the house but instead of tak-ing cover there, I used to run to the church square whenever I heard the air-raid warning so that I could follow the action in the skies overhead. There was always some excitement in store for us: parachutes floating down, dog-fights, barrages from the many batteries around Mosta, a plane trailing black smoke as it plum-meted earthwards... Then when the action got too close we would rush into the church and crouch behind the massive walls.

The pulse of life in the village quickened with the arrival of the refugees and the atmosphere - at least to us youngsters - turned festive. The refugees brought a breath of fresh air with them and changed the tenor of life. The Engerer family from Sliema, with a boy and a girl roughly my age, came to live with us. Many of the girls who came as refugees were smart and tomboyish and knew the facts of life much better than the locals. Boys and girls could now be seen playing together, hitherto something unheard of.

The poor refugees were soon to realise that settling in Mosta was like jumping from the frying pan into the fire. The proximi-ty of strategic sites like Ta' Qali airfield, Fort Mosta and the many anti-aircraft batteries made Mosta a vulnerable place to live in and in fact was one of the most heavily bombed settlements on the island. The number of war victims was quite high, most of the deaths occurring in 1942. The most violent attacks in that year saw a veritable rain of bombs and mines hit the village killing a large number of persons and wiping out a whole family. One of the most memorable days for the people of Mosta was when a bomb smashed through the dome of the Rotunda fortunately without exploding. Many people were in the habit of taking cover in the church during air-raids and, had the bomb exploded, the death-toll would have been staggering.

On the 21st of March 1942, Ta' Qali was attacked by seventy-five bombers; at about half past two in the afternoon a tremendous explosion rocked the village. The entrance and the emergency exit of the public shelter in Gafa` Street had each received a direct hit, the blast killing a large number of people taking

Dome of Mosta church
pierced by bomb which
failed to explode.

cover there. At the same time a fire broke out adding to the disaster. (I heard people say that a quantity of petrol had been stored in the shelter.) The place was cordoned off while the dead and injured were being removed; I remember being impressed when some people remarked that the bodies of victims who had been killed by the blast had shrunk by half.

Bomb Disposal Squad with unexploded bomb.

Among the incidents which have stuck in my memory is when a gang of pilferers were caught stealing from Government stores after apparently having engaged in this type of activity for a long time. The story goes that some of those pilferers were very wealthy by the end of the war, except one who was so upset at being caught that he shot himself. There were also rumours that a few persons in high places used to raid bombed buildings to carry away things which caught their eye. If my memory serves me right, one or two such cases subsequently came up before the Courts..

The "Mosta Miracle"
commemorated.
(Photo N. Genovese).

I do not think that we, in our immaturity, appreciated the full significance of the war and its attendant horrors, and I suspect that quite a few people of my age look back on the war years as being an exciting, and on the whole, pleasant period of their life. Sometimes when I am with friends of my age and the conversation falls on those days, I wonder if it could be a touch of nostalgia that creeps in!

LILIAN CAMILLERI

My father died three years before the outbreak of war, leaving my mother with seven young children. My sister and myself were placed in Ta' Bugeja Institute at Fleur-de-Lys and when the buildings of the Institute were taken over as Police Headquarters we were transferred first to the Rabat school and then to Verdala Palace at Buskett. Sharing the Palace with us were children from another institute, like us about forty in number. I was then twelve years of age.

We had normal lessons at Verdala just as if we were at the village school. The Misses Witton, Busuttil and Manche`, all occupying important positions in the Girl Guide movement also lodged in the Palace. There was no proper shelter at the time and during air-raids we were herded down into the cellars of the Palace. When an air-raid was in the offing I used to hear people say, "They are coming! They are coming!" and I would feel terrified not quite understanding who "they" were. Only a handful of bombs fell in the vicinity of Buskett. One day a woman and her daughter who lived in one of the caves nearby were terrified when bombs fell in the neighbourhood and the two came running to the Palace. The girl was struck by a splinter and died. The girl was brought in and laid on the sofa which, I remember clearly, got stained with the girl's blood. I was deeply impressed with that sight.

The upper part of Buskett was occupied by soldiers who were billeted under canvas. The soldiers often gave us sweets and chocolates. I do not think that we were ever starving although certainly there were times when I wished to have more bread but had to do without. Throughout the war my mother used to come to see me and my sister once a month; she lived at Msida and sometimes had to walk all the way to Buskett, occasionally getting a lift for part of the way. When we were at Fleur-de-Lys, my mother saw us every Sunday.

I lost my eldest brother, Ovvie, during the war. He was a steward on the *Royal Oak* which was sunk by enemy action in October 1939, that is before Italy's declaration of war. He had just turned nineteen. An uncle, Gużeppi Mangion, also perished in that same action.

LINA CIARLO`

I was twelve and had just taken the Secondary School entrance examinations when war broke out. My family consisting of my parents and nine children lived in a large house in Old Mint Street, Valletta with grandparents and uncles and aunts - seventeen persons in all. Underlying the house was a large cellar which was reached through a flight of steps in the courtyard. As long as air attacks were carried out by Italian raiders, we stayed on in Valletta, taking cover in the cellar whenever there was an air-raid warning but when the Luftwaffe took over, the bombardment grew in intensity and the risks rose accordingly, especially since our house was too close to Marsamxett Harbour. We therefore moved to Rabat as refugees and settled - all seventeen of us - in two rooms. Crammed as we were, the situation was becoming intolerable and some days later my father, my grandpa and an aunt returned to the Valletta home and the rest of us tried to carry on as best we could.

Having passed the examinations, I began to attend the secondary school in Valletta. The bus took us as far as Porte des Bombes and I had to walk the rest of the way to the school in Merchants Street. One fine Sunday morning, my mother and my aunt took me and three of my brothers to Valletta so that we could spend the day with my father. The weather was fine and there were no air-raid warnings. At about four in the afternoon, my father and I accompanied my mother and younger brothers to the bus terminus to see them off, having arranged that my elder brother and I were going to spend the night in Valletta with my father. When the bus left we walked back at a leisurely pace, and being in no particular hurry lingered for a while in Kingsway (Republic Street), pausing for some minutes opposite the Regent Cinema, where now stands Regency House. My brother was standing beside the florist's kiosk, and was preparing to get into the cinema for the five o'clock performance. I asked my father to let me go with my brother, but instead he called my brother and told him to go home with us. Muttering under his breath my brother joined us and we had just taken a few steps in the direc-

ion of our home when the deafening sound of gunfire and of aircraft engines shattered the peaceful evening. Everyone ran in the
direction of the shelter in Queen Square. Terrified out of my wits,
I ran with the crowd. Suddenly there was a tremendous explosion, followed by the sound of breaking glass. The Regent
Cinema had received a direct hit, and death and destruction lay
around.

Many were the dead and injured and throughout the night and
the following day soldiers and policemen strove to save those
trapped under the fallen masonry. It was a long time before I
could remove that harrowing scene from my mind, and even
now, many years after the event, I can remember every detail.

Mgr ALWIĠ DEGUARA

Before beginning to say Mass, the parish priest broke the news
that the country was in a state of war and exhorted the congregation to pray for peace. He then proceeded with the Mass but
halfway through, I who was serving as an altar boy heard the
sound of distant gunfire. The parish priest seemed to stumble
over some of the words and hurried to conclude the Mass, and
then turned to the congregation and told them to go home
because the bombardment had started.

The rumour soon went round that the safest places to be in
were the caves. We tried my aunt's cellar but it was not large
enough to take us all. Our neighbours left their home to take
refuge in a large cave in the Gerbulina area and soon others,
including all my family, began to follow their example. We
grabbed some bedding and other essential articles and made our
way to the cave. Our stay there however was to be short-lived
because by the following Sunday, everyone had left the cave and
gone back to their homes. An unusual sight met us as we
returned: the refugees were arriving at Mġarr. You could tell by
their accent that they were from the Cottonera area as they tried
to find families ready to take them under their roof. Some found
accommodation in the stores underlying the church, others set-

tled down in farm buildings or in the neighbouring caves. A woman who lived next door removed the fowl in the hen house and in their stead put up a family with four children. From Zabbar alone, no fewer than seven hundred refugees settled in Mġarr not to mention the many others from the Sliema area.

The headteacher of the local school, Mr Ġanni Cilia, and the parish priest, Father Edgar Salomone chose me to be the village town crier. At around noon every Saturday I had to pop in at the Protection Office where I was handed the news as issued by the Valletta headquarters of the Information Office. On the Sunday, after the evening church service, I would stand at the base of one of the pilasters and read out the news; at that time Mġarr was not

Fr Edgar Salomone, parish priest of Mġarr during the war.

(Courtesy A. Deguara).

18

yet provided with the public address system. After spending some weeks at this job I was told to report at the Information Office in Valletta for instructions. I was asked to get hold of a small room in the village and convert it into an information bureau to be open to the public on certain specified days of the week. Father J Micallef gave me a room in the Catholic Action premises so that I could show posters and distribute leaflets, naturally all with a strong pro-British or pro-Allies slant. The news bulletins which I read out were placed in a notice board along with other propaganda material. One poster comes to mind: a bulldog draped in the Union Jack with the caption "Chins up!" I also made use of a large board with a map on which little flags marked the advances and retreats of the armies of the warring nations. I used the board to show pictures of anti-personnel bombs so that farmers and children would take due care; such devices had killed or maimed a number of people from Mġarr,

Trying on gas masks at Mġarr.

(Courtesy A. Deguara)

Group of residents and evacuees with Fr Salomone and other priests.
(Courtesy A. Deguara).

including a great friend of mine. For all my pains I was paid the handsome sum of 32 shillings (Lm 1.60) a month.

On the spiritual side, I became a rather important person in the public shelter because I was made to lead the occupants in their devotions, probably on the strength of my town crier role.

The first bombs to hit Mġarr were dropped in April 1942, on Maundy Thursday, killing three people and injuring several others. Other bombs landed in the village after that, including one which badly damaged our house causing some roofs to cave in. There was one scene which left a deep impression on us children. An Italian bomber was hit on its way back to Sicily after dropping its load and was leaving a trail of black smoke behind. We were cheering wildly when the plane turned back and seemed to be coming down on us. When it was almost over the church, the pilot baled out just at the instant that the plane caught fire and crashed in the fields behind the church. Some farmers and members of the Volunteer Corps grabbed their shotguns and marched

ı the direction of the place where the pilot managed to land. The
ɑarish priest and some regular soldiers hurried there too and suc-
eeded in protecting the terrified pilot from the wrath of the
ɒcals. The pilot, Franco, was carried to the village school and
reated for minor injuries. At least two other planes crashed in the
ıicinity of Mġarr: one at Gnejna and the other near Zammitello
ɔalace.

When the invasion of Sicily was in the offing, Malta became
he assembly point for all sorts of armament. The streets of
Mġarr, the church square and the fields around were occupied by
hundreds of heavy trucks and tanks; for the first time we children
saw huge ten-wheeled transporters. Even the parvis had its share
of armaments. At the insistence of the parish priest the parvis was
cleared for one evening so that a church feast could be celebrated; on that occasion the Roman Catholic chaplain of the forces
was invited to lead the service and the procession. After the ceremony the military vehicles were wheeled back onto the parvis.

Fr ĠUŻEPP FENECH

I was a Third Former at the Lyceum when Mussolini brought
Italy into the war; the Lyceum then occupied the premises of the
Hamrun primary school near Fra Diegu Square. Examinations
were coming up but, with schools closing prematurely, had to be
cancelled. When schools re-opened in October, I spent the best
part of a day to find out where exactly I was supposed to attend.
I first tried Hamrun: there I was told that I should go to Rabat. At
Rabat I was informed that I should attend the school at Attard but
there, again, I drew a blank. Finally I got to the end of my quest:
Form Four was housed in premises in Balzan. So to Balzan I
went but only for a brief period because our class was soon transferred to Attard. The following year we moved back to Hamrun
but this time it was in the Victoria Avenue (now G Pace Street)
school building.

Not infrequently, as we travelled by bus, an air raid warning
would sound. On such occasions the driver would stop and we

would alight and scurry for the nearest shelter. I remember once having to lie flat on the ground as German fighters opened up with machine gun fire. Another time we were sitting on a low field wall waiting for the bus when we felt the ground under our feet shudder. There being no air raid in progress we thought it must be an earthquake but later learned that a heavy calibre time bomb had gone off in Lija killing several people; the date was the 3rd of November 1942. At that very instant Mass was being said in the parish church; the priest who was officiating had about half an hour before been looking at the unexploded bomb along with some of his parishioners and he must have counted it as one of his lucky days that the device did not explode then!

What worried us most as students besides the food shortage was the unavailability of books and paper as well as the constant interruption of our studies. We spent long stretches of time in the shelters and we were under continuous tension especially when Ta' Qali was under attack. One night German bombers kept up the bombing hour after hour. Here one must keep in mind that at the beginning of the war there were no proper shelters; instead people had to make do with trenches covered with timber beams (incidentally provided from the cargo of an Italian merchantman which had been seized in the Grand Harbour on the day war broke out) or take cover in cellars. Later on proper bomb-proof shelters were dug out of the solid rock. My father and our neighbours agreed to excavate a shelter in the garden and, to keep his part of the agreement, my father used to spend every free minute digging away underground. We began to use the shelter when it was only half finished. One night during an air raid, half the family went down into this shelter while the rest took cover in a neighbouring cellar. We had barely settled down when a loud explosion rocked the shelter. We were all terrified because obviously the bomb had landed in the immediate vicinity and we were very worried about the fate of the rest of the family who were in the cellar. My father went up to investigate and saw that three houses next to my aunt's house were razed to the ground. He made his way with great difficulty to the cellar and found its occupants frightened out of their wits but mercifully unhurt; their

st reaction on seeing my father was to ask about us. Two of my
cles who lived in a house across the street were also lucky to
rvive the incident.

After the first few air raids refugees began to arrive in their
undreds, mostly from the Three Cities area, fleeing to the com-
arative safety of the countryside. At one stage the population of
ja rose to over four thousand souls and accommodation had to
e found in the chapels and clubs of the village. Father Karm Lia,
e parish priest worked incessantly to find accommodation for
e poor refugees.

A regiment from Basutoland, brought over for the planned
vasion of Sicily, used to be quartered in the vicinity of the vil-
ge cemetery. A number of these soldiers were Roman Catholics
nd it was customary for them to attend the evening service in the
arish church and sing African hymns. I noticed that when leav-
ng church they would walk backwards to avoid giving their back

VE Day Parade in Kingsway (now Republic Street) Valletta.
(Photo W.J. Jones)

23

"VE" DAY IN MALTA

The "V-Crowd" that greeted His Excellency when as His Majesty's representative, Sir Edmond Schreiber addressed His Majesty's Subjects in Malta yesterday evening. Every face in the massed crowd has a very special "V-smile".

Right: Lieutenant-General Sir Edmond Schreiber taking the Salute from the People of Malta.

STALIN'S THREE ORDERS OF THE DAY

(Reuter's Service)

MOSCOW, May 8.

Olomouc in Moravia, has been captured by General Eremenko's forces, says Marshal Stalin in an Order-of-the-Day tonight .

Olomouc, which is described as an important bastion in the German defences on the Moravia river, is 50 miles south-west of Moravska Ostrava.

DRESDEN:

In a Second Order-of-the-Day tonight Marshal Stalin announced that Dresden, the only big German city remaining in German hands has been captured by Marshal Koniev's armies.

The Order adds that Dresden was captured after a battle lasting two days. It is an important communication centre and the capital of Saxony.

A third Order-of-the-Day tonight announced that Znoime, in Czechoslovakia, south-west of Brno, was captured by troops of Marshal Malinovsky.

desired for their children and for ours.

"This is the task to which now honour binds

His Excellency the King's Representative, with His Grace, the Lieutenant-Governor and the Services Chiefs, addressing the People of Malta from the Palace Balcony.

the Sacred Host. A few men from the regiment were also baptised in the church having as godparents parishioners from Lia. I can clearly remember one such ceremony.

On being promoted to Form Five, I had to attend school in Valletta, first in Villa Messina and then in the large house which nowadays has become the premises for Lombard Bank. Lessons were held both in the morning and in the afternoon and those of us who wanted to could have a meal at the Victory Kitchen.

Lessons were often interrupted by air raids but we only went down into the shelter when the red flag was run up at the Palace Tower. Some of our teachers insisted on continuing with the lessons in the shelter. I remember once during those schooldays some British officers were entrusted with the conduct of the annual examinations. I never played truant at school but once when the convoy was entering harbour all of us students left in a body and went on the bastions to wave at those brave seamen who had risked their lives to help us survive.

On my eighteenth birthday I was called up for military service but was exempted so that I could continue my studies at the Major Seminary and when VE Day came on the 8th of May 1945 it was at the Seminary that I heard that the war was over. I do not think that I was ever as happy as I was on that day.

GUIDO LANFRANCO

When I was nine and a half, we moved house to Gzira. From the roof of that house my father used to point out various places of interest, among them the monitor HMS *Terror*, with her deck bristling with gun turrets, moored in Lazzaretto Creek. We often heard the sound of gunfire, which as my father explained, meant that military manoeuvres were in progress. A few weeks before the declaration of war, my father glued strips of brown paper on all the window panes, telling us that this was to prevent splinters of glass flying around if the panes were shattered by the vibrations caused when the monitor fired her guns.

I sensed that something was wrong when my grandmother

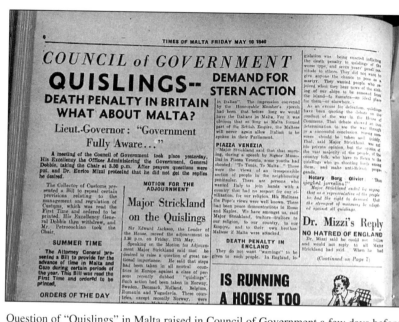

Question of "Quislings" in Malta raised in Council of Government a few days before the outbreak of war.

came to live with us and I heard my father say that Mussolini had declared war. Peeping from the balcony I saw some neighbours being escorted out of their house because, as we were later told, "they were pro-Italian." The following morning we were rudely awakened by the sound of heavy gunfire from HMS *Terror*. My father told us to go downstairs because the war had started. Glued to the inside of our front door was a holy picture and my mother was soon saying prayers with grandma which made us children even more frightened. There were several air raid warnings after that.

In the evening, with people excitedly talking about the effects of the bombing, we decided to go to live with a relative in Balzan. I remember the family joining a procession of refugees walking or riding on horse-drawn carts in the direction of Msida. We carried baskets, sacks and pillow cases packed with food and clothing and on arriving at Msida we were led into the church of the

Immaculate Conception, part of which was excavated out of the living rock, and told that we were to spend the night there. My father, however, managed to hire a taxi which took us to Balzan. The following day we moved on to Fleur-de-Lys and shared the house with another family. With raids becoming common, people began to get complacent; we got used to the routine of taking cover of some sort whenever the siren went. After a few weeks my father decided to take us all back to a house in New Street, Sliema; our shelter there was the area under the stairs. An architect from the Public Works Department had, some time before, inspected the house and suggested that we build a blast-wall under the stairs. As I said complacency had set in but one day in January 1941 changed all that. On that day, early in the afternoon, the gunfire was unusually heavy and the sound of enemy aircraft engines more ominous and menacing. My mother was terror-stricken and took us children to the neighbours' private shelter. As we ran, I looked up and saw the sky covered with puffs of ack-ack fire in and out of which large numbers of planes were flying and diving. This was the Island's first experience of the Luftwaffe blitz tactics, now directed at the *Illustrious* berthed in the Grand Harbour. As from that day we never missed taking cover at the first sign of an air raid warning. The neighbours took the precaution of connecting their shelter to that of their next-door neighbours; the public shelter was also connected to another. We were constantly hearing about various disasters such as that of March 1941 in which twenty five were killed and thirty injured when bombs fell on St Rita Street. In the following May, a parachute mine landed in the grounds of Villa Portelli but failed to explode when the parachute got tangled in a tree. In June we spent interminable hours in the shelter when Italian E-boats attacked the harbours. August saw the complete destruction of the vestry of the Sacro Cuor Church and of the grounds of Capua Palace. In December the Gozo ferry boat was attacked off Dragonara Point.

One day in April 1942 we emerged from the shelter to find our house badly damaged; we could only with great difficulty pick our way through the rubble to reach it. My mother was frightened

Prince of Wales Street, Sliema after air raid of 7 March 1942.

(Photo Times of Malta courtesy Ch. Grech).

death and pulled us along to the Salesian Fathers' shelter. riends of the family asked us to spend the night with them. As we ere walking there, with my mother and father carrying my broth- r Robert in a cot, stepping over the fallen masonry, there was an ir raid warning. A few moments later, we heard the whine of a illing bomb and we thought that was the end of us all. The bomb urst into balls of fire - it was an incendiary device - and we some- ow were unharmed. One of our neighbours, Mrs Maria Spiteri ffered to share her home with us until we could find a house to ive in. The shelter became our dormitory and I remember scoop- ng the clay out of the rock to make little figures; in the night I used o lead the occupants of the shelter in reciting the rosary. Gradually ve got used to the searchlights sweeping the night sky overhead, o cooking on the *kenur* (wood-fired stone stove) and to queuing ip for every imaginable commodity, including Victory Kitchen meals. Once a week we would go up to Msierah (San Gwann) in the hope of being able to buy eggs or milk.

When eventually raids became less frequent, my father took me to Gozo where one of my aunts lived. I remember seeing on going down from Mellieha to Ghadira walls constructed in a labyrinth-like manner intended, as my father pointed out, to obstruct enemy tanks in case of an invasion. On the way back we were stopped by a police squad and half-a-dozen eggs which my aunt gave my father were confiscated, one policeman explaining that this was being done to eradicate black market practices. The policeman did not elaborate as to what was going to happen to the eggs....

Midway through 1943 preparations were in hand for the inva- sion of Sicily and Gzira was transformed into a beehive of activ- ity. Troops were massing in Malta and the streets were packed with tanks, amphibious vehicles, self-propelled guns and huge lorries. Trucks could also be seen driving towards the airfields loaded with German prisoners-of-war to carry out work. Sometimes young women would throw chocolate bars to the pris- oners-of-war.

Once in 1943 when air raids were few and far between, a classmate by the name of Lino Vella, did not turn up for lessons.

The day after we learned that together with his father he had bee
killed by a bomb. One of our teachers placed a bunch of flower
in Lino's place and wrote on the blackboard "In loving memor
of Lino Vella". Sadly there were also other friends of mine wh
did not survive the war.

In the summer of 1943, we could clearly see from the roof o
our house ships of the Italian navy lying at anchor in Marsamxet
Harbour after surrendering. The war could be considered over as
far as we were concerned but not for the two brothers Giorgic
who perished in April 1944 when a mine exploded on the Fond
Ghadir foreshore.

For children of my age the war was like a baptism of fire: we
suffered the pangs of hunger and the stress of daily bombing, but
we also knew a time when all Maltese were united. The war made
us grow into young men unspoilt by an easy life.

MARGERITA LUCIA

My father was an Italian citizen. On the day that Mussolini
declared war the police called at our house and took my father to
Villa Portelli at the top of Savoy Hill. Along with other Italian
nationals he was asked whether he would like to be repatriated or
whether he preferred to remain in Malta as an internee. My father
chose the first alternative, returning to Rome where he took up
the teaching of music in the same college in which my two brothers had studied music before coming back to Malta in 1939.

Meanwhile my mother, with me and the three children who
were still under age, were taken to the internment camp at
Corradino. I remember being led into a large hall crowded with
women and children who were in the same plight as we were. I
remember also those present being served tea out of a bucket
while attendants handed out slices of bread with butter. We did
not touch anything at all. My mother evidently firmly believed
that the police had no real grounds for interning us and she
demanded to see the camp commandant. She put her case quite
forcefully, saying that she and her children were as Maltese as

yone else, and within a few hours we were released. I was a girl
fourteen at the time and I took this as being some kind of
venture, but I must say that at one time I felt terrified when
ti-aircraft guns opened up in the immediate vicinity.

I was a student at St Joseph School in Valletta and in spite of
y father's nationality most of my schoolmates kept up their
iendship with me. But two or three of my classmates, I noticed,
gan to avoid me, a kind of behaviour which I am sorry to say
as encouraged by one of my teachers who was heard to say to
me girls, "Don't stay near the Italian girl." When we went, as
fugees, to live in St Paul's Bay we had no problems with the
eighbours who respected and helped us in all sorts of ways even
ough it was common knowledge that my father was Italian and
at he was living in Italy. I can only recall one exception: one
ay as we were taking cover in a shelter during a particularly
eavy air-raid, a man started making comments which were
bviously aimed at us.

A certain Grezz used to come and stand on our doorstep dur-
g air-raids in the belief that the Italian pilots knew about us and
ad instructions to avoid dropping bombs on our house. Poor
oman! The only bomb that landed on the village killed her hus-
and as he was engaged in digging a shelter.

Of course our father was constantly in our thoughts and as we
earned later he was worrying a lot about us especially when the
talian propaganda machine was daily announcing that Malta was
n ruins. Throughout the war, however, our father managed to
eep a measure of contact with us by regularly sending messages
n the Vatican radio, and, in some way which I have never real-
y fathomed, through Mabel Strickland. With twelve children to
ook after, and without a husband to give a hand, my mother must
ave had a very hard time indeed. The food shortage did not
worry us unduly; one could always get the essential commodities
n the black-market. We had a small chicken farm and a goat
which, of course, helped too.

In the last stages of the war, most of the action was in the north
f Italy and my father took the opportunity to travel down to
Syracuse. Soon after the invasion of Sicily, my brother who was

in the KOMR, was sent there and he managed to meet my fath
we have a photo of the two of them together. My father was bar

The Sliema War Memorial

(Photo N. Genovese)

y recognisable and one of my sisters was so taken aback by the
change that had come over my father that she would refuse to
look at the photo before going to bed.

Fr ANTHONY F SAPIENZA, SJ

The first bombs to land on Gzira fell a short distance away
from our home. I remember that incident well enough. My mother was feeding my youngest sister, Aunt Violet who lived with us
had just gone to buy some vegetables and my father was sitting
in a corner looking very preoccupied. He must have been thinking that with four young children and bombs falling around the
prospects were likely to be bleak. That must have been the
moment when he decided that the family must move to some
safer neighbourhood. But that was easier said than done! My
father must have realised months before that war was in the offing and he had over the weeks piled up a veritable store of commodities under the stairs. There was a sack of rice and another of
sugar, a crate of tinned milk, a large box packed with green laun-
dry soap, a tankful of kerosene and lots more. An upstairs room
had been turned into a gas-proof chamber with blankets over the
windows, ready to be soaked in water as per official instructions;
even as a boy of seven I used to wonder whether we would be
able to breathe in that room.

Apparently my father had not considered the probability that
houses situated in strategic areas, like ours, would be destroyed
in the bombing. Sliema Creek was packed with destroyers and
other naval units. HMS *Terror*, her decks bristling with guns, and
likely to be the target of repeated attacks, was moored in the
creek. It was Zanzu, the greengrocer, who provided the solution
to the problem. My father asked him whether he knew of some
place in the countryside to which the family could move for the
duration of the war. Zanzu's brother-in-law, Indri`, did have such
a place and it was thus that we found ourselves in a small farmhouse in the San Gwann area on the road which then ran between
Sliema and Birkirkara. Transport was provided by Zanzu himself

who put his horse-drawn cart at our service. Grandpa Frank and grandma Nellie joined us in our new lodgings.

A few days after settling down in the two rooms which were put at our disposal, my father persuaded Indri` and his wife Mari` to have a shelter dug in the grounds. My father took his turn along with Indri` and two neighbouring farmers to wield the pick. The shelter was soon ready and we now felt prepared for all even-

H.M.S. *Terror* in Sliema Creek.

(NWMA Collection)

tualities. A few weeks into the war two anti-aircraft batteries sprang up in the vicinity, one at Tal-Qroqq and the other at Ta' Giorni and we found ourselves right in the centre. My father thought it wise to dig down deeper into the rock and so we had a cubicle which was definitely bomb-proof and in which one could sleep the night through without a worry.

Our apprehensions were well-founded. Grandpa Frank, whose father was English, would never dream of going down into a shelter and preferred to run up to the roof whenever he heard an air-raid warning. He said nothing gave him greater satisfaction than seeing German and Italian planes going down in flames. One day he was too engrossed in watching some action over the harbours to notice that some planes had broken off from the main formation and were about to attack the Tal-Qroqq battery. Two bombs landed, one on each side of the farmhouse, and the explosion covered him from head to toes in reddish soil. For once he was shaken and for the first time in his life ran down into the shelter where we were huddled together. In the dim light my grandma thought that he was covered in blood and began to scream; when the truth came out we broke out into loud laughter.

Towards the end of 1940 there was a lull in the bombardment and my father felt he could occasionally take me with him to Valletta. Three doors away from my father's bookshop lived Mr Arrigo, "the Elephant" as he was called, who held the post of Special Constable for the neighbourhood. One day in January 1941, there was an air-raid warning. Mr Arrigo, sporting an armband with the initials *SC* displayed prominently, ordered everyone to lock up and to proceed immediately to the corridor running along the church of St Francis. This particular corridor had a massive barrel vaulted roof and, with its entrance protected by sandbags, was considered to be bomb-proof. No sooner had we crowded into this "shelter" than an unprecedented massive bombardment began; this was none other than the epic *Illustrious* blitz. The noise was deafening; the scream of diving *Stukas*, the booming of explosions, the crash of collapsing buildings, the rapid ack-ack...

Meanwhile inside the shelter one of the most frightening scenes of my life was being played. The constable who was supposed to be controlling the situation went berserk and began to bang his head against the wall as he screamed and wept. Some men grabbed him to prevent his getting injured. My father tried hard to turn my head away as I looked, spellbound, at this scene. I heard people explain that the man had lost a son through enemy action...

For us children life in those days was one long exciting adventure remembered with nostalgia in our old age. In another farmhouse just across the road lived one Moses, who used to let us run into his fields to play. The highlight of those days was the harvesting of the wheat crop, an entirely new experience for us town children. Moses would lift us up to ride the mule and the donkey as these went round in circles on the threshing floor. Fifty years later I can still taste and smell the fresh warm grain piled up in small golden mounds.

JOHN E SCERRI

Ours was one of the few families which did not leave Zabbar during the war. I was nine and a half when, in June 1940, Italy declared war. On the first day of the war we were awakened by the sound of anti-aircraft fire. People took that for military manoeuvres at first but when Italian planes were observed flying at a very high altitude, they realised that this was war. That was confirmed a little later when it became known that bombs had been dropped and that people had been killed.

People were advised to take certain precautions in the event of any air-raid; a table covered by pillows and mattresses was said to provide a measure of safety for those taking shelter under it. We were also told that another safe place in the home was in doorways. It was soon evident however that such measures were useless against bombing and later on, when air attacks became heavier and more frequent, underground shelters were built. We spent long hours in these rock-hewn shelters, scrambling down whenever the warning signal was given from the police station and running up at the all-clear.

An anti-aircraft battery, St Mary's, was built on the outskirts of Zabbar and when its guns engaged enemy raiders, the noise was ear-splitting. We used to admire the bravery of the gunners who, with warplanes diving over them and dropping bombs around, kept on firing their guns.

I missed many of my friends who left Zabbar to go as refugees with their parents to other localities in Malta, or in some cases,

Improvised shelter: watercolour by A. Gerada.

(Courtesy A. Ganado)

Gozo but I made a number of new friends who came to Zabbar from the Three Cities.

The games we played in those days reflected the reality going an around us. We played at soldiers and armed ourselves with a length of wood crudely shaped like a rifle and imitated the drill routines which we saw the soldiers go through. I was dubbed "the captain" and I had to see to it that everyone did his drill satisfactorily. We built a small hut, our "guard room", in one of the fields and each of us had to take his turn to mount guard. Other boys from Zabbar had their own "units" and occasionally hostilities would break out with stones flying in all directions. The highlight of each day would be when, after school was over, we would take our slice of bread and eat it with great relish in our "guard room".

With food getting scarcer and scarcer, our play began to include another routine. I would march my "men" armed with their "rifles" to St Mary's Battery and watch the gunners and their officers troop into the canteen; usually luck would be with us and we would manage to get from them bits and pieces of bread, cheese, butter and jam. I think that the soldiers could see clearly that we were starving.

The primary school had a shelter attached to it and at every air-raid warning our teachers used to lead us down in an orderly fashion. When not at school, we often "forgot" to take cover during air-raids and instead watched with great excitement the dog-fights in the skies. We were spellbound as we saw *Messerschmitts* and *Hurricanes* and, later, *Spitfires* go through intricate aerobatics to evade or engage the enemy plane. During dog-fights spent cartridges would rain down and we would scramble over the field walls to retrieve them still warm from the gun barrel. Most boys also collected shrapnel which could be picked up practically anywhere. Some had their favourite large shrapnel with which they intended to strike the first German or Italian who happened to cross their path. War had turned us boys into hard-hearted savages.

One scene is marked indelibly in my memory. During a dog-fight a *Messerschmitt* was hit by a *Spitfire*; as the former went down in flames, the pilot ejected and we watched as he slowly floated down with his parachute. It seems that there were many other spectators besides us boys because suddenly men seemed to spring out of nowhere and, as they ran to where the pilot would land, loaded their shotguns. The pilot would have got short shrift had not a young man firmly and persuasively told the angry farmers to spare the young German's life and hand him over to the military authorities.

Another memorable scene, perhaps less dramatic but equally vivid, is that of my mother sharing out the day's bread ration at the height of the food shortage. She would take out the scales and carefully measure out the share of each of us children and give the rest to my father which meant that she would herself go without any bread.

MIKE SULTANA

When the war broke out, I was a nine-and-a-half year old boy living with my family in Xaghra, Gozo. The village school was immediately requisitioned by the military and converted into barracks for the Hampshire Regiment. Before the war, part of our house, situated in the main square, was used as a guest-house patronised mainly by Maltese bird-hunters. This part was now given over to some men of the same regiment who occasionally also had their meals with us. When we cooked for them it was usually eggs and chips, there being few other commodities available. The family owned some land and we never lacked potatoes and eggs. The men of course used to pay for their meals but they would often provide us with certain "delicacies" like chocolate and canned ham which were otherwise unobtainable. Sometimes instead of paying cash, the men would pay in kind, say a blanket or a coat, which like food were very hard to come by in those days. The police had instructions to carry out inspections in private houses to look for Army clothing and we therefore regularly took the precaution of packing such articles in a large bag which we kept suspended in a deep well in the house.

Air-raid warnings in Malta also applied to Gozo but we in

Grunju Street, Nadur, after the air raid of 3 January 1942.

(Courtesy D. Camilleri)

Gozo knew an air-raid was in the offing even before the air-raid warning sounded. Enemy raiders regularly flew in from the north, that is from over Marsalforn and we could identify whether the aircraft was friend or foe by the sound of the engines. Gozo was bombed several times and houses were demolished and people killed. Xagħra was one of the villages hit, presumably not because it had any military importance but more likely as the result of bombers dropping their load to lighten the plane when attacked by RAF fighters.

Some incidents readily come to mind. A *Messerschmitt* swooped low to strafe passengers in a bus going from Rabat to Nadur but when the pilot tried to pull the plane out of its dive, he miscalculated and it crashed into the Xagħra hillside, bursting into a ball of fire on impact. Several boys, including myself, who were watching raced to the spot hoping to get some parts of the plane as souvenirs. As we arrived I saw members of the crew burning in the wreckage, a scene which persists in my memory to this day.

There was another experience which made a deep impression on me. After nightfall curfew regulations made it a crime to walk in the streets without special permission. On this particular occasion, I was at my grandmother's house which was quite near our house and being absorbed in some kind of activity I did not return home before the curfew. As I was about to leave I saw a policeman on duty in the square and did not dare leave the house. I went up to the roof to watch the constable's movements and when I thought that the coast was clear, ran out of the house. Somehow the policeman caught sight of me and chased me. I was terrified.

During the war my sister married a soldier from the Hampshire Regiment and when the regiment was transferred to Malta she followed her husband there. I began to cross over to Malta fairly frequently, partly to give some support to my sister and partly to carry some potatoes and eggs, which we were never short of, to her.

EDWIN ZAMMIT

From Senglea, where we lived until war broke out, we were evacuated first to Birkirkara and then to Naxxar. We were six in the family: my father, my mother and four children. My father was a Dockyard worker and getting to work and back day in day out was too much of a nuisance for him. My parents therefore decided to go back to Senglea, come what may.

On returning to Senglea we found that daily life had more or less got back to normal. The *Illustrious* blitz soon changed that!

The first air-raid warning of the day sent us down into the shelter as usual. What followed then was not the usual, however. Tremendous explosions rocked the shelter as never before. Soon the word went round that many people had been killed and a large number of buildings were razed to the ground. Another rumour had it that a sewage pipe had burst and flooded a shelter so that the occupants were up to their knees in the liquid. We dared not get out of the shelter and spent the night cooped up there. When on the following morning we emerged a scene of devastation lay before us; everywhere buildings lay in ruins, mounds of rubble lay all around and the streets were blocked. My mother, rather fearful by nature, had by now become a bundle of nerves, almost paralysed by terror. There and then my father went to our house, collected a few things, lifted my mother up to take her through the fallen masonry and informed us we would be going to Gozo immediately.

The decision to go to Gozo was taken because one of my aunts lived there. My aunt was not expecting to see us at all but she took us in until we found another place. We rented a small house and felt that life had begun again for us. Those were very happy days for me. I stopped attending school; for me it was one long, long holiday and the troubles of war were forgotten. For my father, it was a different story. He could not be with us as he had to report for work daily at the Dockyard. Every evening after work he used to go to St Philip's Priory in Senglea where he was

Scenes of destruction in Senglea.

given a bunk. For his daily needs, like washing and so on, he used our house which was quite near and which was still standing. On Saturdays, when weather conditions permitted, he would cross over to Gozo to see us.

As far as bombing was concerned Gozo was much safer than Malta. I remember, though, one episode in which a German plane swooped down and opened fire on the people. My brother and I were in the fields and we could see clearly what was going on. Something seemed to go wrong for the pilot because instead of getting out of the dive, the plane crashed into the hillside and exploded. We scrambled towards the spot and I can still see the members of the crew lying among the wreckage.

Every night a spectacle awaited us. From a vantage point we could see Malta in the distance and above it a web of searchlights, with puffs of white smoke dotting the sky. On their way to their targets in Malta, the bombers with their deadly load flew in over Gozo and we could tell by the sound of their engines that they were labouring under a heavy load.

About a year after our move to Gozo, bombs fell on Nadur and my mother, probably anxious to go back to my father, told us, "This doesn't seem to be very different from Senglea; if we are to die, we can just as well do it under the same roof with your poor father." That was final. We went back, this time taking up residence in Paola near the parish church.

During our stay in Paola, there was a heavy raid in which heavy calibre bombs were dropped over Paola, mostly in the Paola Square area, causing havoc and killing a number of people. I remember many horses and mules which were used by the military lying dead in the square and lots of blood, human and animal, spattering the kerb. One bomb smashed through the roof of the reservoir underlying the square causing it to cave in. Subsequently a man fell into the roofless reservoir and drowned.

IEQAF MINUTA JEKK JOGĦGBOK!
MA' MIN IŻŻOMM?

MA' DIN ?

JEW MA' DIN ?

JEKK L-UNION JACK HI L-BANDIERA LI ŻŻOMM MAGĦHA, INTI TKUN QIEGĦED TGĦIN BIEX IŻŻOMMHA TPERPER IŻDA JEĦTIEĠ LI

TAĦSEB QABEL MA TITKELLEM

IFTAKAR LI T-TPAĊPIĊ U X-XNIGĦAT FIERGĦA HUMA PERIKULUŻI.

ŻOMM IL-FEHMA TIEGĦEK; KOMPLI SEJJER BIX-XOGĦOL TIEGĦEK. U GĦIN ĦALLI TIĠI MIRBUĦA L-GWERRA.

MAĦRUĠ MILL-INFORMATION OFFICE—MALTA.

"Beware of Idle Talk ......"

(Courtesy J. Borg Bonello)

44

II. Adolescents

MOTHER ALOISIA BAJADA

I had always wished to become a cloistered nun but as I lived with my family in Xaghra, Gozo and since there was no Order of such nuns in Gozo it seemed unlikely that my dream would ever come true. One day, on the feast day of St John the Baptist, I was attending a service in the parish church of Xewkija and heard the preacher, an Augustinian friar, talk about virgins who left all worldly matters behind and took up the cloistered life in the service of God, which was precisely what I wanted to do with my life. After the sermon, with a friend of mine who shared my vocation, I struck up a conversation with a woman from Sannat who invited the two of us to her home. I was then sixteen years old.

Once inside the house, the woman began to show us samples of the kind of needlecraft which the sisters from the cloistered Order of St Catherine had done. The nuns had only a few months before evacuated their convent in Valletta and moved to Ta' Ċenċ close to Sannat. On the spur of the moment I begged the woman to introduce me immediately to the Mother Superior. The latter welcomed the two of us with great kindness and hinted that the war was going to be the means by which we were to join the Order. Thereafter, my friend and I used to walk regularly from

Xagħra to Ta' Ċenċ to meet the nuns. To make doubly sure that mine was going to be a responsible decision, I went several times to the spiritual director who lived in Rabat. There were few buses in those days and we had to do the trip to Rabat and back on foot, and it was on one of these trips that we nearly met our end.

An air-raid warning had just sounded and we kept walking up the hill to Xagħra when a German fighter suddenly appeared out of nowhere and flew in our direction with its guns firing. We could only watch helplessly as there was no possibility of taking cover and I was sure that we were going to be killed. I had just started reciting the Act of Contrition when an Air Force fighter appeared out of nowhere and chased the German away.

In the war years Xagħra was a second home to many servicemen who were billeted in private houses requisitioned by the military authorities. I remember the occasional soldier begging for a slice of bread, and being given food of some kind by the villagers. During the years when food was very scarce, my father worked as a clerk in a small firm which had its offices in Mġarr and I remember him telling us that he had heard his boss say that the population in Malta was on the verge of starvation.

In January 1944 the nuns left Ta' Ċenċ to return to their convent in Valletta and shortly after my friend and I received an invitation from the Mother Superior to join the Order as novices, which we, of course, accepted without a second thought. I can confidently say that it was the war that helped me fulfil my long-standing dream.

Dr GEORGE BORG

At the age of eighteen I was attending the Sixth Form at the Lyceum and was about to take my final examinations prior to entering university. Mr Brennan, one of our teachers, was constantly drumming into our heads, "War or no war education must go on". I was then living with my family in Gudia and on schooldays, promptly at half past six in the morning, I would regularly walk to the Annunciation shrine on the outskirts of Tarxien and catch one of the Kalafrana or Żejtun buses going to Valletta, or, when the Lyceum moved there, to Hamrun.

Tragedy struck on the 19th of April 1942. That was the day on which my father asked me to accompany him to Qormi to call on a certain dealer who went by the nickname of "Onions". My father used to buy flour wholesale from this dealer and then distribute the flour among the bakers in Gudia and the neighbouring villages.

During the last few weeks, "Onions" had begun to be somewhat difficult and did not supply my father with the usual consignment. My father's customers, the bakers, were soon complaining at being left without flour and on that fateful day, he decided to go to Qormi to demand an explanation from "Onions". I agreed to accompany him in spite of the constant air-raids to which we were being subjected in those days. Before leaving Gudia we heard Mass at the parish church and then set off in the pony trap. To avoid the Luqa airfield area, then a prime target, we took the roundabout road through Tarxien, Paola and Marsa. We had scarcely done a mile before there was an air-raid alert which however did not stop us. As we passed the Corradino Prisons and made our way down to Marsa, there was a second air-raid warning and before the sirens were silent, bombs started falling around adding to the thunderous sound of anti-aircraft guns. There was nowhere to take cover as we saw the *Junker 88*'s diving over the Dockyard area. I was terrified but my father seemed unruffled and tried to laugh off my fears. "We'll push on towards the Civil Abattoir where there is a proper shelter and take cover until the all-clear", said my father.

With bombs falling around, we reached the gate of the abattoir and I alighted and was tethering the horse to the iron bars of the gate when I heard the whine of a falling bomb. I threw myself flat on the ground, my father instinctively threw his body across mine to shield me from danger. A split second later, an ear-splitting explosion... splinters of rock flying around... a cloud of dust and choking smoke... and the sensation of being struck by flying stones. When the air cleared a bit I made an effort to rise and looked around for my father; he was nowhere to be seen, nor was the horse. The buildings around had also disappeared, reduced to so much rubble. I caught sight of the horse, dead, some twenty yards away with the shattered cart nearby. Between me and the horse lay my father and as I staggered towards him, realised that blood was flowing from my leg and my clothes were in tatters. I knelt beside my father and saw that he was still alive. I heard him mutter, "Son, I'm dying" and I saw that he was pale and in a state of shock. He was bleeding profusely from a wound in the chest caused by a splinter. He was evidently in a bad state but fully conscious, and I asked him to join me in reciting the Act of Contrition.

Moments later, another stick of bombs hit the ground and though there was nobody in sight, I started calling for help. From

Antonio Borg *(sitting)*.

George Borg as a medical student

(Courtesy G. Borg)

the shelter attached to the abattoir six men emerged and looked shocked at the sight of me and my father. I was grabbed by the shoulders and dragged to the shelter. "What about my father?", I screamed and one of the men said, "How can we expect to carry him?". My father was a six-footer and very well-built. Some five minutes passed and then there was silence. We crawled out of the shelter and I ran to where my father lay. When he saw me he said, " I'm dying, George, but I saved your life". A police constable stopped a man who was riding by on his bicycle and told him to go for assistance to the ARP post in Marsa. It was almost an hour before the ARP personnel were on the spot, because, as they explained, the roads were all blocked with debris from the devastated buildings. When the ambulance arrived my father and myself were carried inside along with other casualties.

All the while, I was spitting blood and I asked for some water to drink. I felt very faint and I thought I was going to die. On arriving at Ta' Bugeja hospital, I was told by Professor Peter Paul Debono to walk upstairs and to leave my father to be looked after in one of the wards on the ground floor. I was laid on a bed in a ward which was crowded with casualties. By sheer coincidence, one of the orderlies happened to be my father's godson and it was he who told me that my father's condition had taken a turn for the worse and that I had better go to see him. On reaching his bedside, I found my father stretched on a bed with blood all over his chest and with a priest standing by. My father breathed his last soon after. A fortnight after my discharge from hospital, I took my final examinations in St Dominic's Priory in Rabat, and in spite of all the vicissitudes I had been through, was successful.

JOE BORG BONELLO

In the wake of the first bombing attacks followed a veritable exodus from the Cottonera area with large numbers of refugees moving to Birkirkara, my home town, to seek shelter. The refugees streamed in carrying mattresses, clothes and other belongings, some on trucks or buses, others on horsedrawn carts or on foot. Some seemed to be in a state of shock, others were weeping openly, as they begged to be taken in. In most cases the locals received them with open arms and welcomed them into their homes. Among the refugees was a girl from Valletta who was eventually to become my wife.

I was then eighteen years of age and the cubmaster of the Birkirkara Scout group. Soon after the war started, I was one of

Signalman Joe Borg Bonello.
(Courtesy J. Borg Bonello)

a number of scouts recruited to serve as runners in the censorship and information office which was housed in the Auberge d'Italie in Merchants Street, Valletta. The officer-in-charge was a certain Mr Tench with a number of Maltese on his staff, among whom I can clearly remember Gorg Pisani, Guze` Chetcuti and Godfrey Zarb Adami. Shortly after, Father Hersey, OFM, who was the Island Secretary of the Boy Scouts Association, invited me to join a group of coast watchers who were attached to the Royal Navy. I readily accepted and was posted to Fort St Angelo while others were stationed at the Palace Tower, Fort tas-Silġ, Lascaris, the Red Tower and the Auberge de Castile. We were given intensive training in the use of the semaphore and the Aldis lamp, but our duties included also other tasks depending on one's posting. For example if you were attached to the War Room at Lascaris, you had to deliver messages and man the telephones. In the coastal look-outs the duties were somewhat different: you had to sweep the horizon constantly through binoculars to detect the slightest suspicious movement or floating objects like, for instance, mines.

When the Germans unleashed their first attack in January 1941, I was stationed in Fort St Angelo and had just gone off duty and crossed the harbour to Valletta, minutes before the first bombing in the *Illustrious* blitz. The German bombers dived repeatedly at a very steep angle and then skimmed the surface of the water. Although the din was terrific, I do not think I was really terrified and I watched spellbound the spectacle unfolding before my eyes.

One night during my off watch rest, I was relaxing in the company of some seamen near the Captain's House in St Angelo when there was an air-raid alert. As the enemy warplanes approached, the searchlights opened up and picked out some strange objects drifting down slowly from the sky. Our first guess was that they were paratroops but the explosions which rent the night when they landed left us in no doubt that they were parachute mines. I can still see in my mind's eye the flames shooting up into the sky from St Elmo and Floriana. We immediately signalled to all craft in harbour, including ferries and Gozo boats, that engines were to be turned off and all harbour crossings to be halted. I also remember seeing, from a vantage point on St Angelo, the church of the Annunciation at Vittoriosa receiving a direct hit; only a few hours before I had been hearing Mass there.

Ours was, without a shadow of doubt, a significant contribution to the war effort and our officers appreciated it and trusted us blindly. There was however one occasion which left a bitter memory and even now after all these years I still recall it with a feeling of anger. I was stationed on watch duties at the Palace Tower, sometime in August 1942, when we had a visit from some high-ranking Navy officers. In the tower was a large notice board on which were posted lists with the names of ships, including those belonging to the Merchant Navy. I overheard one of the officers giving instructions to the Chief Yeoman of Signals, "Make sure that this place is out of bounds for messengers". That made me curious and I moved closer, being all the time very careful not to appear disrespectful. I very soon got to know that the officer's order was related to the imminent arrival of the Santa Marija convoy. The scene of the convoy entering the Grand Harbour is also one of my unforgettable memories, especially when the battered U.S. tanker *Ohio* hove into sight, supported on either side by other ships. We were soon passing on messages of congratulations to the crews of the ships which had managed to make harbour.

During one of my stints at Lascaris, a merchant ship moored at the Ras Hanżir wharf caught fire and was soon enveloped in flames. As I looked on, an officer turned on me and said scornfully, "We risk our lives to get food through to you and this is what you do to us in return!", by which remark he meant to say that this was a case of sabotage. I cannot, of course, state categorically that that was impossible but to this day, I feel fully convinced that sabotage could have been ruled out. It could easily have been an accident - as one of the men standing by suggested. There can be no question about the loyalty of the Maltese during the war. I was hurt by the officer's snide remark and could not stop myself retorting, "First of all you have no grounds for saying that and secondly I would like to remind you that the foodstuffs which you risk your lives to provide go also to British servicemen and their families with, however, one important difference: you get the whisky and the chocolate while we get candles and beans." And the story ended there.

In the middle of the summer of 1943, while stationed at Lascaris, I got to know that a message had just come in about a massive operation which was going to involve everyone from the

MEMORANDUM.

Malta Communications Staff will shortly have
to compete with probably the heaviest load of operational
traffic that has ever been dealt with by any headquarters.

2. I realise that conditions are far from ideal
and difficulties considerable. A large number of extra
Naval and Army staffs have arrived which means extensive
additional distribution; new cypher and coding personnel
have recently joined the staff and have had little time to
settle down. Ventilation is bad and the weather hot.
The ventilation I hope will be improved very shortly.

3. Nevertheless, we have somehow got to produce
the answer. Upon our ability to deal rapidly and
accurately with the vast volume of traffic that will be
passing in and out of Malta, will depend the success of
operations vitally affecting the war.

4. This means that every member of the
Communications Staff, whether W/T operator, Cypher Officer,
Signal Officer, Coder, Messenger, Typist, Signalman,
Transmitting Room Watch-keeper etc. etc. has to go all out
to achieve this. I am sure it will be done.

Commander.
Fleet Signal Officer.

6th. July, 1943.

Distribution

S.S.O.X
P.S.O.   3 copies.
Duty Signal Officer
    (and for Warrant Tel.)
Cypher Office
C.C.O.
J.R.A.
O.i/c Signal W/T
I.C. Communications Office
Auxiliary W/T Office

Memorandum from Commander Fleet Signal Officer issued a few days before the
invasion of Sicily.

(Courtesy J. Borg Bonello)

most high-ranking officer down to the lowliest messenger. On that same day we had three prominent visitors at Lascaris: Eisenhower, Montgomery and Admiral Cunningham. The War Room had never seen such frenetic activity before and we soon learned that the planned operation was none other than the invasion of Sicily.

I cannot say that I was ever on the verge of starvation in the same way as some sections of the civilian population were. Although I was not a regular serviceman, I could always count on that little bit extra. During the war I was courting the girl who later became my wife and during breaks, I used to pop over to see her and her family who then spent most of their time in the public shelter in Marsamxett. My future in-laws had a wireless set in

M. Geraldo who presented music programmes on the BBC dedicated to countries in the British Empire.
(Courtesy J. Borg Bonello)

the shelter and I was never tired of listening to the BBC, whether it was the news or *Geraldo and his Band*. This Geraldo used to dedicate his programmes to various countries in the Empire but never to Malta prompting me to write to him complaining about

Office of Commander in Chief,
Mediterranean Station,
MALTA.

13th July, 1943.

Dear Sir,

Thank you very much for your letter of 10th July in which you send your congratulations to us all in the Navy.

It is a great delight to me to be back in Malta, in which gallant island I have spent so much time, and even more so is it a joy for the Navy to be once again using Malta as a main base from which our sea activities against our enemies can be carried out.

There were months when the Navy was most anxious about your island and her people but thanks to the help given by our comrades of the Army and Royal Air Force, that period has come to an end and with the ever ready assistance of the people of Malta I am sure the island will soon regain its former active commercial position in the Mediterranean.

Yours faithfully
A.B. Cunningham

Mr. Joseph Borg Bonello.
149 Valley Road,
Birkirkara,
MALTA.

"There were moments when the Navy was most anxious about your island and her people".

(Courtesy J. Borg Bonello)

the omission. He wrote back to say that he would be more than willing to dedicate a programme to Malta provided that I would give him some indication of the kind of music preferred by the locals. With his letter in my hand I hurried to the *Times of Malta* premises where I was shown into Miss Cutajar Beck's office. On reading the letter Miss Cutajar Beck was as pleased as I was and she soon busied herself making up a list of classical and light music and later wrote a feature for the paper on the subject. The requested programmes were launched on the 23rd April 1943.

One of my hobbies during the war years was writing to prominent people, especially the main actors in the defence of Malta. It was not only the autographs that I hankered after but also the

---

ARCHBISHOP'S HOUSE,
WESTMINSTER, LONDON, S.W.I.

January 10th. 1941.

Dear Mr. Bonello,

Thank you for your letter of Dec. 11th. which has just reached me. May God keep you all in safety and grant us peace through justice and charity. We are confident that the courage of the people of Malta will do very much to secure victory and lasting peace.

I send you, and through you the Island of Malta, my best blessing and my congratulations on your bravery and endurance.

Yours devotedly in Christ,
A. Cardinal Kinsley
Archbishop of Westminster.

"We are confident that the courage of the people of Malta will do very much to secure victory and lasting peace."

(Courtesy J. Borg Bonello)

56

brief comments in answer to my request. Surprisingly, more often than not, these people obliged in spite of what must have been very busy schedules and I still have in my possession letters from, among others, Cardinal Hinsley, Air Marshal Park and Admiral Andrew Cunningham.

Unfortunately as time went by relations between us and the staff at Lascaris soured especially when we were made to do menial work such as sweeping and scrubbing floors. My colleagues and I decided to refuse to do such chores and I was delegated by the others to talk to the officer-in-charge. When I went up to him it was like preaching to a stone wall and his only reaction was to remind me that while we were refusing to sweep the

The striking group of Maltese coast watchers who were attached to the Royal Navy.
(Courtesy J. Borg Bonello)

IMPORTANT—This Enlistment Notice must be regarded as a personal document which is to remain in the possession of the person on whom it is served, until he has been "attested" or "exempted".

Enlistment Notice No. *15933/F-D*   Address:— *149 Vally Rd*

Index No. *5519.*   *B'Kara.*

NATIONAL SERVICE.
Enlistment Notice (Reg. No. 7).

In accordance with Regulation No. 7 of the National Service Regulations 1941, published under Government Notice No. 58, of the 19 February, 1941, the undermentioned Recruit of whom particulars are hereunder given, is required to report at

to Rupert 13th/8/43 at 9 a.m..

PARTICULARS OF RECRUIT.

Christian Name *Josf*   Surname *Borg Bonello*

Nickname —

Date of Birth *21 years.*

Trade *Coartracker.*

Father's name *Benjamin (C)*   Mother's name *Angela (C)*

Date *7/8/43,*   Height *5* ft. ins. *3.*

_____

REMARKS BY D. M. P.

floor, others were in the front-line facing death every minute. At this we resolved to resort to strike action; the strikers included a man who operated the high speed Morse machine. On the morrow we were marched under a naval escort to Fort St Angelo to appear before the Captain. I was the first to be called up and when I began to explain our stand, I was summarily silenced. I then respectfully asked to be heard but the Captain refused to have any explanation. I was thoroughly disconcerted and I blurted out, "I thought there was only one Hitler!" The Captain immediately said that I was to consider myself discharged as from that instant. My colleagues were called in one at a time and I am glad to say that we kept a united front.

We had scarcely stepped out of St Angelo before we were handed the notice to report for compulsory national service. I was instructed to go to the recruiting officer at Fra Diego Institute at Hamrun the following morning. There, Colonel Bartolo listened to my story, and seemed to sympathise and understand. Father Hersey, to whom I had recounted the strike episode, had apparently talked to the colonel before. I asked to be exempted from military service because I had to look after my aunt. My request was accepted on condition that I found employment within three months. I eventually began to work at St Francis Hospital, in Birkirkara, one of the hospitals which had been hastily improvised to deal with war casualties, and I remained involved in hospital work without a break until 1980.

My admiration and appreciation of the Boy Scout movement have never waned and I have also maintained my interest in trade union activity. In spite of the occasional problem, I have consistently admired the British.

FRANCIS X CORDINA

I was a sixteen year old student at the Lyceum and a member of the Boy Scout movement when Italy declared war on the Allies. My first job was in the Harbour section which was in charge of lighters but later was promoted to tally clerk. My duties involved going on board ships in harbour, for which I was paid a pound a day, a princely sum in those days considering that I was still in my 'teens. But more important than the money was the fact that working at the Marina where ships were unloading their cargo gave me the opportunity, now and then, to get some extra foodstuffs which were virtually impossible to come by in those days. An element of danger was always present, however, especially when I was on board during an air-raid on the harbour.

Travelling daily to and from Żebbuġ where we lived was something of a hardship to me especially when I knocked off in the early hours of the day and I had to walk all the way in pitch darkness by myself. Before moving to Żebbuġ, my family spent a brief period living at Hamrun with my aunt.

✝

IN LOVING MEMORY
OF MY SON 82 628

JOE CORDINA

SANITARY INSPECTOR
WHO LOST HIS LIFE
AS A RESULT OF ENEMY ACTION
ON THE 26ᴛʜ JUNE 1940.

Heart of Jesus most worthy of all praise
Have mercy on his soul.

HIS FATHER

Joe Cordina one of a number of passengers who were killed when the bus they were travelling in was hit by a bomb in June 1940.

(Courtesy FX Cordina)

On the 26th June 1940, barely fifteen days after Italy's declaration of war, tragedy struck my family. My twenty-one year old brother, Joe, had three days previously been promoted to sanitary inspector, and at the end of that day, having left his office in Senglea, walked to Vittoriosa to get some clothes from our home there. He boarded the bus which should have taken him to Hamrun where we had taken up residence as refugees. On arriving at Marsa Cross, the bus was struck by an incendiary bomb and caught fire. My brother managed to scurry out of the bus in time and took cover in a nearby store. The next instant the store received a direct hit and my brother was struck by a flying splinter which pierced his heart and left him lifeless. His body was removed to Ta' Bugeja Hospital. We were completely unaware of all this at the time and were waiting for him as usual. When hour after hour passed and my brother did not turn up, we rang up my father who was on night duty and told him that we were getting worried about Joe. My father came home at dawn and by that time word had got round about the Marsa Cross tragedy. My father, an elder brother and myself hurried to Ta' Bugeja Hospital. A harrowing scene met us there: in the main ward were rows and rows of corpses of the men who had perished in the bus and of others who had been killed in other incidents on the same day. Our hopes started to rise because we could not see my brother among those lifeless bodies. We then went into the mortuary and there the scene was similar. Mutilated and burned bodies were laid all round. My father immediately recognised my brother's among the other bodies and broke down weeping and it was only with great difficulty that we managed to tear him away from that place.

As we made our way home, we agreed not to tell my mother about the fate of our Joe; instead we told her that he had been injured and that for the moment no visitors were being allowed. To make sure that she would not suddenly decide to go and see him in hospital we moved to Żebbuġ and by the time my mother learned of Joe's real fate, he had been buried for many weeks.

HELEN CUELL

By 1940 I had completed my schooling and had found a job as a salesgirl with *Grech and Hicks*, shoe dealers, in their Valletta branch opposite St John's Co-Cathedral. One fine morning, on going to work as usual, I was shocked to discover that the shop and the buildings around it were reduced to mounds of rubble. I was therefore told to report for duty at the firm's other branch at Rabat and subsequently at the Hamrun outlet but when the supply of leather dried up, the firm started closing down their shops and discharged their employees. My sister Betty, two years my senior, was employed as a plotter at RAF Lascaris and it was she who suggested that I put in an application for a similar job. I was

A near miss for St. John's
Co-Cathedral.

called up for interview and employed. That was in June or July of 1942. There were some sixty Maltese girls employed as plotters at the time as well as a few British girls who had worked as artistes before the war and had decided to stay in Malta when the war began. Among the latter I remember two by name: Christina Ratcliffe who was later awarded some military decoration and Melita Rustidge who as *Auntie Melita* subsequently took part in Father Born's children's programmes on the Rediffusion.

We worked in a large hall with a large table on which was fixed a map of the Mediterranean area; we used the map for plotting the position of enemy planes flying towards the Maltese Islands and picked up by the radar installations. We wore headphones through which the Island's radar stations constantly relayed information concerning the number of planes, whether

Christina Ratcliffe

Operations Room, Lascaris

(Courtesy H. Cuell)

Plotters and other members of staff at RAF Lascaris. H. Cuell is second from left, top
row.

(Courtesy H. Cuell)

they were friendly or enemy craft, the height at which they were flying, the direction and whether they were fighters or bombers. The plots were marked by perspex arrows. From the adjacent Operations Room the RAF Controller marshalled the available fighters at Luqa and Ta' Qali, giving the order for pilots and crews to take off to intercept enemy aircraft before reaching the coasts of Malta. Also present in the Operations Room and directing the anti-aircraft batteries was the Army Controller, alerting the batteries about the approaching raiders.

We worked in shifts round the clock: 8.00 a.m. to 1.00 p.m., 1.00 p.m. to 6.00 p.m., 6.00 p.m. to 11.00 p.m. and 11.00 p.m. to 8.00 a.m. We used to live in Paola in those days and, as long as public transport was available, travelling to Valletta was not a problem but when buses stopped running, my sister and I had to walk all the way, as a rule going down to Marsa and proceeding by way of the harbour road. Curfew was in force and we had special passes to show if stopped by military patrols. We were often overtaken by air-raids on the way and we knew the location of every shelter by heart. At night roads used to be in pitch darkness and even the striking of a match was forbidden; besides that, the road lay through an area which was often under attack. Sometimes we used to hire a *karozzin* to take us to Valletta; the fare was five shillings (25 cents), a hefty sum when one remembers that our weekly wages were thirty shillings. I do not think we were doing that job for the money but because we felt that our country needed us. Our job was a very sensitive one and before we were employed we had to declare under oath that we would under no circumstance divulge any information seen or heard in the course of our duty.

On entering the plotting hall one day, I noted that the level of activity was much higher than usual. I was asked to leave my place at the table and move on to another task. The highest Army, Navy and Air Force authorities seemed to be all over the place and I could not understand what was going on, but eventually I learned that the Santa Marija convoy was about to enter the harbours.

In spite of the war social life for us girls was quite hectic, with lots of dances organised for every imaginable reason. The dances were usually held in the afternoon, as a rule between 3.00 and 6.00 p.m. and the venue was generally the Vernon Club, now occupied by the Central Bank. Malta at that time was literally packed with servicemen. If the walls of the Vernon Club could speak they would tell stories without number of the nice time we had there, in spite of the rigours of war. There was an abundance of nice boys. Air-raid warnings used to send us scurrying down to the shelter in the old railway tunnel and as soon as the all-clear sounded we would all be back on the dance floor. When the war began to recede from our shores, I began to frequent the Catholic club of the Knights of St Columba at Pieta`, where we also enjoyed every moment.

Hundreds of bombs fell on Paola and a large number of buildings were destroyed. Our house remained standing but it suffered a lot of damage so that we had to move out and go to live in a smaller house in the neighbourhood.

Like most Maltese we suffered the pangs of hunger, in fact, probably we suffered more because we could never stomach the Victory Kitchen meals with the possible exception of tinned tuna. We never got any food from service people; I think they were as badly off as the rest of us.

Looking back, I feel that the Operations Room was a key factor in the defence of Malta and although everyone contributed his or her share to the war effort, I think Malta owes its survival mainly to the RAF.

ANTON FARRUGIA

In the scholastic year 1939-40 I was a Fifth Former in the Seminary, Floriana but on the outbreak of hostilities, those of us who were, like me, boarders were sent to live with their parents. I remember that when I went back to Żebbuġ, refugees were already settling in in ever increasing numbers. The first air-raid caught us unprepared and many thought that the sound of gunfire was merely some military exercise in progress.

I cannot at this moment recall all the vicissitudes through which Seminary students passed in the war years but I clearly remember that when a bomb landed in the courtyard the Seminary building suffered great structural damage with not one window pane left unbroken. Premises had therefore to be found elsewhere. At first we moved to St Aloysius College in Birkirkara but, as time went on, more and more of the College rooms were given over to be used as hospital wards. Our next move was to the Old Oratory in Birkirkara, and later still we returned to our Floriana premises which we now had to share with a section of the Law Courts. Incidentally it may be of some interest here to say that it was at the Seminary that the trial of the Maltese, who were eventually to be sentenced to internment and exile, took place. Somehow I had at the time obtained a full list of all the Maltese involved and the autographs of many of them.

An old bicycle, probably dating from World War I, which was rusting away in a junk room at home, provided me with some means of transport between Żebbuġ and the Seminary. One morning as I was pedalling in the stretch of road between Żebbuġ and Attard on my way to the Seminary, a low flying *Messerschmitt* swooped in to strafe the anti-aircraft battery sited at the roadside. I threw myself flat on my face on the ground and escaped injury. I had another narrow escape when parachute land mines were released over Żebbuġ. On that occasion, while the air-raid was in progress I stole out of the shelter to watch the action. One of a stick of bombs exploded a few metres away from where I was standing and I was struck by a splinter which fortunately caused only a superficial wound to my right hand.

During the war, a large number of troops - from Britain, Mauritius and Basutoland - were billeted in and around Żebbuġ, and it was only natural for young men like myself to make friends with them. I had some friends among the soldiers manning the San Blas anti-aircraft battery and one day, I was invited along with another Maltese refugee, to attend a concert which was being held in the fort. We were enjoying the concert, laughing heartily at the jokes, when an alert sounded and the concert was brought to an abrupt end with all the soldiers and officers scurrying to action stations. A sergeant hurried us into a slit trench running between gun positions, but when we realised that the trench was packed with ammunition rounds, we decided to leave the "shelter" and return to Żebbuġ, accompanied all the way by the din made by the San Blas guns and the diving enemy aircraft.

Civilians had strict orders to take cover during air-raids but I never took kindly to shelters. Our house was very close to the police station and I knew some of the policemen on duty there so that during air-raids I would often walk across to chat with the men. It so happened that an old woman, Kunċett, lived next door to the police station and this woman, like me, had never seen the inside of a shelter. During an air-raid she would sit on a box by her doorstep, reciting the rosary, looking absolutely unruffled. One evening, a small bomb landed and exploded metres away from the police station but luckily none of us happened to be there on that particular occasion, not even Kunċett. Somebody up there......

A number of men from the Buffs regiment were billeted in Baron Azzopardi's palace near the *ta' l-Abbandunati* chapel in Żebbuġ. I had struck up a friendship with one of those soldiers, Tommy, a thoroughly well-informed and articulate young man who spoke very clear English. I was very interested in the English language in those days and I welcomed every opportunity to practise it. We used to meet on the village main square practically every evening, mixing with the crowds of villagers and refugees promenading until an air-raid warning would send everybody scurrying to the shelters.

FRANCES FAVA

Until its demolition by a direct hit, the old Auberge de France housed the Central School which as a sixteen year old girl I was attending at the outbreak of war. My father, a teacher, was appointed Protection Officer for Qormi, the village in which I lived with my family. I was enrolled with the ARP after undergoing a First Aid course. We were issued with a white armband carrying the letters ARP and our duties included patrolling the streets to check that doors were properly locked, and, after nightfall, to make sure that no lights were visible in any house.

On the day that Italy declared war, my father hurried to take down a picture of the Sacred Heart which used to hang on one of the bedroom walls and place it prominently on the sideboard in the dining room. That evening the family gathered around this picture, before which my father had lighted a candle, and recited the rosary. We could not tell what was in store for us and we were very apprehensive about the future. On the morrow, the 11th June, I was getting dressed when the sirens sounded the air-raid warning. The whole family ran downstairs and gathered around the holy picture and began to say our prayers. In the course of the day, the refugees began to arrive from the Cottonera region. We took in some people for the night, and spread bedding on the floor for them to sleep on. Confusion reigned on that first day of the war; many people did not bother to cook the usual meal. Our evening meal on that day, I remember, consisted of corned beef.

A Rediffusion loudspeaker, set up in St Francis Square, used to attract crowds of people who gathered round to hear the latest news. Qormi did not experience the heavy bombing which other places in Malta, such as Cottonera, suffered but the raid which took place on the 10th February 1942 still stands out in my memory. That day, the feast of St Paul, was a school holiday and I was having a siesta in the afternoon. At about five, there was an air-raid warning followed almost immediately by the all-clear. A few minutes later there was another warning and I hurried downstairs only stopping to put a jacket on. When I stepped on the landing, a couple of roofing stone slabs came crashing down. One of the slabs landed on my foot and for the following two and a half months, I had to go around with it in plaster. The fanlight over the door was wrenched from its place by the blast and hurled against a bookcase in which my father, then in charge of the circulating library, had stored away hundreds of books. The back door was also blown in by the blast but miraculously the holy picture on the sideboard was not touched, nor was the lit candle put out. We were terror-stricken and rushed out of the house and into the nearest shelter. We later learned that during that raid, the school had also received a direct hit, destroying the school chapel which served as an emergency hospital.

To me the war is synonymous with hunger, poverty and suffering. Fortunately people showed solidarity in those difficult times and those who were comparatively well off were always ready to share with those who were in need. With so many bakeries in Qormi, we always managed to have an adequate supply of bread, though of course one had to pay black-market prices for it. Once my father paid forty pounds for a sack of flour and my mother used to make spaghetti for the family.

The war was the cause of much social mixing between the refugees and the locals and I think that on the whole this mixing was beneficial, but I am afraid the locals picked up a number of undesirable habits from the refugees...

LUCY GENOVESE

Shortly after the war started, my mother - a widow - with the nine of us children left Sliema as refugees to go and live in one room in Rabat. Very soon my mother could not stand the crowded conditions any longer and we went back to Sliema to live with my sister. At first life went on more or less normally until a family argument led to my mother going back to our house in St Rita Street. On the very day that we moved, tragedy struck the family. During the night there was an air-raid warning and my mother took my brothers and sisters to a nearby shelter. Three of us, however, decided to stay at home: my twenty year old brother Ninu, my sister Mary aged seventeen and myself then aged sixteen. Even now I cannot remember the events of that night except that I was sleeping in bed when it all happened. I woke up suddenly to find myself buried under the rubble. I heard my sister cry out "Mum!" and my brother screaming. I blurted out, "Tell them I'm here," and then, after a few minutes' silence, I heard lots of voices, among them my mother's, shouting. ARP personnel and

Mary and Alex Grech

(Courtesy L. Genovese)

a number of sailors had come to give assistance. I was hauled out by Father Born, OP, and I was made to stand but I collapsed and was rushed to hospital in an ambulance. When I collapsed, I heard someone say, "Poor Lucy, she's broken her spine; it would have been better for her if she had died."

Throughout all this, and after arriving at the Blue Sisters Hospital, I was fully conscious of what was going on around me. A doctor came to look me over; my body was covered with bruises. At about three in the morning, my brothers and sisters came to see me. They were all asking me how I felt and I told them that I did not feel any pain. Then they told me that my sister Mary had been killed at home and that Ninu had multiple fractures; at the news I broke down in uncontrollable weeping. I then learned that my brother Alex, fourteen, was dead too; he had gone down to the shelter barefoot and my mother had sent him back to get his shoes because he had a cold. The bomb had exploded just as he stepped into the house.

I need hardly say that this was a terribly hard blow for my mother. For many nights after this episode, she would wake up with a start and scream, "They are killing my children." It is a miracle that she kept her sanity. When she went to see a psychiatrist, he gently told her, "If weeping could get your children back, I would be the first to weep with you; you've got to get over it somehow." Time eventually exercised its healing powers and she got better but to the end of her life she was constantly mentioning Mary and Alex.

Our family was not the only one to be struck by tragedy on that fateful night. Twenty three people were killed in that raid.

My stay in hospital was quite brief; I was discharged after a week though it was a long time before I got over the shock and the backaches. My brother Ninu's stay at the Blue Sisters' was longer because his fractures were complicated. As you may imagine, after that experience, we were always the first to take cover. My mother got into the habit of spending most of the day sitting on a stool at the shelter's entrance and passing sailors, who had got used to her habits, would playfully whisper "Air-raid warning" to her at which she would grab the stool and dive into the shelter.

JOE MICALLEF GRIMAUD

Two years before completing my secondary schooling which would have taken me up to the Senior Oxford Certificate - then the passport to a teaching career - I dropped out and began to look for a job. My main reason in doing that was to avoid being called up for national service, because the rule was that if you had an important job, you would be exempted from having to join up. A friend of the family, an architect who was "in the know" and knew what important jobs were available, urged me to apply for a post in the Public Works Department. I took his advice and was soon given a job as overseer in the construction of shelters in the

Msida and Pieta` area. My duties consisted mainly in checking the volume of excavated rock, surveying, checking attendance, effecting payment to the labourers and generally keeping track of the work in progress. After about a month on the job, I met our friend, the architect, and asked him about the chances of my being called up. "None", he said. When I confessed to him that I had left school simply to avoid the draft, he strongly advised me to go back to school to complete my studies.

After some soul searching, I decided to follow the architect's counsel and in November 1940, I went back to school. Six months later, in April 1941, I was asked to report to the engineer-in-charge at the Power Station who informed me that I was being offered the post of writer, which post seemed to me to be more worthwhile than that of overseer and timekeeper. I took the job and congratulated myself that I needed not worry about military service. I was soon proved wrong, however, because in March 1942 I received the draft notice informing me that I was to report for the medical and then to proceed to Fort Ricasoli. I opted for service in the RMA and after a two month gunnery course, I was attached to the 3rd LAA (Bofors) Regt., RMA. The 15th Battery in which I was to serve had just been formed and had only one gun which was used for training purposes. The headquarters of the 15th Battery was at Marsaxlokk.

I quickly learnt all there was to know about the Bofors and I soon got a promotion. My duties now consisted of training recruits in gunnery practice. By this time we had got some guns, with our first Bofors being mounted in a new gun position on the heights of Delimara. The gun crew of this first Bofors was made up of a number of keen youngsters, myself among them, all eager to see action. Fate however decreed that a tragic episode was in store for us.

One evening, when the sun was setting and bathing the rocky heights of Delimara with a warm red light, the gun crew were standing to, a routine exercise in getting ready for action. For the exercise, live ammunition was used, but No. 4 (the man who would normally lay and fire the gun) had to put into operation the safety catch so that the gun would not fire. While we were engaged in this exercise, a cheerful young man who was on sentry duty and therefore not part of the gun crew, was looking intently at us, singing as usual, as we went about our routine.

The gun crew had got to that part of the exercise where the gun is traversed, elevated and depressed as if following a target. The procedure was that when No. 7 and No. 8 both called out "on target", the sergeant gave the order to fire. At the very instant that the sergeant cried "Fire!" the gun happened to be pointing directly at the sentry and our No. 4 stepped on the firing pedal without operating the safety catch. Tragedy followed. The first victim of our brand new gun was to be one of our own men.

That episode which marked the baptism of fire for the 15th LAA Battery RMA was soon to be followed by another tragic mishap in the village of Marsaxlokk. At about four in the afternoon, in the course of an air-raid, a dog-fight between fighters was raging over our heads. Our cooks were busy preparing our supper of tea and sardines when one of them got it into his head to leave his post and go outside to watch the dog-fight from the middle of the village square just opposite the parish church. He seemed to be spellbound as he followed the action, now turning one way, now the other. All of a sudden someone noticed that the man, a certain Vella, was sprawled on the ground holding his back. One of our men rushed out and as he reached the injured man's side, he started screaming for help. The dying man had been struck by a stray bullet. Someone ran to fetch the parish priest who was soon on the scene to administer the last rites.

So there we were, most of us barely out of our teens, witnesses to two tragic deaths which should never have happened. Two young lives were thrown away - an experience which still haunts me fifty years later...

JOHN A MIZZI

My childhood was dominated by the threatening clouds of war. In 1935, at ten years of age, I remember myself standing before the family wireless set, listening to the news that

Issue of gas masks to children of Hamrun.

(Photo W.J. Jones)

Mussolini was making attempts to grab Abyssinia. Malta was one of the places that the Fascists claimed to be Italian territory and in their numerous mass rallies placards with *Malta - Mare Nostrum* were paraded regularly. Among the Maltese there was a general fear that in the event of war breaking out, Malta would be one of the first targets.

Before the war started, manoeuvres were held routinely by the services. At night searchlights would sweep the dark sky to search for British planes flying around to provide practice for the searchlight detachments. During the day, ARP personnel used to give demonstrations to the general public about the use of gas-masks and about precautions in case of aerial bombing.

At that time Malta was split into two factions, one uncompromisingly pro-Italian and the other fanatically pro-British, both sides showing their allegiance with the same kind of outward

PRAYERS FOR AN ALLIED VICTORY

THE MIRACULOUS CRUCIFIX JUST OUTSIDE THE GATE OF THE OLD CAPITAL OF MALTA, MDINA

THE PILGRIMAGE AT MENSIA, WHICH TOOK PLACE AT THE SAME TIME AS THE PILGRIMAGE AT RABAT.

ARCHDEACON MGR. CANON JOSEPH APAP BOLOGNA, Ph.D., J.C.D., S.T.D., DOM PREL. TO HIS HOLINESS THE POPE, DELIVERING HIS ADDRESS TO THE PILGRIMS, URGING THEM TO PRAY FOR PEACE WITH JUSTICE.

THE GREAT CROWD AT THE SAQQAJA, RABAT, ON SUNDAY.

Malta's Reply To Rome Demonstrations

SCENES DURING COUNTER-DEMONSTRATIONS ON SATURDAY, IN VALLETTA AS A REPLY TO THE ANTI-MALTESE DEMONSTRATIONS HELD IN ROME. (LEFT) A SCENE IN THE STREETS. (CENTRE) POLICE GUARDING THE ITALIAN CONSULATE (RIGHT) THE REMAINS OF THE TABLET TO DR. FORTUNATO MIZZI IN SDA. ZECCA.

The *Times of Malta* report on Mussolini's speech from Palazzo Venezia.

manifestation that we associate nowadays with football supporters. Families and friends were often split by these allegiances.

On the morning of the 10th June 1940 word went round that Mussolini was to address the nation from the palace in Piazza Venezia in Rome; in the evening, most Maltese gathered around public loudspeakers and private wireless sets heard Mussolini with his usual bombast and histrionics declare that Italy was at war with Britain and France.

I was roused from sleep early on the following morning by the sound of gunfire and ran up to the rooftop. Clusters of white puffs dotted the sky left by the exploding anti-aircraft rounds and, like so many tiny specks, were a number of airplanes flying at a very high altitude. Columns of smoke and dust were rising from the harbour area and Luqa airfield. The monitor HMS *Terror*, moored in Msida Creek, opened up with its deafening guns. On that day the war claimed its first victims, civilians and soldiers, in Valletta, Gzira, Cottonera and the Porte des Bombes area.

The presentation of *Faith* by the RAF to the people of Malta on 3 September, 1943.

(Photo W.J. Jones)

Fleur-de-Lys road, where I lived, was the scene of what looked like a mass exodus with hundreds of people carrying their belongings on every kind of transport imaginable, from prams to lorries. This exodus went on during the days that followed, while high-flying Italian warplanes flew overhead, usually coming in towards nightfall. For the first time, we saw a British fighter, the *Gladiator*, taking off to challenge the enemy aircraft; the *Gladiators* had been brought over in crates and assembled in the Hal Far workshops. The first three *Gladiators* were given the names of *Faith*, *Hope* and *Charity*.

Our house was provided with a "shelter" built by the Public Works Department; this consisted of one of the rooms having its roof reinforced by scantlings. It was not long before it was realised that this sort of shelter was ineffectual. Stuck to the front door of our house was a notice saying SHELTER, and whenever

Before shelters were dug out in the rock people took cover in rooms which had their roofs reinforced by scantlings; drawing by Guido Lanfranco.

there was an air-raid neighbours would flock into our house, crowd into the "shelter" and spend most of the time reciting the rosary and other devotions.

As time went by, proper bomb-proof shelters were excavated out of the living rock and people felt safer, and soon life seemed to be returning to normal. I went back to my school, the Lyceum, which had as its premises the building now occupied by Lombard Bank in Republic Street, Valletta. I was then aged fifteen and I could follow the news pretty well. France had fallen and Britain was under constant hammering from the Luftwaffe, but we never doubted that Britain would carry the day in the end. That certainty was somewhat shaken in mid-January 1941 when the aircraft carrier *Illustrious* was made the target of a blitz by *Stukas* and *Ju 88*'s flying over from airfields in Sicily, where the Italian forces had recently been bolstered up by the arrival of German units. Apparently Mussolini's men did not have much stomach for soldiering and his German allies thought it prudent to reinforce the Southern Italy front. Be that as it may, on that memorable January day, the Luftwaffe devastated the Three Cities and parts of Valletta but could not stop the *Illustrious* from giving them the slip and sailing out of the Grand Harbour, bound for Alexandria, under her own steam.

The frequency of German air-attacks increased rapidly, the targets being generally the airfields at Luqa, Ta' Qali and Hal Far, the last-named being the base for Royal Navy torpedo planes which were proving to be a veritable thorn in the side of Axis shipping. The submarine flotilla accomplished much useful work from its base in Marsamxett harbour and in March 1941 *Hurricane* fighters were brought over in one of the convoys. In the meantime Malta was being subjected to incessant bombardment, and food supplies were running dangerously low leading to even stricter rationing. With fuel supplies getting scarcer and scarcer, public transport operated for a limited period every day and the horse-drawn omnibus, with its two long benches facing each other, made its re-appearance on the streets. We attended school regularly, lessons only interrupted by air-raids when we would be led to a nearby shelter.

The second half of 1941 saw a lull in the bombardment as German forces were rushed to the Russian front. Evenings became more relaxed; villagers and refugees took out their chairs on the pavement and chatted while children played in the streets, then, of course, devoid of traffic. I enjoyed darting around on my roller skates which incidentally I have still got. When off duty, pilots often came down to Birkirkara from their billets in Rabat and we older boys made friends with them; they were only two or three years older than we were. Some of those friendships lasted for many years after the war, and I have on many occasions both in Malta and in England met those pilots.

On the morning of the 16th July 1941, I was rudely awakened by the sound of heavy gunfire. This time it was not the anti-aircraft guns that were being called into action but the heavy coastal defence batteries. That was the day in which intrepid Italian E-Boat units pressed an attack on the Grand Harbour. This daring exploit failed, and practically all the naval units and the supporting air-cover were wiped out.

The Luftwaffe increased its presence in Sicily in November 1941 and the bombing by day and by night started again. German fighters swooped low and machine-gunned everything in sight. The constant state of alert began to have its toll; men were going to work half asleep. Weather conditions also took a turn for the worse, with a constant drizzle and low clouds. Sometimes I wonder how, through all this, we still attended school regularly although I must say that lessons were more often than not disrupted. At the sound of an air-raid warning we used to troop out of the school and make our way to the public shelter near the Palace and at the all clear we were normally allowed to go home, usually walking there all the way. Once while we were taking cover in the Palace shelter the building received a direct hit. The explosion made the shelter shudder and we could easily tell that the explosion was in the immediate vicinity, which we confirmed when we emerged from the shelter and saw that a section of the Palace was in ruins and that a number of dead were lying on the ground.

The months of February, March and April of 1942 were the most terrible as raid followed raid with fearful regularity through the day. During that period I left school and got a job in the Birkirkara Protection Office having as my main duties the registration of people for rationing purposes, distribution of the coupon books and making the necessary arrangements with grocers. I was soon transferred to the Qormi office and more often than not had to walk all the way there and back. The road to Qormi took me past the anti-aircraft battery at Fleur-de-Lys which seemed to be engaged in action all the time as enemy planes often passed overhead on their way to dropping their loads on Ta' Qali or Luqa, sometimes skimming the rooftops and opening up with machine-gun fire. I was often terrified and years after the war was over, I would wake up with a start in the middle of the night dreaming that I was taking cover behind a field wall with bombs raining down and exploding around me.

In mid-1942 Victory Kitchens were set up to cope with the food shortage; the meals consisted generally of potatoes, beans and mutton or goat meat. Vitamin deficiency, the result of the poor nutrition levels, manifested itself in scabies. When Lord Gort arrived in Malta to take over the governorship from General Dobbie, plans for surrendering the Island were apparently being considered, but the former on sensing the spirit of the defenders resolved to hold on until the last cartridge and the last morsel of food. Intelligence reports that gliders were assembling in Sicily confirmed that plans for an invasion by Axis seaborne and paratroop divisions were well in hand and in Malta, the invasion was expected to take place any moment. Reinforcements to the garrison came in the shape of more *Hurricanes* and, for the first time, *Spitfires.* The German raiders were getting more and more daring and destroyed several of the newly arrived fighters on the ground as well as ships moored in the harbours. On the 15th of April, King George VI awarded the George Cross to the people of Malta.

Four months had barely passed when the Santa Marija convoy dropped anchor in the harbour and people breathed a sigh of relief. At about this time I was playing with a friend of mine when this friend decided to go and hide behind a field wall. Nobody paid much attention when a small explosion was heard; such explosions were commonplace ever since the Germans had got into the habit of dropping "butterfly" anti-personnel devices. Members of my friend's family later came to ask if I had seen him and I said that the last time I had seen him was when he disappeared behind the wall. His body was soon discovered, lifeless, killed by one of those devices. Sadly, with violent death having become an everyday experience, he was soon forgotten by the rest of us.

From his base in El Alamein, General Montgomery attacked and swept aside the German and Italian divisions in Libya and the Mediterranean was opened up for convoys. Tripoli fell to the Allies and within days American troops and aircraft began to assemble in Malta in readiness for the impending invasions of Tunisia and, later on, Sicily. The wind of victory was beginning to be felt, when poliomyelitis suddenly struck. Cinemas which had opened their doors throughout the war, were now to close down as a precaution. Simultaneously, a typhoid epidemic killed off a large number of people who had survived starvation and bombardment..

By the time that the war had come to an end, my boyhood was over and I had become a man and I found myself in a new world.

PAWLU SALIBA

Our house was in the Manderaggio in Valletta but after the first air-raids we moved to our shop under the Marsamxett bastions and lived there through the war. My married sister, with her children, came to live with us. As a protection we filled up a lot of sugar bags with sand and piled them up in front of our shop. At first, we were the only people living in that part of Valletta but gradually others began to excavate shelters in the solid rock base of the bastions and we decided to do likewise. I was then fourteen years of age and quite capable of handling a pick and shovel and did my part of the digging, but we were not used to that sort of work and progress on the shelter was very slow and my father had to get some proper workmen to finish it off. The monitor HMS *Terror*, a veritable floating battery bristling with guns, was moored across the water, a few hundred metres away and when her guns opened up the ear splitting thunder shook and rocked our shelter.

The destroyer flotilla had its moorings in the Marsamxett harbour and the large number of sailors kept the grog shops on the waterfront very busy. We were never short of custom and sailors would drop in at every opportunity.

A Bofors gun was mounted a short distance away, near the police station, and the gun crew was made up of Maltese soldiers. One day the Maltese gun crew was relieved and a Scottish detachment took over. On the following day the gun site received a direct hit and most of the men were killed. As usual, whenever there was an explosion in the sea in our vicinity, I used to take the boat out and collect the dead fish floating on the surface; that day I saw a badly mutilated body floating and recognised it as that of the Scottish sergeant.

Many wartime incidents come to mind. One of my cousins was in his father's store together with a Gozitan friend, when a parachute mine exploded nearby. The two of them were buried

Valletta boys playing at sailors during the war.

under the masonry and we managed to extricate them alive but the Gozitan died within a few hours. I also remember the day when Italian E-Boats attempted to force their way into the Grand Harbour.

Before the war I used to attend the school attached to the Church of St Augustine, but when war broke out the school closed down, although the church kept functioning normally and I carried on in my role as an altar boy. The church was patronised by the few people who stayed in Valletta. With some friends I used to spend long hours playing with a wooden plane which I had made; the plane would be run up and down a long wire attached to the top of the bastion, while we would try to shoot it down. We once built a small "turret" from which we used to run up flags just like the sailors used to do on their ships. One day while we played in this fashion an air-raid warning sounded, and for the first time ever, my mother called me and insisted that I go with her to the shelter. We had just got inside the shelter when a bomb landed near the "turret" shattering it into smithereens; you can see the scars on the bastion to this day.

Colonel de Wolff was in the habit of coming down to Marsamxett every day to take the ferry to Sliema and before boarding the boat he used to stop for a few minutes near us, we would "present arms' and after giving us the salute he would proceed on his way. He seemed to enjoy our little performance and sometimes he gave us a tin of cheese.

A little later I got a job as a boy messenger and then a telephone operator. I was drafted into the Army in 1945 when the war was practically over. I spent one and a half years in the RASC and then returned to civilian life.

The food shortage did not really affect us at all because before the war my father ran a grocery shop, and when he closed down the business we had a lot of foodstuffs stored away. The only commodity we ran short of was bread and this problem was solved by turning to the black market.

Auberge de France
(right) before it was
destroyed by enemy
action. *(Photo W.J. Jones)*

JANE SPITERI

When, in 1939, Germany declared war I was a sixteen-year-old Fifth Former in the Higher Secondary School which occupied part of the palatial building then called "Ta' Bugeja" in Hamrun and which now houses the Social Welfare Centre. In October 1939 the school was transferred to Birkirkara. We were then living in Hamrun but within a few days of Italy's declaration of war we went over to Żejtun where my aunt had a spacious and comfortable house near the parish church. Thousands of refugees from the Cottonera region came flocking to the village, changing

Auberge de France after the Easter Monday 1941 raid.

(Photo W.J. Jones)

overnight the pattern of daily life for the locals. Schools closed down and students had a break from the grind of tests and examinations. We were due to take the Oxford school certificate examinations for which we had been preparing hard, and our parents had already paid the registration fees when the examinations were cancelled and the fees refunded. When schools opened again in October 1940 we had to start all over again; I was now attending St Louis Central School in the Auberge de France which stood on the site now occupied by the headquarters of the General Workers Union. The first thing we used to do when we met for morning assembly was to look around to see whether any of our colleagues were missing. One of my schoolfriends from Tarxien died when the shelter she was in received a direct hit killing most of the occupants; we learned about the tragedy the morning after.

I was terribly frightened every time the air-raid warning siren went and you could count on me being the first to take shelter, yet I was never absent from school. With the constant interruptions from air-raids, lessons were rather erratic. When taking cover in the shelter, we never had lessons; instead we would do a bit of praying, a bit of chatting and singing, recount experiences and crack jokes. Easter Monday of 1942 was a school holiday. That was the day in which the Auberge de France was wiped out when a stick of bombs landed on the place and we could not help imagining the tragedy that would have struck us if we had been at school. After that, I stopped going to school since we had taken our examinations before the Easter holidays. Then started the anxious waiting for the postman to deliver the envelope with the results!

Those weeks were the most critical in the whole siege. Provisions were running dangerously low and the Victory Kitchens were launched to mitigate the situation. Clothes and shoes were as scarce as food and we had to make do with sandals made of cloth uppers and rope soles. With kerosene being strictly rationed, people took to cooking on the traditional *kenur*, a kind of wood-burning stone-stove, using fuel usually obtained from among the rubble of bombed buildings. Smokers used to improvise "tobacco" by drying and shredding vine leaves, sometimes even potato skins. People spent the night in shelters sleeping on mattresses consisting of straw-filled sacks, which used to end up wet through with the damp and had to be taken up to dry out in the sun the morning after.

For light we used to make oil-lamps, usually improvised out of an empty milk tin half-filled with kerosene or oil, with a cotton string for a wick; I must have read scores of books by the light of such lamps!

One day I was asked to enrol as a helper in the Victory Kitchens. I was appointed supervisor of a newly opened Kitchen in St Mary Street, Żejtun. I was later transferred to the Kitchen in St Gregory Street where I was responsible for preparing about a thousand meals a day. When the St Marija convoy reached the Island we had barely a few days' provisions left. With the arrival of the convoy the situation immediately took a turn for the better with, simultaneously, a decline in the frequency of air-raids.

However, when things seemed to be looking up, a new threat appeared. A bomb which landed in the Balzan area broke a sewage pipe which resulted in the contamination of drinking water and in a few days a typhoid epidemic was raging, causing the death of hundreds of people.

With the closing down of Victory Kitchens, some of the supervisors, including myself, were posted in the head office at Balzan. I was soon struck down by the sickness and for a time it was touch and go for me and I seemed to be heading for an appointment with my Maker. The last sacraments were administered to me. On the same day, I received the letter of appointment as teacher. A few days later, I was out of danger and I slowly recovered. On the 8th of September 1943, the day on which Italy surrendered, I took my first walk outside and a week later, I took up teaching at the primary school in Żejtun.

M'GHANDEKX...

Din ███ magħmula **għalik**, aqraha, ftakarha, għaddiha l-ewwelnett lil ħbiebek u l-iktar ħaġa meħtieġa fuq kollox hija li

M'GHANDEKX TAGHTI WIDEN LIX-XNIGHAT
Inti jkollok l-aħbarijiet kollha li jinteressawk, tajbin jew ħżiena, fil-gazzetti. Kull ħaġ'oħra li tisma' la temminhiex, b'mod speċjali aħbarijiet li jqajmu l-biża'. It-tieni ħaġa li għandek tiftakar hija li

M'GHANDEKX IXXERRED INFORMAZZJONIJIET
Inti tista' tkun taf li fil-għalqa ta' ħdejn il-ġnien tiegħek hemm moħbi bi ħżunija kanun kontra l-attakki mill-ajru. Iżda din mhix raġuni li għaliha inti għandek tgħid lil ħaddieħor; jista' jasal f'widnejn min ma għandux ikun jaf b'din il-ħaġa. Inti tista' tkun taf bil-movimenti ta' xi wieħed mill-bastimenti Ingliżi tal-gwerra, iżda żomm dak li taf għalik. Jekk din l-informazzjoni tixxerred ma' ħafna bnadi, dan jista' jikkaġuna t-telfien tal-ħajja ta' bosta nies.

LA TITLIFX RASEK
Fi kliem ieħor, uri wiċċ daħkani. Xejn ma jiswa billi inti kull fejn tmur turi wiċċ ta' buri; b'hekk tagħmel ħafna ħsara lil nies li jibżgħu mix-xejn u li mhumiex bħalek. Għaldaqshekk jekk qatt taqa' xi bomba fit-trieq tiegħek, ħaġa li ma tantx tista' tkun, uri ruħek daħkani.

LA TISMAX MINN NIES LI JHOBBU JBEŻŻGHU
Inti għandek dejjem issib madwarek nies li jħobbu ibeżżgħu. Gib ruħek magħhom bħalli kieku kellek tiltaqa' ma' kas tal-ġidri- Itlaq iġri. Il-għadu iħobb ixerred ix-xnigħat. Biċċa mill-kampanja tiegħu kienet li jqajjem il-biża' fostna, u huwa jibqa' jittanta l-istess ħaġa għalkemm qata' jiesu.

LA THALLIX ILLI FOLOL TA' NIES JINGABRU
Il-Pulizija għandha x'tagħmel biżżejjed. Jekk tara n-nies jinġemgħu u ma hemm ebda raġuni li tiffolla magħhom ibqa' sejjer. Fi ftit kliem ilħaq xogħlok.

U fuq kollox la tinsiex il-qawl ta' żmien l-1914-1918. **Kun fommok sieket, kun bil-għaqal, widnejn il-ghadu qeghdin jisimghuk.** Issa imxi 'l quddiem, agħmel ix-xogħol tiegħek u la tinkwietax ruħek.

"Do not believe all you hear..... Do not spread rumours...... Do not panic.....Do not let others scare you ... Avoid crowds...."

(Courtesy J. Borg Bonello)

90

III. Housewives

GUZA BONDIN

My husband whom I married a few weeks before the war started was a gunner in the 1st Coast Regiment RMA. As a young man, he used to help his father who was a fireworks maker. He got very little money for his pains and so when we decided to get married, he joined the Army as a volunteer, starting on a weekly wage of nine shillings (45c) in the first week rising to ten shillings (50c) as from the second week. Of course things were much cheaper in those days and a couple of shillings would go a long way. My husband was stationed at Fort St Rocco overlooking Rinella Creek and he used to come home for a couple of hours and then go back to his post. On the 10th of June, the very same day on which Mussolini declared war, he was due to spend his first night at home since our marriage. We had settled down for the night when, at eleven, he received orders to go back to his station at once. When he protested that he did not have any transport, he was curtly told to walk and he had no alternative but to obey orders.

A couple of days later, that is after the first bombing raids, refugees started moving to Zurrieq from the harbour area and getting accommodation of sorts in the houses of the villagers. My sister-in-law took in two families who packed themselves into two rooms as best they could. I rented my house out to a family from Paola and went to live with my father.

Our first child, a daughter, was born in October 1941 but her life was to be cut short by enemy action when she was barely nine months old. I shall never forget the events of the 23rd of July, 1942. On that day I was due to get the baby's milk ration from the grocery in St Michael Street; I took my daughter along with me and as usual I intended to stop to spend a few minutes at my father's shoemaker's shop. It so happened that on that particular occasion the shop was closed because my father was paying a visit to Captain Parnis England commanding the Special Constables. The time was around half past five in the afternoon and as I turned the corner, I heard a deafening explosion. In the morning a number of delayed action bombs had been dropped over the village, and this must have been one of them. I squeezed myself against a door and covered my child with my body to pro-

The war memorial at Zurrieq. On the left a woman weeps over the lifeless body of her child.

(Photo N. Genovese)

tect her from the stones that were raining down. In spite of my efforts my child was struck in the head by a flying splinter. All I can remember is that some ARP people came and took the baby from my arms. She was unconscious and she died just as we took her home. I was later told that she had died from the effects of the blast from the explosion. Other people died in the same incident; there were two priests, Father Joe Cuschieri and Father Joe Zammit, the village apothecary, Joe Saydon and others whose names I cannot recall after all these years. The cursed bomb had lodged in a small garden near the church and began to tick away loudly. Two young girls went to peep to see where the ticking was coming from and at the instance in which they raised their heads above the wall, the bomb exploded, killing them on the spot. Seven people lost their lives on that day and several more were injured.

The lifeless body of my daughter was taken to hospital. My husband was on duty on that day and I had no idea as to his whereabouts. He heard about our daughter's death from my brother who was also a soldier. I never saw my child again. Some relatives went to the hospital to see to her burial. All I know is that she lies buried at the Addolorata Cemetery but I have no idea as to where her grave is. I could not afford to bring her body home because hiring a hearse and buying a coffin would have been beyond my means. On that day I lost not one child but two because at the time of the incident I was seven months into my second pregnancy and I miscarried. That trauma was the cause of another four miscarriages in succession.

I also lost an uncle through enemy action. He died as he was leaving his house to go to Mass when a bomb brought the building down.

Such were the first years of my married life. I kept my sanity because of the support I got from my relatives.

ĊENSA BONNICI

I lived at Senglea and was employed in the local health clinic as a nurse with ten years' experience. In addition to myself, there was the doctor in charge, Dr Jaccarini and two sanitary inspectors, Mr Imbroll and Mr Soler. Later on we were joined by another nurse, Dolly Barber. We also had a maid who served us with food issued by the Government. My father and mother were both dead and I was, as yet, unmarried. Some relatives of mine also lived in Senglea but when we started having air raids, they moved to a safer district and asked me to join them but I preferred to stay behind with Dr Jaccarini who was like a second father to me.

In the first days of the war practically all the residents of Senglea moved out of their town but most of them gradually trickled back over the following few months and when the *Illustrious* drew the enemy's fire, they were caught on the wrong foot. In that blitz, several inhabitants lost their lives and many more were injured; many of the houses were reduced to rubble and the entrances to some of the shelters were blocked with fallen masonry leaving the occupants buried alive. Immediately after

Cardinal Spellman visits Senglea on April 15 1943.

(Photo W.J. Jones)

the *Illustrious* attack, there was a second exodus from town but Dr Jaccarini and a few others including myself decided to stick to our post. We had special permission to spend the night in the Admiral's rock-cut shelter in the Dockyard, a privilege also extended to the parish priest, Fr Manuel Brincat. Our services were called upon frequently both inside and outside the Dockyard.

Fr. Emanuel Brincat, Senglea archpriest during the war.

I had almost forgotten the barmaids who were understandably reluctant to leave the harbour area with its myriads of sailors and servicemen; the bombs did not scare them off and after each raid they would emerge from the shelters and take up where they had left off.

We were bombed out of our clinic three times and each time we would find another building. We collected our pay packet from the Head Office in Valletta, going there on the harbour ferry or, when the service was suspended, getting one of the boatmen to take us across. We used to be terrified when we were caught in an air raid while making the crossing.

I first met my future husband at the Dockyard where he was employed. At first he and I would exchange glances whenever we met until one fine day, in January 1941, he came to Senglea and proposed to me. Two months later we had our engagement and in November of the following year we were married. There was a shortage of anything you would care to mention and it is hard to-day to imagine the difficulties I went through before I could get a decent dress and a pair of shoes for the wedding. Anyhow on the appointed day we repaired to the vestry, which was the only part of the church that was still standing, for the wedding ceremony. As we made our entry and proceeded to the altar, a relative of the parish priest played the *Ave Maria* on the harmonium. There was a small congregation which disappeared into thin air when an air raid alert sounded just as the officiating priest was about to begin the service leaving us, the happy couple, the two witnesses and the priest alone in the vestry. The witnesses were two of my brothers-in-law who had come from outlying villages in a *karozzin.*

The wedding reception was a party in name only; there was just one cake, baked and presented to us by a neighbour, a few cups of cocoa, a bottle of Vermouth given as a wedding present by my husband's uncle and a bottle of rum which my husband had bought from a serviceman and which was liberally mixed with water to make it go further. After our marriage we went to live at Paola, renting a half demolished house with every window pane broken and with canvas keeping out the wind and the rain.

I kept my job for some three months; I was posted at the Tarxien clinic where the doctor in charge was Dr Paul Schembri. But by then I was on the way to starting a family, and I thought that the family should have my undivided attention and so I resigned my post.

LUCY CHIRCOP

In 1940 I was a married woman with six children, living at Paola. My husband was a Petty Officer in the Royal Navy on duty overseas. I kept a small shop, selling cloth, crockery and giftware. During air raids we used to take shelter in the Hypogeum at Hal Saflieni, a short walk from our home but after some six weeks we followed the example of many of the residents of Paola and moved out of that village. We took up residence in a large house at Qormi together with some of our relatives. In addition to myself and the six children, there was my sister with her husband and their six children, my father and mother, and those of my sisters who were still unmarried. I took with me bales of cloth and other objects from the shop and I set up a little business there. Sometimes I bartered cloth for foodstuffs like bread and potatoes which were otherwise quite difficult to come by.

We soon found out that though the house was fairly large, there were too many of us - twelve children and almost as many adults - and decided to return to Paola. That was in January 1942. We had been back for just a few days when there was a very heavy bombing attack, which left several people dead at Paola. On that day, I remember, I had gone to Valletta and was returning to Paola in a horse-drawn cab when, as we were going through Marsa, there was an air raid warning. We naturally stopped, got out of the cab and went down into the nearest shelter. At one point, someone came in and reported that several bombs had fallen on Paola. You can imagine how worried that made me! I had left behind me my children and I could not help fearing the worst. As soon as the raid was over we resumed our trip and as we drove up Paola Hill and were going past the Corradino Prisons, I caught sight of my children who were waiting for me. They were terrified and they too had been very anxious because the news had spread that a bomb had exploded within yards of a *karozzin* coming from Valletta. I realised that that *karozzin* had left Valletta a few minutes before ours and I could not help thinking that I had escaped death by those few minutes. The scene at Paola square was appalling and unforgettable.

I must confess that when the food shortage started making itself felt among the general population, I was not too badly off as I could resort to barter - cloth for bread and other food stuff.

Occasionally I had to buy necessities on the black market. One deal I can remember clearly: I gave a zinc wash-tub to a baker from Qormi in exchange for a loaf of bread supplied to me every day for a period of weeks. There was another occasion when I got a sack of potatoes for a man's suit. I could not bear to see my children go hungry.

My husband had been posted overseas a few weeks before Italy's declaration of war. At first he was in South African waters and then was transferred to the Port Said station. I rarely received news about him and there was one long stretch of nine months during which I did not have a single word from him. On that occasion I went to the Vernon Club in Valletta and tried to contact some officers so that I could have some news. Apparently they took some action because after a few days I was informed that he was safe and sound and that I would be soon receiving a letter from him as in fact I did within the week. In his letter he asked me to send a photo of myself with all the children because, he wrote, "I am not sure that I will ever see you again".

Meanwhile I got my business going again. Traders like me were given our quota of cloth which I used to collect from the large building which now goes by the name of the Mediterranean Conference Centre at the lower end of Merchants Street. The amount of cloth which you were allocated depended on the number of customers registered with you; cloth could only be bought against coupons that were issued to each head of the family in proportion to the size of the family.

In 1943 my husband returned to Malta after an absence of three and a half years. The children and myself could not contain our joy at the prospect of being reunited and one of my daughters was so excited that she passed out. Being parted from your nearest and dearest, as so often happens in wars, is unbearable.

JINNY DARMANIN

My husband whom I married in October 1939 was a seaman on board HMS *Protector*. We had been married for just six days when he received orders to report for duty; the *Protector* steamed out of harbour to its destination, Alexandria, taking away my husband whom I was not to see for the next three and a half years. Once, during the war, he was due to come home on leave but shortly after leaving Alexandria, the ship was attacked by units of the Italian Navy and had to limp back to harbour with several of its crew killed or wounded. After looking forward so eagerly to seeing him again, I broke down and wept when I got the bad news. When he eventually came back, he stayed for a whole month before sailing out again. During those interminable three and a half years it was the letters which I got regularly from him that kept me going.

When, with Italy's declaration of war, the bombing started I left Vittoriosa where I had settled after my marriage, and went to live with my relatives in Siġġiewi. I was not happy there at all and early in 1941 I went back to Paola, a move that coincided with the worst days of the war. Several bombs fell on that village and a few doors away from mine a number of houses were razed to the ground killing some of the occupants. I remember another bombing which left several victims and in which I had the narrowest of escapes. I had just managed to get into the entrance of the shelter and was about to go down the first few steps when a bomb exploded some yards away. The food shortage did not bother me as much as the bombing; I was never short of money and I could always buy essential commodities on the black market.

When I look back I cannot help feeling angry that I had to spend what should have been the happiest days of my married life separated from my husband, alone in an empty house…

CONCETTA FALZON

When war broke out I had been married for some ten years and I was the mother of four children. Two days after Italy declared war, we moved from Paola, where we lived, to Rabat. We were given two rooms in an old house and in those two rooms were packed myself, my husband and four children, my sister with her husband and two children, and my brother and his wife: in all three families and twelve persons. Our move to Rabat started badly. As the truck which was carrying us and a few belongings was driving through the old archway at Fleur-de-Lys, it was involved in a collision. We were rather badly shaken and we were taken to the Police Depot which was then housed at the Bugeja Institute and given a cup of hot tea. Our belongings were then shifted to another truck and we made the rest of the trip in a bus.

After one or two weeks my family found accommodation in another part of Rabat in the neighbourhood of the chapel of St Sebastian. We shared the house with the owner, who was an acquaintance of my husband's; we had one room at ground floor level and the cellar below it.

My husband was employed as a chargeman at the Dockyard. Transport to and from the Dockyard was not a problem at first but difficulties arose when fuel supplies became scarce. There was a period of time when buses going in the direction of Rabat stopped at the bottom of the hill to save on fuel. There were instances when my husband and one or two others would hire a horse and cart to make the trip.

Although there were occasions when bombs fell on Rabat, I do not think that we were ever in any great danger especially when shelters became readily available. We had a small cubicle dug out in the public shelter; we had to pay a lot of money for it. In the worst part of the war, we used to sleep in it, using hammocks and straw mattresses. Every morning we used to take up the mattresses and place them in the sun to dry out the humidity. What with people chattering and others praying at the top of their voices or singing, shelters were noisy places and quarrels broke out frequently.

One of my worst experiences was when we went down into a small shelter, an old catacomb, and so many people crowded into it that the air inside turned foul and people could not breathe. The flames in the few oil lamps and candles began to flicker and finally went out. People were gasping for breath and screaming hysterically, "We are suffocating!" and started rushing out. For some

Queueing outside one of the many *Victory Kitchen* outlets which had been opened on the Island.

(NWMA Collection)

time we sat on the pavement until we got our breath back. That experience was a real nightmare.

When we first moved to Rabat food was plentiful and cheap. You could buy a hen for practically nothing and we used to eat very well. But then, suddenly, all this came to an end and hunger pains began to be felt. Sometimes I used to buy a bit of meat under the counter from a neighbour at black market prices, but at least we had something to eat. Eggs, when you could find any, cost half a crown (12c5) each and oranges were about as expensive. On some days I used to take the road to Buskett pushing the pram with my youngest child in the hope of finding something to buy. When, on rare occasions, I managed to buy a few potatoes I would hide them under the baby because at that time you could be stopped and have the food confiscated if you bought anything outside your ration. Of course more often than not I returned home empty-handed.

When the Victory Kitchens started functioning we used to get some food in exchange for ration coupons. A close friend of my husband's, a middle-aged bachelor, used to give us his coupons so that we were able to get an extra portion. All my cooking used to be done on the old kerosene stove with three wicks. Kerosene was rationed too and you had to present the coupon before you could be served. My eldest daughter used to go and stand in the kerosene queue; sometimes when she came back with our ration, she would go again and when the kerosene seller asked her for the coupon she would start weeping and say that she had lost it and that she would get a beating when she got back home which, of course, was not true. And then the kind man would take pity and give her another ration. There was a scarcity of everything not just foodstuffs. For example it was impossible to find clothes and shoes. I used to make shoes, or rather sandals, for my four children. Further down the street from where we lived the Strickland family used to run a small weaving industry. I used to buy a few lengths of rope which I would sew on to a foot-shaped piece of canvas, add a few straps and there's your pair of sandals! Most of that kind of work was done in the shelter in the light of oil-lamps or candles.

We spent some three years in all at Rabat. We returned to Paola on the day that Tripoli fell to the Allies. By that time, air raids were getting less and less frequent and seemed to be petering out. But there was another problem making itself felt: scabies. All four children caught the disease but my husband and myself were spared. Catching the scabies was almost as bad as having bombs dropping around you.

ANNE HOCKEY

Three days after the outbreak of hostilities my parents, my brother Willie and myself left Senglea where we lived and moved into a garage at Żebbuġ which had been rented to us by our greengrocer. My other brother, Joe, was in the Royal Navy, posted overseas and he was never out of my parents' thoughts. Occasionally I would catch my father shedding a tear as he mut-

Blitzed street in Senglea.
(Photo Times of Malta)

tered, "We are gathered here in safety while Joe is risking his life night and day". Letters from him were few and far between and when one day my brother Willie happened to hear someone say that the *Devonshire* had been sunk, you can imagine how worried that made us. But it transpired that it was the *Dorsetshire* that had gone down.

When the *Illustrious* attack came I happened to be in Senglea where I had gone to buy a wedding present for a friend of mine. My brother had warned me the night before to keep away from the harbour area because the aircraft carrier had steamed in and was lying-to in the Grand Harbour but I was not in the mood for listening. I remember it was a Thursday afternoon; no sooner had the siren stopped wailing than the deafening thunder of hundreds of guns firing broke out. On the Senglea waterfront there were some warehouses and together with another woman I hurried into one of them for shelter. With every bomb explosion the gate of the warehouse would fly open and I would slam it shut again. I have never been so terrified in my life as I was on that day; I felt certain that I would never see my family again. For me it was as if the end of the world had come.

B'TIFKIRA U B'GIEH
LIS-SENGLEANI
LI TILFU HAJJITHOM
MATUL IT-TIENI GWERRA DINJIJA
1939-1945

"In memory of the people from Senglea who were killed during World War II."
(Photo N. Genovese)

104

Then as suddenly as it had started, the noise abated and we crept cautiously outside. An English serviceman stopped us and warned us to take cover immediately because a second wave of raiders was on its way; we took his advice and made our way to a proper shelter. We had just settled down when the silence was shattered by bomb explosions and the deafening sound of gunfire. This second attack appeared to be even more ferocious than the first. The lights went out and the shelter was shuddering with every explosion. Adults and children were screaming and weeping in terror. Then abruptly the thunderous noise stopped and a man came down and told us that it was safe to go out. On emerging into the daylight, we saw a scene of complete devastation. The buildings in Our Lady of Sorrows Street were now masses of rubble; electricity cables were hanging down from bent poles and people were running aimlessly about. Then rumours began to fly around...the Theuma family killed...the canon and his family killed... I wanted to get away from all this and I made my way through the Dockyard to Cospicua where I was hopeful of getting transport to Żebbuġ. All around I saw people trudging along carrying bundles; everyone seemed to be deserting Senglea. I heaved a great sigh of relief as I found myself back in Żebbuġ.

For me that was the worst experience of the war. I never expected to come out alive and I count myself lucky that fifty years have gone by since then and I am still alive. The wedding gift that I bought that day is still in my possession. In the confusion which reigned on that unforgettable day, I left the gift with a friend who agreed to pass it on but she never did and after some time she returned it to me. I suppose you could say it is a souvenir of the war now...

ANTONIA MIZZI

I was standing along with several other people in the square at Vittoriosa listening to the news on the public loudspeaker: Mussolini had declared war. On hearing this I hurried back home to my husband and five children. I had been married for ten years and my husband was a Dockyard worker. The following morning, at about seven, we had the first raid. I pulled my children out of bed and pushed them under the large dining table as we had been advised to do should we be bombed. I was at my wits' end; I was alone in the house as my husband was on the night shift and had not returned yet. The following day we collected a few belongings and made our way to Gudia.

There were quite a few of us in that house at Gudia: my husband, myself and the five children, my mother-in-law, a sister-in-

Cooking became an ordeal when kerosene was in short supply; water colour by
A. Gerada.

(Courtesy A. Ganado)

law and a brother-in-law, another sister-in-law with her three children, and various cousins and friends - all of us packed into a small house. At first we did not bother to go down into shelters but when the Luftwaffe came, we soon got into the habit of taking cover whenever we heard the siren. I kept a watchful eye on my children but the two eldest would come down with me through one entrance and go straight out through the other without my being aware.

In September 1941 I gave birth at home to another child. Once when the baby was a few days old there was an air raid alert during the night; I grabbed the baby wrapped in a woollen shawl and hurried to the nearest shelter. My husband was on the night shift and the other children had already gone to the shelter with their aunt. When I closed the front door the shawl got caught in the door and I could not pull it free. So there I was with bombs raining down and me pulling at the shawl. The street was deserted. Suddenly a man went hurrying by and when he saw me he said, "What are you doing out here?" When I explained my predicament he took out a flick-knife and cut the shawl through, freeing me and saving the child from catching pneumonia.

The war was the cause of a great deal of hardship for us all. But of all the hardships, the worst was the food shortage which became very acute when we returned to Paola. My children used to collect firewood from among the fallen masonry; that went for cooking on the *kenur*, the old-fashioned stove made of stone which had come back into daily use because of the kerosene shortage. Even the hen-house which we had in the yard was eventually broken up for firewood. We made every effort to obtain food; I often went up to Tarxien in the hope of buying eggs which were then selling at two shillings and sixpence (12c5) apiece - a great deal of money when you remember that my husband's wages were two pounds a week. When my mother passed away at the hospital in Qormi, I failed to report her death. Before going into hospital my mother lived with me and therefore her ration was included in our entitlement; I therefore kept having her ration for many weeks after her death. With the regulations in force at the time, I could have been given a prison sentence if I had been found out. But the situation was so desperate that I was prepared to go to prison if that was the price of feeding my children. Like many other mothers sometimes I would go hungry so that the children could have my share.

We suffered a great deal in the war, especially when we were on the verge of starvation, but on the whole I was quite happy - I was young then. Now I am in my eighty-eighth year and I feel old.

DOLORES PENZA

We used to live at Cospicua and my husband was the head-teacher of the primary school there. On the very first day of the war every window pane in our house was shattered but the building was otherwise undamaged. We took the hint and thought it would be wiser to move away from the Dockyard area and so, before night fell, we were already settled down in a house which my husband had rented at Zabbar.

However before the month was out we went through exactly the same experience at Zabbar: during an air raid a bomb which fell nearby shattered the panes in our house and we decided there

Joseph Penza, BEM, Luqa
Protection Officer.
(Courtesy D. Penza and K. Cini)

and then to move to Luqa where my in-laws lived. We were given the large stable where the family used to keep the horses. My husband and his brothers soon set about digging out a shelter in the large garden at the back of the house and built a room in a corner of the garden to be used for cooking and eating. Every night we would take our bedding down into the shelter and sleep there. It was a very large shelter and we often asked neighbours to come and share it during air raids. There was also an area where schoolchildren could be taught. My husband and his brothers, stone masons by trade, had done a very good job of it; it was quite comfortable as shelters go and we even had electric lights installed.

The shelter had one drawback, however; water used to seep through after every heavy downpour and flood the place. I would often get up in the morning and step into large puddles of water. My two children, one aged six and the other seven, were often given the task of drying it out. Another problem was rats; they would come down into the shelter from the garden and gnaw at everything including the bedclothes. Once as I was getting out of the shelter I spied a monster of a rat waddling down the steps; I grabbed the handrails on either side and drew my feet up to let the creature pass.

On moving to Luqa, my husband took up the duties of head-teacher at the local primary school but with the school being requisitioned by the military authorities, the pupils had been placed in a number of private houses. During air raids, the pupils were taken down into the nearest shelters and I know of at least two other shelters, besides ours, in which pupils had their lessons. Interruptions to their schooling were therefore kept to a minimum. During one air raid, as we were taking cover underground, there was a terrific explosion and when we emerged out of the shelter we were stunned to see that the house, together with the garden and the small room in the corner, were a total wreck. But we could consider ourselves somewhat lucky for, on moving to Luqa, we had stored our furniture in my cousin's house at Żejtun so that at least something was saved!

With the constant bombing, Luqa was far from being the ideal

No. 2417/36.

LIEUTENANT-GOVERNOR'S OFFICE

Malta, 31st December, 1943

CONFIDENTIAL

Sir,

I am desired by his Excellency the Governor to inform you that he has received an intimation from the Secretary of State for the Colonies to the effect that His Majesty The King has been graciously pleased to approve of the award to you of the Medal of the Most Excellent Order of the British Empire, Civil Division.

2.   His Excellency desires me to offer you his congratulations on this well earned distinction, of the conferring of which he has learned with the greatest satisfaction.

I have the honour to be.
Sir,
Your obedient servant,

Lieutenant-Governor.

Joseph Penza, Esq., B.E.M.,
Protection Officer,
Luqa.

In recognition of services often rendered "in the face of great danger."

(Courtesy D. Penza and K. Cini)

Colonial Office,

Downing Street, S.W.1.

1st January, 1944.

Dear Mr. Penza,

I should like, if I may, to offer you my warm congratulations on your recent award.   The services you have rendered as Protection Officer in Luqa, so often in the face of great danger, are fully deserving of this tribute.

Yours sincerely,

place to live in and several villagers were killed. I would say that in the war, and as far as we were concerned, the bombing was the worst experience. The food shortage did not really hit us because my in-laws had a grocery and they had managed to put aside a large quantity of foodstuffs before the war started. In addition to that my husband was the local Protection Officer and in that role was in a position to help a lot of people. My husband had a few British servicemen among his friends and sometimes he invited these to our house so that we could treat them to some home cooking.

One of my husband's jobs was to organise the rationing and distribution of food in the village. Before that, people would congregate in large crowds at the shops but with the rationing system everyone was sure of getting his or her share.

As regards clothing, we managed to get by; the clothes which we had bought before the war, with a bit of mending here and there, saw us through without any great problems. I only remember buying a length of cloth once during the war. Sandals we used to make ourselves; the sole was made of coiled rope with cloth straps for the uppers.

We remained at Luqa throughout the war. My mother and my sister had moved from Sliema to Rabat where they found accommodation in the Franciscan priory. Occasionally my mother would pluck up courage and come to visit us at Luqa. I used to go to church every Sunday to hear Mass and when the parish church was bombed, Mass began to be said in one of the apses which was left standing. At the end of the war my husband was awarded the B.E.M. (British Empire Medal) for his services.

INEŻ PORTELLI

On the first day of the war, towards evening, my brother called at our house in Vittoriosa and took us to Siġġiewi to live at his house. There was quite a crowd in that house for there were other families besides ours, and it was not long before we made up our mind to move elsewhere. So with my husband and four children we found another place in Siġġiewi and I soon got fond of that village especially as that area was practically free from bombing. But in spite of that I still carry with me the scars of war because I lost an arm in an incident at Rabat.

It happened like this: on the 10th of October 1942 my daughter was staying at my sister's house at Rabat where she had gone to spend a few days. On that fateful day I got a message from my sister saying that my daughter was running a temperature and that there was not as much as a spoonful of sugar or a drop of milk in the house. That message had me very worried and I decided there and then to hurry to Rabat on foot taking with me some sugar and a bottle of milk from the goat which we kept in the house. My son would not let me go without him and I took him along. I had never been to my sister's before and so the first thing I did on reaching the Saqqajja was to ask the way. After I had trudged through many a street, I eventually found the place and much to my surprise the door was opened by my brother-in-law who happened to be on leave on that day and who told me that my sister had gone to church taking my daughter with her. This appeared very strange to me because I was expecting to find my daughter in bed. In the meantime there was an air raid alert and I hurried with my son and my brother-in-law to get cover in the nearest shelter. Before I had gone down two or three steps, a terrific explosion sent us all reeling. Suddenly all was confusion. Panic-stricken people were screaming and running aimlessly around and as I looked out I saw people lying on the ground, motionless while others were crawling away or writhing in agony and moaning. My arm had been nearly torn away but I did not feel any pain. My brother-in-law took one look at me and fainted. I was laid on a stretcher and taken to the infirmary at Santu Spirtu Hospital where my arm was bandaged. I was carried into a van with some six other persons of whom two were dead and the four others badly injured. Although I was in a state of shock I never lost consciousness and knew all the time what was going on around me. When we arrived at the Ta' Bugeja Hospital in Hamrun I was examined by the doctor on duty. He stuck a needle into my arm; I felt no sensation and I heard him mutter to an assistant that my arm was "dead".

I was taken into the operating theatre and when I came to in the morning I realised that my arm had gone. Later on in the morning the hospital chaplain administered the Last Sacraments to me and I knew that there was little hope for me; I was so shocked that I begged them to let me die but the chaplain gently asked me whether I had any children. "Yes, four", I said. Then he said, "You will still be able to look after your children somehow with one arm but if you are not there, anything could happen to them". Those words struck home and I was determined to go back to the family. I spent a month convalescing at the hospital and then I went back to Siġġiewi. I remember my little daughter of four greeting me with "It's better to be alive with one arm missing than to be dead."

That was forty-nine years ago. My four children are now married and I have also fostered another child. Little by little I learnt to do everything with my one remaining hand: cooking, sewing, cleaning... everything. After the war came to an end I stayed on at Siġġiewi for some twenty years because I had grown fond of that village and the people with whom I got on very well and who were always ready to help me in my hour of need. In fact I can say that my children never went to bed hungry because I used to get food from the kind villagers. You can say that at times I was penniless but there was never any want of necessities at home.

RITA ZAMMIT

I was married in 1938 and when the war broke out I had a daughter and another child was on the way. We left Tarxien and went to live at Mosta with two elderly spinsters who knew my husband's relatives and who gave us two rooms on the first floor. In those two rooms, in addition to my family, there were other relatives: my father-in-law, his bachelor brother, my mother and sister, and so on: some fifteen people in all. We partitioned one room into two sections and resorted to the traditional arrangement with men sleeping in one part and the women in the other;

the second room was for eating, cooking, washing and so on. We had no toilet facilities other than a bucket in a small room downstairs. As you can easily imagine we soon found the situation unbearable and after some three months we decided to move back to our house at Tarxien.

As was the custom in those days, my first child was born at home but when my second was due I had to go to hospital as the midwife who served at Tarxien had gone elsewhere as a refugee. During the twelve days which I had to spend in hospital, I left my baby daughter with a friend from Hamrun. I would normally have left her with my mother but she was living in the old railway tunnel at Valletta, certainly no place for a baby.

In February of 1942 - perhaps the worst period of the war - I had my third child. She was born on the day that a parachute mine fell within a stone's throw from our house. I found my neighbours a great help in those terrible days. Whenever there was an air raid, one or another of my neighbours would call at my house and take the children down with them into the shelter while I stayed at home washing nappies and the baby clothes. (In those days we did not have disposable nappies!) There were times when I would barely have time to wrap the babies in a towel before handing them over to the neighbour, especially if I happened to be bathing them. I was of course running a great risk by not taking cover during air raids. In fact people died by enemy action a few doors away. On one tragic occasion seventeen people were killed in a shelter a short distance away from our house.

We coped with the food shortage pretty well because though the children were very young we could get an adult's ration for each of them. For instance they were each entitled to a quarter *ratal* (about 200g) bread per day and since they were too young to eat that we were left with more than enough for myself and my husband and sometimes we could afford to give away some of the bread ration to needy neighbours or barter the bread for something else. We used to get powdered milk for the babies. Eggs were in very short supply and you had to pay through the nose for them; we therefore kept a few hens in the backyard so that at least now and then we would have an egg or two to give to the chil-

The war dead of Tarxiern commemorated.

(Photo N. Genovese)

dren. During the worst part of the food shortages my husband used to cycle all the way to Rabat to buy potatoes or flour on the black market. Some farmers would only accept gold objects in payment.

One of my worst experiences of the war was when a mine fell on the Lampuka palace. It seems that the Germans saw a whole procession of lorries packed with soldiers belonging to the *Devons* (the Devonshire Regiment) and the *Dorsets* (the Dorsetshire Regiment) making its way through Tarxien and released this mine at the instant that the column was going past the palace. Several soldiers were killed in that incident. On another occasion, during the night we were in bed when we heard someone knocking on the window shutters. It was one of our neighbours who was worried when she realised that we had not left the house for the shelter. We got out of bed and on going outside saw that the night had almost been turned into day. Several parachute flares were floating down slowly and lighting up the whole area. One of the flares ended up in our backyard and to this day one can see still the scorching marks on the floor tiles.

My husband made a lot of friends from among the soldiers billeted in the neighbourhood and some of them used to come to him for private lessons in the Maltese and Italian languages. Some of those soldiers often came to our house; I think they were homesick, poor lads! We sometimes asked them to share a meal with us because we felt so sorry for them when we remembered that they were so far away from their homes and families. One of those soldiers is still a friend after almost half a century. Before his wife died she confided in me, "I feel so indebted to you and your family for making my husband feel at home when he was feeling lonely and depressed."

IV. Schoolteachers

MIKIEL ANĠ BONNICI

I was appointed teacher in the primary schools in 1934. Up to 1940 I had been teaching at Qrendi; then on the outbreak of the war I was transferred to my home town, Zurrieq. At first the school practically closed down. The premises were taken over by the authorities: the boys' section by the military and the girls' by the ARP. The classes were re-allocated in a number of places: one class remained in the original premises, three classes were housed in St Catherine's Band Club and two others in the Oratory adjoining the parish church. The remaining classes were dispersed in a number of private residences and the sisters' convent at Nigret. The headteacher had no fixed office but constantly moved from one place to another. In the event of an air raid before eight in the morning pupils were exempted from attending school; an air raid after eight would mean that the pupils were to be kept under the supervision of their teachers. We had to escort them into the rock shelters and try to have lessons as best we could. If the raid was still on after two in the afternoon the pupils would be with us until the "raiders passed" was heard. We were strictly enjoined not to send any child home during an air raid even if he or she lived just across the street.

I was teaching Standard V pupils in a classroom which was formerly the bar room of the local band club. The following year I moved to the main hall of the same club; this was a much larger room which however I had to share with another teacher. The two classes were arranged back to back so that hopefully the pupils' attention would not wander too much. Another class was held on the stage at one end of the hall. The year after that I had to move again, this time to the old charnel house beneath the parish church. On occasion the lesson would be interrupted by the gravedigger who would sidle up to me and whisper, "Excuse me, but I have to clean up one of the graves; I hope you won't mind the smell." Then, with every child's eyes fixed on him, he would lever up the slabs and proceed to remove bits and pieces of bones and rotten coffins. I recollect one particular class inspection in the course of which the gravedigger put in an appearance. The inspectress was shocked! She could not stand that scene, what with graves and skeletons and exclaimed, "How can you permit such scenes to take place right in front of your pupils?" I could only reply, "What else can I do, madam? The children have by now got used to such things."

I must say that I managed to avoid being called up for national service by the skin of my teeth. I had been told to report at the drafting office but before I did so I went up to the Director of Education, Dr Laferla. He told me to put my mind at rest on the matter because he had already made arrangements for conscripted teachers to be released from the Army. My main reason for wishing to avoid conscription was that I was in line for taking up a scholarship in England which would ensure my promotion to headteacher; if I got caught up in Army life I would run the risk of missing that opportunity. In addition to teaching, I served as a part-time Special Constable (SC). The Director of Education always insisted that every teacher had to make some contribution to the war effort. One of my responsibilities as a SC was to see that people took shelter during air raids and that no lights were shown at night. I was under orders to report any person breaking those rules; even striking a match at night in the open was considered to be a criminal offence. Curfew regulations had also to be observed to the letter and in the event of a person refusing to comply we had instructions to call in the military who were authorised to use arms if necessary. Fortunately I never had the need to resort to such measures.

I was itching to go to England to proceed with my studies and whenever I could I called at the Education Office to enquire about arrangements. At the time the Office was at Fleur-de-Lys and I had to bike all the way from Żurrieq. (That reminds me of the Governor of the time, Lord Gort, who used a bicycle instead of motor transport to get around thereby saving fuel.) On these trips I occasionally got caught up in an air raid and I had to seek some form of shelter. More often than not I took shelter in one of the many roadside G-Shelters which were designed to protect one from splinters and shrapnel. In wartime public transport was very restricted, generally to the hours between eight and ten in the morning and after four in the afternoon and those who had to travel outside those hours had to walk or use a bicycle or perhaps a horse-drawn cart or *karozzin* (cab). In a few places one could also come across an old omnibus!

One day I went to Valletta with a friend of mine and when it was time for us to return we hired a *karozzin* which we shared

The omnibus became a familiar sight on the roads during the war.

with a couple of men from Luqa. I remember the fare was half-a-crown (12c5). The road cut across the aerodrome and as we drove through, time bombs were going off around us with the result that the horse panicked and we were sure the cab would turn over. The next instant my friend and I were hurled out of the cab. Luckily the cab driver managed to rein in the horse and we eventually resumed our journey to the accompaniment of intermittent explosions around us. I don't think I have ever been so scared in my life and to this day I count myself lucky to have survived the experience.

For some time I used to work as Assistant Protection Officer (APO) in the afternoons, taking time off from my teaching duties. The Protection Officer, Dr Carmelo Caruana, placed me in charge of the distribution of flour to the bakeries of the district, by no means an easy job as I was soon to discover. I rarely left the office before eight in the evening and all the time I was on tenterhooks to proceed to England. Thrice I made my way to the aerodrome at Luqa expecting to get on a flight to England and every time the plane did not turn up. Finally, towards the end of January 1943 I succeeded in getting a berth on a mine-layer. The Senior Transport Officer, a Mr Zerafa, was an evacuee at Zurrieq who knew I was trying to get a passage to England and one morning he called me up and said, "If you are ready to leave to-day make sure that you are at the Customs House by 2.30 this afternoon. For security reasons I cannot tell you the name of the ship." My luggage had been packed for quite some time before and I turned up at the Customs House at the appointed time. At 4.00 p.m., just out of harbour, we were called to the canteen and given a cup of tea and some food; I was really amazed at the amount of food laid out on the tables when people back home were on the verge of starvation. I was the only civilian on that mine-layer. Off the coast of Pantelleria we were attacked by enemy aircraft but we were not hit. Our first port of call was Gibraltar and I welcomed the opportunity to spend six days ashore. The second leg of my journey was on the *Ile de France*, a liner which had been converted to carry cargo and now was one of a convoy of twelve ships bound for English ports. In the Bay of Biscay we were attacked by U-boats; there were huge seas running and I was doubly scared. The ships in the convoy kept zigzagging to avoid becoming easy targets. Finally we got to Glasgow and I hurried to meet the principal of the college. His first words after I had introduced myself were, "Are you mad, my son?"

As it turned out that question was more than justified for a few days later flying bombs began to fall around and I had a near miss myself when while I was in the company of a Maltese woman a flying bomb crashed down in front of us. I instinctively threw myself flat on my face and covered my head with my suitcase. A thick pall of smoke rose slowly and suddenly hundreds of people were running about. Within minutes we were packed into an ambulance and rushed to hospital. My companion was injured in the leg. After the necessary treatment we were handed a tot of whisky and discharged. After Malta, England was a veritable haven. The only problem was the bombing; though some commodities were rationed, food was relatively plentiful and you could have as much coffee and bread as you fancied, quite a different situation from that in Malta. And, I may add, for as little as five shillings (25c) you could have a three course meal.

VINCENT CARUANA

In September 1939, on the eve of the declaration of war between Germany and Britain, I was in the company of a group of pilgrims travelling to Lourdes. On our arrival in Rome we happened to come across another group of Maltese led by Dr Albert Laferla, the then Director of Education, returning from a cultural visit to London. Dr Laferla regularly organised such tours for teachers in the summer holidays. He pulled aside the leaders of our group and advised them to cut their tour short and return to Malta at once because, he told them, "War is about to break out." We took his advice, caught the first train to Syracuse and there boarded the *Knight of Malta*. A large crowd of relatives and friends greeted us on landing because the news had already spread.

At that time, my family had just moved house to Marsa from Valletta in the belief that should war break out, that locality would be safer. I was then teaching at the primary school in Vittoriosa, having received my appointment as teacher in 1930.

The day following Italy's declaration of war saw my family moving again, this time to Rabat where we found accommoda-

Dr Albert V. Laferla LL.D. OBE, Director of Education.
(Courtesy MB Amato)

tion at the Saqqajja with some people. Later on in the year, we moved once more, this time with a woman who lived in College Street and who rented out to us a couple of rooms. Rabat was overflowing with refugees who had left their homes in the harbour area and some of those refugees found shelter in the Franciscan priory. My brother belonged to the Franciscan order and I too found a place in the priory.

In the meantime, like other teachers, I was engaged as a Special Constable. At nightfall, because of the curfew, people were not allowed to leave their home and we had to see to it that these regulations were strictly followed. We had other duties as well: for instance we had to carry out supervision in school premises which had been converted to accommodate refugees. We were more or less in charge of those premises and we had to see to every need and every complaint of the inmates. One incident stands out clearly in my memory: I was on duty at Villa Messina which stands opposite the church and priory of St Dominic and on the road leading to Dingli. The building was packed with refugees and when, in a night raid, bombs started falling around the residents suddenly panicked. I was the only person with some official authority and it was no easy task for me to bring those people to their senses and restore order.

When schools re-opened after the summer vacation, I was posted to the primary school housed in the old Governor's Palace in the main street of Mdina. This was one of the several premises used for teaching the children living at Rabat whose number had more than doubled due to the large influx of refugees from the harbour areas. I was given the Lyceum class, that is boys who would be taking the Lyceum entrance examination that year. As teachers we used to do our utmost to avoid disrupting the day's lessons. Of course, at every air raid warning we had to take our pupils down into the shelters where we would carry on with the lesson as best we could; sometimes, we would have to switch to another lesson, such as, for example, general knowledge or similar subject when one could manage without a blackboard. People sharing the shelter would often listen in to what was going on. We still had regular inspections from time to time, sometimes from the Director himself. Dr Laferla visited my class on several occasions and would show his pleasure whenever the boys used correct English to answer his questions. The Director was well known for being a staunch supporter of the Empire and anything British.

Some bad experiences still stand out in my memory. There was the incident when, with bombs falling around, I ran as fast as I could to get into a shelter; as soon as I reached the entrance I was caught by the blast of an explosion. I was unhurt but two people who were immediately behind were injured. When the all clear sounded and I made my way out of the shelter, a scene of utter destruction caught my eyes: the Hotel Point de Vue, in which were billeted a number of airmen, had been made the target of that raid and many men, who instants before were playing the piano and having a singsong, were now lying dead or injured......

On another occasion in the company of a number of friars, I was on the roof of the Franciscan Priory watching an air raid in progress in the distance. We used to do that sort of thing regularly; it was fascinating to see the play of lights as searchlights

Point de Vue Hotel after it was bombed on 21 March 1942.
(NWMA Collection.)

swept across the dark sky made even darker by the black-out which was being very strictly enforced at the time. This fascination was tempered by the realisation that what was going on was deadly serious and men's lives were in jeopardy. I think that I am by nature somewhat claustrophobic and I could never feel comfortable inside a rock shelter; I much preferred to be killed off by a bomb to being buried alive underground. That night, as we were watching, a blinding light like a flash of lightning shot out from the far side of the priory followed by a deafening explosion. A bomb had hit a house next to the priory. I rushed down to see whether I could be of any assistance and as I entered what remained of the building the balcony dropped down, narrowly missing me by inches. In the house, lying dead, was a friend of mine, a certain Galea from Valletta. On that same night an Augustinian novice also lost his life.

As a member of the adult section of the M.U.S.E.U.M. society, I often had to go to Dingli, more often than not walking there and back from Rabat. Several times as I was walking I would hear an air raid warning and see planes hurtling from the skies. M.U.S.E.U.M. activities were regularly kept going throughout the war even though some of the premises had been requisitioned to house refugees. When premises were not available we used to find some other place where we could teach catechism to children - usually the parish church would be made available to us. At Rabat we instructed children either at the "College" which also housed the Protection Office and the Special Constables unit or in the chapel standing opposite the parish church.

As members of the adult section we used to meet more or less regularly but certainly not as frequently as we did before the war. Our founder, Dun Gorg, was living as a refugee at Żebbuġ with some members of the Society who lived in a small community. With him was his sister and a maid who used to look after their daily needs. Dun Gorg was in rather low spirits during those days because his brother had been interned. Dun Gorg could never come to terms with that. From time to time some of us would take the road to Żebbuġ walking all the way to pay him a visit and seek his advice. He, in his turn, used to try to organise plenary meetings for members of the adult branch of the Society as often as possible.

One day Dun Gorg called a meeting for all senior members at St Joseph's Institute at Hamrun to introduce the revised statute of the Society. Also present at the meeting was Bishop Emanuel Galea, then Vicar General of the diocese. At the end of the meeting, I left with a colleague, Censu Mula from Sliema, to make our way back to Rabat. We walked through Attard, passing the Tal-Mirakli chapel and took the road cutting across Ta' Qali. By that time it was getting dark and as we emerged on the Rabat road, a soldier stopped us and told us to follow him. We were carrying an empty box each which we had used to carry some food for the day. One can easily imagine our apprehension, especially as we were afraid that we would be caught in one of the many air raids to which Ta' Qali was being subjected daily. We were taken in before an Army officer who interrogated us at some length. We had presumably been taken for spies! The officer reached for the telephone and called up somebody at Army Headquarters at Castile. When he rang off, he said, "O.K., you can go," and accompanied us part of the way. Then he bade us goodnight and left us. Of course we got home much later than expected and we found our families worrying to death about us.

I lost some very good friends during the war; one of them, a Turu Farrugia from Bormla, was riding in a bus when it was literally incinerated by an incendiary bomb near Marsa Cross. Incidentally Turu was on the pilgrimage to Lourdes to which I referred before. On our way back to Malta he had told me that when things returned to normal we could do the Lourdes trip with an easier mind. He was, as far as I know, the first member of the adult section of the Society to lose his life as a result of enemy action.

ANGELO GRIMA

With Malta's involvement in the war appearing inevitable we took the precaution of renting a house in Mannarino Road, Birkirkara. When Italy did in fact declare war on the 10th June and bombs soon started raining down we hurried to move to Birkirkara from Senglea where I lived with my family and where I had been teaching at the local primary school for the best part of eleven years. My sister and brother, with their families, came to live in the same house along with my family so that we were quite a crowd.

Teachers who moved from their home town were obliged to go and report for duty at the school where they were now living and therefore I hastened to report at the Birkirkara school where the headteacher was Mr Anthony Valletta. The school premises had practically been taken over to accommodate the large number of refugees and I had to teach in the chapel dedicated to St Anthony, practically next door to the local police station. My class was made up of ten pupils. After a few weeks, my class was transferred to the vestry of the old parish church; things were a bit better there: I even had a blackboard at my disposal! Nevertheless the system could at best be only described as makeshift with little or no sense of direction and was a system in name only. Pupils turned up for lessons or not as they chose and discipline was generally lax. I never gave lessons when we were in the shelter.

During the war teachers were paid a pittance and if you had a large family like me you had to do something to supplement your wages. I started giving private lessons at home and did some bookkeeping for a few traders. When the war ended I was transferred to Senglea primary, temporarily housed in a large house in St Ursula Street, since the school proper was in ruins as indeed was practically the whole of that town.

IRENE LUCIA

Just before the war I used to teach at the Valletta primary school, a stone's throw away from Fort St Elmo. Then came a brief spell of teaching at Floriana, and then when war broke out, the school term came to a premature end. When schools reopened in September I was transferred to the girls' secondary school in Valletta, a very inconvenient arrangement for me as by that time my family had moved lock, stock and barrel to our summer residence at St Paul's Bay. I thought that it would make more sense for me to seek a placement nearer home and so I applied to go back to the primary schools. Luck was with me and I got a transfer to the primary school at St Paul's Bay. The teaching was then taking place in private houses leased to the Education Department and it was due to this arrangement that I began to teach at home. Two of the rooms in our house had been converted into makeshift classrooms: I was teaching in one and my sister Iris was teaching in the other. You cannot imagine how pleased my mother was to see the two of us so conveniently set up! In those days that was much better than travelling to and from your place of work. Later on however the teacher who had taken over my duties at the Valletta secondary school got married and as was the practice at the time had to resign. I was asked to take her place and this time I accepted, my subjects being Italian, Religion and Nature Study.

The school, officially designated *School for Young Ladies*, was an old building in Merchants Street. Whenever there was an alert we used to take shelter in one of the crypts under St John's Co-Cathedral. Although times were far from normal, students were rarely absent. When raids became more frequent and more devastating the Valletta premises were closed down and the students were placed in two villages, Hamrun and Lija, and I found myself teaching in a private house at Lija. The Lija "school" consisted of four classrooms, one on the groundfloor and three upstairs.

Getting to Lija from St Paul's Bay meant having to get up very early in the morning. We lived practically next door to the police station where there was a bus stop. On several occasions by the time it got to that stop the bus would be filled to capacity and I would find myself stranded. To make sure of getting a seat I used to walk all the way to Xemxija. I remember that sometimes when I boarded the bus men would comment, "What's that girl doing here? Why doesn't she stay at home?" or something to that effect. Sometimes I missed the bus and I would then have to try to get a lift on a military lorry or jeep. Getting back to St Paul's Bay often proved to be more problematic and I had to use any means available such as military motor cycles or trucks or, failing that, walk part of the way. During this period a British soldier was trying to strike up a steady friendship with me and one day he was driving a lorry and stopped to pick me up. But I thought my mother would not be pleased at all if she saw me with a soldier and so I had to get off the lorry as soon as we reached the outskirts of St Paul's Bay, precisely near Villa Chapelle, and walk the rest of the way.

During the war, the education system was a shambles. Inspections became a thing of the past and at every alert lessons were interrupted so that we could scramble down the nearest shelter. Social life, too, was one of the casualties of war. Our only amusement consisted of country walks in winter and bathing in the summer months. Of course compared with people in some parts of the Island we were not too badly off and to the best of my knowledge St Paul's Bay was only bombed once. I remember that occasion quite clearly: my brother was on the roof top catching up on his studies, when he saw a badly damaged German bomber dropping bombs as if they were confetti. He screamed down to us to take shelter which we promptly did. One of the bombs killed a man who was at that very instant digging out a rock shelter. My younger sister, Margaret, was injured in the leg in the same incident but the wound was superficial and she was soon up and about.

Before we went to St Paul's Bay, we used to live in a house in Republic Street, Valletta from where my father conducted his business. At first my mother refused to leave the Valetta home for the one at St Paul's Bay hotly maintaining that the house was bomb-proof and perfectly capable of withstanding anything that the Germans could throw at it. Had we so desired we could have moved up to Mdina where a friend of the family, a monsignor, had a house which he was ready to share with us. My mother was not willing to share any residence since there were twelve of us, brothers and sisters, in the family. But when a bomb fell opposite St John's our house was declared to be in a dangerous state and we had, willy-nilly, to move out.

FRANCIS MEJLAQ

We used to live at Senglea and I had been teaching for just one month at Zabbar when schools closed down on the first of June 1940, that is six weeks before the usual time. On the morning of the 11th just before seven I was startled by the sound of gunfire. I rushed to the balcony to see what was going on . An Air Raid Warden wearing a steel helmet and with a gas mask slung over his shoulder immediately spotted me and shouted, "Get in! There's an air-raid on." I said, "Are you sure this isn't some sort of manoeuvres?" That was of course the first air-raid, but none of us knew precisely what an air-raid, or a real war for that matter, was like. On that first day there were some eight bombing attacks, I think. Many people left Senglea in search of a safer place. We lingered a bit longer but eventually we thought it wiser to follow their example. We were instructed to move into Tal-Mirakli chapel in the vicinity of Ta' Qali where another two families, also from Senglea, were already housed. Together with my married sister, we were given the use of the vestry while the others lived in the chapel proper.

Although we were terribly crowded, the place was in the middle of open countryside and the surroundings were very attractive to us who had always lived in a densely populated town. During night attacks, mostly over the harbour area, we used to climb up the chapel belfry and watch the proceedings. I remember one incident when some soldiers told us we were under arrest and charged us with sending light signals to the Italian planes. We strongly protested our innoCence. It transpired later that a village goatherd used to go regularly at night to feed his flock in an enclosure near the chapel, using an electric torch in the process. A serious warning from the military authorities quickly put an end to that practice.

When schools re-opened I was given just six pupils to teach. The stage in the main hall of the local band club was improvised as a makeshift classroom without as much as a blackboard. I got hold of a sheet of plywood and used that as a blackboard.

In November 1940, the Air Force moved some of its aircraft to Ta' Qali and the place soon became one of the prime targets for enemy bombers. For us refugees this was a case of falling from the frying pan into the fire and we thought we could just as well make our way back to Senglea. The other two families were somewhat luckier: they had a summer residence at St Julian's to which they moved. In the meantime rock shelters had been excavated at Senglea and several refugees felt that it was safe to return to their hometown. In fact they felt safe enough to try and celebrate the town's festa, as in the pre-war days, on the 8th of September 1940. But then the events of the 16th of January of the following year put an end to all that!

That was indeed a memorable day. On that day, I was standing in a naval outfitter's shop, chatting with the owner when the red flag was run up at Castile and St Angelo. As was the practice the owner prepared to close down his shop to take shelter, but a sailor who happened to be in at the time refused to budge at first but was eventually persuaded to leave. We all trooped down into the nearest shelter and it was two full hours before we dared emerge into daylight. The bombers came in two waves; in between, ambulances and first aid personnel stepped in to tend the injured and to extricate people who were buried under the rubble. When the second wave came even ambulances were hit. When the all clear sounded I emerged from the shelter though most people, expecting another attack, decided to stay put. The scene that met me was one of total destruction. The church was severely damaged and Victory Street was reduced to mounds of rubble with electricity poles and cables lying all over the place. I went to the ramparts to have a look at the harbour. Across the water was the *Illustrious* and between us and that warship was "the potato ship" as the locals had dubbed the cargo ship which had the deck covered with sacks of potatoes but which was in reality laden with munitions. Luckily for all of us a bomb which struck the cargo ship in the funnel failed to explode. Senglea was definitely not the place to be in and so, when Sunday the 19th of January came along, with more heavy attacks in one of which the two entrances into the town had been blocked by two powerful mines we decided to call it a day and move to a more peaceful area. That was how we found ourselves at Siġġiewi living in a house which belonged to a friend of my brother's.

At Siġġiewi I taught in a room in the local Catholic Action centre. I had thirty pupils in that room which incidentally was quite well equipped. The headteacher at that time was Mr Nazzareno Pisani. I spent some six months teaching there at the end of which I went to live with my married sister at Paola. My sister had two children and her husband was employed in the Dockyard fire brigade; he was also in the A.R.P. and consequently was often on night shift duties. I was - and still am - a bachelor and my father suggested that it would be a good idea if I were to go and live

The blitzed church of Our Lady of Victories, Senglea.

there and give the family some much-needed moral support. I immediately applied to be transferred to teaching duties at Paola, and as few teachers were prepared to work in that town which was dangerously close to the harbour area, the Director of Education was only too ready to oblige. When I broke the news to Mr Pisani he exclaimed: "Have you gone mad? Do you know what you are letting in yourself for?" So there I was, teaching at Paola, where the pupils were dispersed over at least three different premises: one in Zabbar Road, another in Palm Street and the third in School Street, Tarxien. I was posted to the first-named where there were four classes taught in shifts: one class would attend in the morning and the other in the afternoon.

In spite of the frequent air attacks, we teachers tried to do our best in the circumstances. Lessons were carried out normally and when there was an alert we had to take our pupils to the shelters. We even had regular visits from the school inspector. Many teachers had been called up for military service. I, too, was called up and managed to avoid conscription by, literally, half an inch. The minimum acceptable height was five feet two inches and I was five feet one-and-a-half inches. Teachers were often given other duties in addition to teaching such as those of Protection Officers, A.R.P. and supervisors in public shelters.

Life at Paola during the war was no bed of roses. There was nowhere to go, there was a scarcity of everything and if you wanted something really hard, you had to look for it on the black market and pay exorbitant prices. Pupils were suffering from vitamin deficiency and they were issued with a daily glass of milk and a biscuit for which their parents paid sixpence (2c 5m) a week. My salary at that time was under five pounds sterling a month, and at the end of each month I had to go to the Education Office at the Auberge de France in Valletta to collect my pay packet. That was, of course, until the Auberge received a direct hit. I remember once I was sick for a fortnight and could not report for duty but still at the end of the month I had no deductions from my salary as used to be the practice. When my colleagues came to know about this, they made their way to the Office to complain that in their case, when reporting sick, deductions had been made in their wages. Their complaints were found to be justified and they were reimbursed.

My mother had chosen to remain at Siġġiewi and I used to visit her regularly. A workmen's bus did the return trip from the Dockyard to Siġġiewi and I usually caught it in Cospicua Road. Occasionally I had to make the trip on foot. I suffered a personal loss during the war: the death of my uncle who was travelling on a bus which received a direct hit from an incendiary bomb near Marsa Cross.

Italy's surrender was announced on the 8th September 1943 which happened to be Senglea's feast day. The news, first broken by the parish priest as the statue of the Madonna was being carried into St Philip's church, spread like wildfire and the people spontaneously broke out into cheering and merrymaking.

The statue of Our Lady of Victories (Bambina) being carried shoulder high in Senglea on September 8, 1943.
(Photo W.A. Gatt)

134

JOSEPH MIFSUD MATRENZA

When war broke out I was a Grade III Teacher. The people of Malta had been fearing the worst for months past. Mussolini's speech at six in the evening of June 10th took the ground from under our feet and made us fear what the future held in store for us. A few friends and I were in the habit of meeting outside the *Trocadero Café* before going into the church to hear the seven o'clock mass. On the morning of the 11th we were chatting there when at ten to seven we heard the sirens wailing and, over the public loudspeaker, the warning that an air raid was imminent. A few seconds later came the monotonous but menacing drone of Italian warplanes. I hurried across the street and the next instant was standing in St Gaetano church. The anti-aircraft batteries opened up a deafening barrage which terrified the congregation, mostly women and children, in the church and suddenly there was a general panic. As I was at that time enrolled in the Special Constabulary I hurried to put on my armband with the letters *S.C.* and with the assistance of the parish priest Fr Cordina Perez tried to calm down the situation and stopped anyone from leaving the church.

The parish priest showed great presence of mind: he told them that this was simply a military exercise and there was nothing to be anxious about. But, he continued, if this was a real war they should put their trust in God and pray forgiveness for their sins, and God would deliver them from evil and harm.

Schools had closed earlier than usual and those of us who were teachers were detailed to help Protection Officers especially in the organisation of refugee accommodation. That same evening Hamrun saw the first batches of refugees seeking a roof over their heads; these we put up at Fra Diego Institute and at the school premises in School Street. Each day more refugees arrived and we managed, not without great difficulties, to find accommodation for them.

The refugees, mainly from Valletta, Sliema and Cottonera, pushed up the population of Hamrun to some 26,000 souls and made our task of housing the new arrivals extremely difficult. I will only mention one small detail: on the second day we had to buy the entire output of one bakery to feed those hundreds of refugees. When, after some weeks, people's fear and panic subsided and the situation appeared to be returning to normality, schools were re-opened but because of the shortage of teachers the "double class" system was introduced, that is, each teacher was responsible for two classes teaching one in the morning and the other in the afternoon. The classrooms of the premises in School Street had been taken over for the use of refugees and I had to use a little corner in one of the corridors of the school for teaching my pupils. At first classes had six pupils but very soon numbers rose to nine as refugees asked us to take in their children so they would be close to them.

In April or May of 1941 I was called up and was attached to the RAMC (Royal Army Medical Corps). During the war there were five military hospitals: the 35 General Hospital, the 45 General Hospital, the 90 General Hospital and two field or mobile hospitals. The RAMC enjoyed non-combatant status as defined by the Geneva Convention and my decision to join the RAMC stemmed from the fact that I was a declared pacifist; my intention was to render humanitarian services.

Life in the Army provides one with several experiences, both tragic and comic. Before the providential Santa Marija convoy, the RAMC had set up several emergency posts around the Grand Harbour and I was posted in an underground clinic at Ras Hanzir, Marsa. Each emergency post was fully equipped for any eventuality. On the eve of the feast of the Assumption, three ships steamed into the Grand Harbour and on the following day the legendary *Ohio* limped into harbour with another ship. This, of course, was the crucial convoy which gave the beleaguered Island some much needed respite and which in effect saved Malta from falling to the enemy and changed the course of war.

As we watched the ship which was nearest to us one of my corporals approached and asked me to lend him some money so that he could buy cigarettes for all the staff. He then went up to each of his mates in turn and did the same. By the end of this operation, he had collected a considerable sum of money. He then grabbed a stretcher and, with four soldiers wearing the Red Cross armband, went on board the ship which if my memory serves me right was called *Rochester Castle*. Fifteen minutes later the party returned with a casualty on the stretcher. My heart missed a beat: we were in for a hard day's work, I thought. As soon as the party stepped into the clinic, the "wounded" man leapt out of the stretcher, laughing and dancing, and hundreds of packets of cigarettes and bars of chocolate came tumbling out of his clothes. He obviously liked the exploit and was about to give a repeat performance. But I had to restrain as I was fully aware of the consequences should our commanding officer get wind of the ruse and I did not exactly relish the possibility of facing a court martial. Still, I could not help feeling delighted with the windfall; at the time the only way you could obtain cigarettes was on the black market at fifty times the normal price.

I cannot claim that my four years in the army were very stressful as I was invariably posted in clinics which were at some distance from strategic military targets. We went through a stretch of intensive activity during preparations for the invasion of Sicily when we had to carry out mass injections. On 8th May 1945 Germany surrendered unconditionally and by the end of that week I was back in civvy street, returning to my teaching career.

For me, the war years left me with bitter memories. The scars are still with me, not physical but moral and psychological. The war ruined what should have been the best years of my life, it snatched away my girl friend (she was one of the victims of the typhoid epidemic which broke out when a bomb damaged a sewer and contaminated drinking water), it interrupted my career and kept me away from my best friends. Time and time again I risked catching tuberculosis when I had to look after sick Yugoslav soldiers and I had to endure the company of many unsavoury characters.

MARGARET MORTIMER

When Germany declared war in 1939 I was on a holiday in

England. At the time I was teaching girls at the Higher Secondary School. Although there was a war on when my holiday came to an end, I returned to Malta via France and Italy taking the boat at Syracuse. During that journey I did not experience any untoward incident and one could almost forget that there was a war on.

Within a few days of my return to Malta a circular was issued inviting serving teachers to apply for scholarships in the United Kingdom; apparently some teachers who had been awarded scholarships turned them down because of the war. I was always eager for an opportunity to further my studies and I therefore hurried to send in my application. I was chosen, along with five others, to go to Britain. October 1939 saw me preparing to go back to England to take up studies at University College in Exeter, which at that time was considered to be a safe town. I crossed over to Syracuse and from there travelled by train to Calais to take the boat to Dover. The only problem I met came from the heavy seas running in the Channel during the crossing; the only war-related precaution taken was that we had to stay down below deck because of possible enemy action.

In the meantime the war started spreading to other parts of Europe and when it seemed clear that an Italo-German pact was imminent the British Council, which looked after the welfare of scholarship holders, was preparing to send us back to Malta. However when Italy declared war, we were still in the U.K and we had no option but to stay there. In Exeter months were to pass before we had any first-hand experience of the war, although occasionally we could see German bombers flying at a high altitude over Exeter on their way to bombarding Plymouth. My sister lived in South Kensington, London and I often took the opportunity of visiting her. In London of course one could see all around the devastation caused by the heavy bombing. During air raids we used to take shelter in the basement of the house. Luckily my sister's house suffered no damage from the bombing and not a single window pane was shattered. My sister was a very religious person and she had blind faith in the Sacred Heart of Jesus whose effigy she hung in every window of the house.

Exeter was relatively untouched by the war although, as in

138

every part of the United Kingdom, practically everything was rationed and the blackout was enforced throughout the night. In 1942, like all third year students, I moved out from the college buildings and went to live in digs so that we would make room for the freshers. My landlady was a Mrs Ellis, a woman in her late sixties. One night through my bedroom window I saw bright flares floating down from the black skies reminding me of *festa* time in Malta. I smelt danger and I hurriedly woke up Mrs Ellis and said we should move out of the house immediately. At that instant I heard a loud crack as if something had struck the house; it was an incendiary bomb and before you could bat an eyelid the house was in flames with all that was in it. We had barely enough time to run out into the garden and look helplessly at the conflagration which engulfed even the trees in the garden. Naturally all our belongings were wiped out including my books and lecture notes. We were lucky that the local authority stepped in and gave us money and coupons so that we could buy our essentials.

Though Mrs Ellis's house was a total loss, apparently very little damage was done to other buildings in Exeter and the newspapers gave very little or no importance to the raid. But ten days later Exeter experienced a much more ferocious raid. Incendiary bombs were dropped in large numbers and these were followed by explosives which caused havoc in several parts of the town. People said that the Germans wanted to teach the British press a lesson.

I spent the summer vacations working in the fields. My first vacation was spent gathering peas in North Devon and the following summer I got a job harvesting wheat in Wiltshire.

I kept in touch with events in Malta mainly through listening to the BBC which regularly carried news from every theatre of war including the Mediterranean in which, of course, Malta featured prominently. I wrote regularly to my family in Malta and equally regularly I received letters from them with the latest news. I also managed to send the occasional parcel with baby foods for my brother's children who were then very young. The news from Malta was far from reassuring. The British press was full of praise for the heroic part which the people of Malta were

HM King George VI inspecting a guard of honour at the Customs House Valletta on 20 June 1943.

(Photo WJ Jones)

playing and their guts and loyalty came in for a special mention. One of the College janitors kept a keen eye on news concerning Malta which he would pass on to me and it was he who first told me about the award of the George Cross by King George VI.

I stayed in England until November 1943 when like the other scholarship holders I received a letter from the Colonial Office informing us that transport to Malta was available to those of us who wanted to return. Four of us, two nurses and two teachers, travelled to Liverpool where we boarded a small cargo ship. Our boat stood off for a day and a night and then joined a convoy of about twelve ships. With everything being hush-hush we did not quite know where we were and, with the weather being unusually fine, some of us thought we were already in the Mediterranean. In fact, however, we were somewhere in the Atlantic and after some fifteen days at sea we made port at Gibraltar where much to our surprise after our experience of the blackout in England we saw lights everywhere. We also had our first good meal in many weeks. In Gibraltar we were put on a military plane which flew us to Algiers and two days later we were taken to Tunis for an overnight stay before boarding a military plane which finally landed us at Luqa. With all military movements shrouded in secrecy, our families did not even know that we had arrived.

In the meantime my family had returned to their home in Sliema after spending a couple of years at Lija as refugees. I took up my teaching career where I had left off and was posted at the girls' secondary school in Merchants Street, Valletta. Parts of Valletta were in ruins although in 1943 some effort was already being made to bring the situation back to normal.

The years in England saved me from the bombs, the hazards and the starvation which were the order of the day in Malta but after all was said and done, I was the only one in the family to have been bombed out of my lodgings and to have lost most of my personal belongings as a result of war activity.

SALVINA SAID

Our house in Siġġiewi was quite large and when war broke out several relatives and acquaintances came to live with us. My brother, a notary public by profession, vacated the couple of rooms which he used as offices and moved with his desk and books to one of the landings where he could meet his clients and draw up contracts. Several babies first saw the light of day in our house including two born to my sister-in-law who had married my brother during the war. As a rule I can say that though we were quite a crowd in that house, we lived in comparative harmony, with everyone making an effort to be tolerant and understanding - not always an easy task!

Siġġiewi was regarded as a safe place during the war and consequently drew refugees in large numbers from the harbour area especially Cottonera, Valletta, Floriana and Sliema. As a matter of fact few bombs were dropped on Siġġiewi and those were invariably from bombers which ran into trouble during sorties over Malta. Bombers used to fly over Siġġiewi on their way to dropping their bombs on the Luqa runways.

Lord Gort, VC, Governor of Malta:
4 May 1942 – 18 September 1944.

At the beginning of the war I was a headteacher at Siġġiewi Primary. Teaching duties were carried out normally except during air raids when we had to escort our pupils down into the shelters. I was later transferred to Qormi Primary as the head of that school had been appointed school inspectress. At Qormi life was decidedly different. On one occasion bombs fell on houses next to the school and a number of people lost their lives. The school was also damaged and the school caretaker, Teresa, was badly injured. Incidentally the school at Qormi was serving a dual function: classrooms on the ground floor had been converted into a temporary hospital and hospice for indigent old people while the first floor continued to serve as a school. Looking after the sick and aged were some Franciscan sisters.

When our pupils were taken down to the shelters, some of the teachers would try to go on with lessons but with people chattering away or praying at the top of their voices, that was virtually impossible. One incident which has stuck in my memory was when the Governor, Lord Gort, visited our school, going into each class to exchange a few words with teachers and children. In one particular class the teacher was dealing with "nouns in apposition" and Lord Gort, with a perplexed smile turned to one of his officers and asked him if he knew what a "noun in apposition" was because, he confessed, he himself did not have the faintest idea.

As a rule, my daily trip from Siġġiewi to Qormi and vice versa was done on foot except on the rare occasions when I managed to get a lift with a doctor who lived at Siġġiewi and worked at the hospital or even less likely in an Army lorry or car.

During my term of duty at Qormi I never encountered any difficulties from parents or pupils, and as at Siġġiewi, I found full co-operation at Qormi. I noticed that at Qormi the children did not look quite as lean and hungry as children from other localities: perhaps that was because there were so many bakeries in that town.

Along with others I was involved in the distribution of second-hand clothes and shoes to indigent families living in Siġġiewi. Many women including myself used to spend much of our free time re-cycling - as we would call it these days - old woollen garments, using the wool to knit jumpers and similar things. We used to hand over these to the parish priest who, in turn, would present them to needy persons. The Attorney General's wife, Mrs Inez Galea together with the wife of a high ranking Army officer and a secretary came regularly to Siġġiewi to hand over to us quantities of second-hand clothing so that we could pass these on to families in want. We sometimes managed to organise door-to-door collections of money for the poor. At first those who could afford to gave money willingly but gradually as life became harder, this source of assistance dried up. I have always been the sort of person who finds it terribly hard to go and beg for money and I can say that I did not relish the experience even though it was all done for a good cause.

CARMEN SAPIANO

Before the war we used to live at Paola but when hostilities broke out we took up our belongings and moved to Siġġiewi where two sisters, both spinsters, put us up at their house. I had just been appointed teacher and as was the practice in those days I had to do in-service training at the Training School which shared the premises in Old Mint Street with the infant school.

The 16th of January 1941 is a day I shall remember for the rest of my life. On that particular day as soon as I stepped into the Training School an air raid warning sounded and the red flag was run up at Castile. As usual we trooped into the shelter under the Law Courts. My father who happened to be with me came down too. It was an air raid of unprecedented intensity…bombs raining down and guns keeping up an incessant fire. Some of the infants started screaming in terror especially those whose fathers were manning the guns around the harbour. It was a heartbreaking scene; even hardened men broke down and wept openly.

The war was still on when I was sent to teach at Valletta Primary then housed in the Auberge de Baviere. During raids we used to go down with the children into the shelters. On one occasion we had just finished morning assembly when there was an air raid warning; the raid dragged on for hours during which the red flag was almost continuously at masthead, the sort of raid which wore you down mentally and physically. At about noon a man came down into the shelter carrying a dishful of baked rice. The children, of course, were starving at the time and naturally crowded around him in expectation. The man's reaction was to start weeping as he mumbled to the headteacher, "I haven't even got a spoonful for each of these poor children."

Halfway through the war I was transferred to Paola. Here I found that the school buildings had been requisitioned by the military authorities and the ARP section and what teaching there was was carried out in private houses leased to the Department of Education. I taught in Captain S C Xuereb's large house in Palm Street and at every air raid warning had to lead the pupils into a nearby shelter. Some of the children were quite a handful. A few of them would try to get out of the shelter during an air raid so that they could watch the action - the aerial dog fights, bombs raining down and guns firing away - while others were terrified and would scream for their mothers. I do not remember any serious incidents at the school. After school many of us would spend hours in the shelter sitting on wooden boxes or stools. We were very close to starvation in those days: food was scarce and what little there was was rationed. I remember one particularly moving scene when a five year old boy with tears streaming down his face kept asking his mother for a slice of bread and the mother, weeping, saying, "I haven't got any, my son". What made that scene even more poignant was that none of us there had any food to give him. I used to go with members of my family to the farms lying behind the Turkish Cemetery to try and buy some vegetables, under the counter, as we would say, because farmers were not allowed to sell their products directly to the public. There was one field, I remember, which was covered with cauliflowers and we would ask the farmer to sell us one. "That's ten shillings", he would say, pointing at one, but would not pull it out of the ground before he had the ten shillings tucked away safely in his pocket. Then we would hide the cauliflower so that any passing policeman would not notice.

As for teaching I can say that lessons went on almost normally; we used to have routine inspections and even the school doctor visited the pupils regularly. When the scabies epidemic raged, pupils who had contracted the disease were exempted from attending school so that hopefully the epidemic would not spread.

GUŻEPPI ZAMMIT

On the outbreak of hostilities, we put together some of our belongings and left our home town, Tarxien, to move to Mosta. I was then employed as a teacher and I had to report for duty at Mosta primary school. During the summer holidays we returned to Tarxien and when the scholastic year began I was assigned to teach what was then called Standard IV (now known as Year Six) in a private house leased to the Education Department situated in Zabbar Road, Paola. At that time the primary schools for Tarxien and Paola were amalgamated. The class which I was given had previously been in the hands of a teacher who had been conscripted. A few days after that I too received the draft papers.

A couple of days before, the then Director of Education, Dr Laferla, had paid a visit to the school; after putting a few questions to the pupils he expressed his satisfaction at the progress. I could not stop myself from confessing to him that I had only had the class for a few days and any praise was due to their previous teacher, who was now a regular soldier. "That will make a man of him", remarked Dr Laferla. When I said that I, too, had been called up he said, "That will do you a lot of good!" Dr Laferla was well known for being an enthusiastic supporter of Army life and he was all for teachers doing a stint in the Army. In fact so many teachers joined up that for a time there was a serious shortage of teachers in the schools.

My days in the Army started towards the end of summer of 1941; I was attached to the Royal Army Medical Corps (RAMC). We spent our first month as recruits at St Andrew's. Most of those days were spent in performing the various routine drills and road marches; then came my first regular posting at St Patrick's military hospital. It was a fully equipped hospital with spacious wards housing the sick and the wounded. My mates and I performed the duties of medical orderlies. The nursing was in the hands of British servicemen who, incidentally, were very knowledgeable in the care of the sick. What I found hardest to get used to were the working hours: I used to get home at around half past four in the afternoon and by ten at night I had to be back at the barracks. No transport was available and I had to walk all the way from Tarxien to St Andrew's and back. There were times when I was lucky to get a lift for at least a part of the way.

One particular nasty incident which has stuck in my memory after so many years was when German fighters strafed the Gozo boat which was on one of its trips between Gozo and Valletta; the fighters opened fire when the boat was just off St Andrews. Some

Gozo boat being attacked by a German plane; painting by Tony E. Spiteri.

of those on board were killed and others wounded; these were brought into the hospital at St Andrew's. Subsequently I made a request to be transferred to the Dressing Centre located in Marquis Barbaro's villa at Tarxien. The Dressing Centre was the medical post for military personnel in the neighbourhood and every morning soldiers from billets in the vicinity called for medication or to report sick; when it was not possible to provide treatment on the spot, they were referred to one of the hospitals.

St. Andrew's Hospital in ruins.

In February 1942 I was back in my teaching post after some eight months in the Army. By then the school premises at Tarxien and Paola had been requisitioned by the military authorities and the headteacher asked me whether I had a spare room in my house which could double up as a classroom during the day. I suggested the sitting room, and suddenly I found myself teaching in my own home. In all I had some twelve pupils. Across the street, situated conveniently just opposite my front door was an air raid shelter and whenever an air raid warning sounded all of us - the pupils and my three children - would make our way down the shelter. As teachers we had strict orders not to let children out of our sight during air raids even if the raid were to run into the evening. Pupils were told that they were to stay at home if there was an air raid before eight in the morning. There were days when children did not turn up for school at all because of this rule. Schooling was not at all regular during the war years...

During this time I had a few men from the Devonshire Regiment coming to me for private tuition in the Maltese and Italian languages. Army authorities had offered a prize of ten pounds for the soldier who showed the best performance in the Maltese language, the prize being presumably meant to encourage the British Tommy to fraternise with the local population. The prize was in fact awarded to one of my soldier students. This same man had also picked up a working knowledge of Italian which was expected to be useful during the projected invasion of Sicily. A few soldiers who were billeted in the vicinity used to come to our home to have a chat with the family and play with the kids. Looking back in retrospect I think the men were somewhat homesick and were missing their families. Sometimes they would stay on to share a meal with us; from time to time they would bring along with them some foodstuff - biscuits or a few bars of chocolate - to supplement the meagre family rations. I remember that once, a few days before Christmas, we were presented with a tin of biscuits which my wife used to make the Christmas pudding.

Another incident which I remember vividly was when, just after the stroke of midnight, there was a knock on the door. I opened the door and there was one of those soldiers with a few tins of corned beef; he said he and his mates had been unloading the cargo of a convoy ship and he thought we would find these tins useful. On another occasion, which I remember just as vividly, another man - heaven-sent I thought - had brought me a thousand or so cigarettes.

Incidentally the man who had got the Maltese prize, John Lassels by name, was in the Intelligence branch and after the war came back to Malta to give evidence in the trial of some Maltese nationals who resided in Italy during the war and were being charged with collaborating with the Fascists.

Some of those friends we made during the war years kept in touch with us for many years and occasionally visited us and we reciprocated the visits.

V. Priests and Religious

Fr RIKARD ATTARD

When the siren signalled the first air-raid, I was in the vestry of the Annunciation Church in Vittoriosa preparing to say the seven o'clock Mass. I disregarded the warning and proceeded with the Mass as if it was a normal day probably out of ignorance of the real nature of war. After the Mass I walked to my mother's house in Cospicua and later in the day helped the family to load essential provisions on the mule-cart before leaving for Qormi where, before the war, my mother had rented a house. After seeing them off I returned to the priory for the night.

Within the first few weeks of the war, Vittoriosa became a ghost town with cats and dogs roaming the deserted streets. Then, as air-raids became less frequent complacency set in and people began to make their way back to their homes which they had so hurriedly abandoned in a mass exodus. On the 16th of January 1941, the Luftwaffe showed its teeth in an air-raid the like of which had never been experienced before. The massive and fierce bombardment terrified everyone and crowds flocked to the priory for shelter. I suppose there were close to a thousand persons sheltering under our roof. When the bombs began to rain down, rocking and shaking the walls around us, people were scared out of their wits and one woman became hysterical and began to tear out her hair.

During a lull I went out with some people and heard that hundreds of bombs had hit Senglea. We walked down cautiously to the St Lawrence foreshore (now Xatt ir-Rizq) to investigate but before we had time to do so a second wave of bombers flew in and I hurried back to the priory to calm down the people there. The rest took cover in the Church of St Lawrence. The second raid was as massive as the first but the bombs fell much closer to us this time. When the all-clear sounded I heard people screaming that the church had received a direct hit and I went as fast as I could to render whatever assistance was possible. On arriving there I saw that the church vestry was reduced to a mass of rubble, and I knew at once that many people were buried under that rubble. I remember a young woman who was pinned under some stones but mercifully was still alive. I helped to pull her out; she survived the ordeal but walked with a severe limp thereafter. Among the many helpers I remember Father (later Monsignor) Pawl Galea, then archpriest of the parish. Dun Pawl was speechless with horror, and after we had done all we could I asked him to go with me to the priory, gave him a tot of whisky and invited him to spend the night with us.

In the meantime those people who had returned to Vittoriosa, hastily left again to go back to the refugee homes. Our community stayed in Vittoriosa as decreed by our superiors, a decision with which I could not agree but had nonetheless to obey. Three days after that blitz while the community was in the refectory for the mid-day meal there was an air-raid warning followed by a heavy attack. We ran out of the building to seek shelter near the police station. Bombs were falling around us with ear-splitting and earth-shaking explosions. On going back to the priory we saw that the all buildings with the exception of the church were in ruins; a few days later the church collapsed too. We lost all our possessions in that one raid, including the "treasury", that is, the cupboard with the silver vessels belonging to the friars. I lost two communion-cups and a set of vestments. That same evening we made our way to the Rabat priory. On the following day, a Monday, the Father Provincial Fr Nolan, an Irishman, instructed me to go to Vittoriosa to try to salvage whatever was possible. With the help of some men, I managed to retrieve the statue of St Dominic from among the ruins, as well as a few other articles, all

The church of the Annunciation sustained heavy damage
and had to be rebuilt.

(Courtesy L. Zahra)

of which we loaded on a truck and took up to Rabat.

Some two weeks after that we got an offer from Mr Ignatius
Bonavia, the marble merchant, to move into his villa at Fleur-de-
Lys. The twelve of us who had been bombed out of our convent
home in Vittoriosa gladly accepted the offer and soon we were
giving our services to the residents of the area who now num-
bered, with the influx of the refugees, around five thousand.
Many of the refugees came from the Sliema area.

A stone's throw away from our new home was an anti-aircraft

The damaged belfry and façade of the church of the
Annunciation at Vittoriosa.

(Courtesy L. Zahra)

battery mounting seven guns. One day an Italian fighter crashed
near the battery and I hurried to the site to administer the Last
Sacraments *sub conditione* to the pilot.

I had been through a similar experience way back in the summer of 1940 when I was spending a short holiday in our summer
house at Marsascala. A dog-fight between an Italian fighter and
an RAF plane ended with the Italian going down in flames. I
rushed to the wreckage and found that the pilot was badly
injured. To my great surprise the face was familiar; shortly
before the war I met him a few times in a hatter's shop in

What was once the historical clock tower in the main
square at Vittoriosa.

(Photo W.A. Gatt)

Valletta; he was a sales representative from a firm manufacturing
hats based in Florence. The pilot was rushed to hospital but died
soon after. I learned later that the RAF pilot also perished in the
same action.

After the war, in 1947 to be precise, while travelling in Italy I
made it a point to pay a visit to the Italian pilot's family which I
had traced through the help of a friar friend of mine. It is difficult
to describe the happiness with which the pilot's widow and his
mother heard me describe how I had managed to assist him and
how I had tried to do my best so that he would not be buried in
an unmarked grave.

It was also at Marsascala that I heard rumours that the Governor was about to issue orders for the evacuation of that seaside village, which rumours subsequently turned out to be true. I therefore wrote to the Bishop of Gozo, Mgr Gonzi, to ask him to provide a home for the ninety children of the Cospicua orphanage who had moved to Marsascala. The bishop kindly obliged and offered them a house in Marsalforn.

I counted among my friends a number of influential people, among them the Police Commissioner, Mr Joseph Axisa. When on the 19th of November 1944 the statue of the Immaculate Conception was to be returned processionally to Cospicua from Birkirkara where it had been taken for security reasons, it was due to my persistent pleading that the Commissioner consented to send a contingent of Mounted Police to accompany the ceremonial procession.

Sister CARMELA AXISA

When Italy declared war I was a Sister of Charity living in our convent in Rabat and teaching at the government primary school in Mtahleb. With the other nuns I was hearing Mass when the first air-raid warning sounded. The members of the congregation got somewhat restless and the celebrant, Fr Mikiel Callus had to stop and ask them to calm down and get on with their devotions. We were all terrified and queued up to confess our sins; poor Fr Mikiel was kept busy all morning hearing confessions!

About two years later Mother Provincial gave me instructions to move to our convent in Tarxien and to take up teaching duties at the Birżebbuġa government school. Once as I was returning to Tarxien from BirŻebbuġa in the company of another nun there was an air-raid and the driver stopped the bus. All the passengers scurried out of the bus and dashed to the nearest safe place which happened to be a large store. Inside we came face to face with a number of soldiers. When the all-clear sounded and we were about to leave, one of the soldiers came up to me and said, "Next time you'd better find some other place to take cover in; you've just been inside an ammunition depot". When I got back to the convent and recounted the whole story, Mother Superior was so worried that there and then she said that she could not let us to go on with teaching in these circumstances and she wrote to the Director of Education, Dr Laferla to that effect. The latter promptly wrote back insisting that we continue with our teaching duties. But she was adamant. "Dear Director," she told him, "the schools are yours but the sisters are mine." And that was that.

Although I was no longer teaching, I stayed on in Tarxien. It was a time when bombing was frequent and heavy, but luckily we had a very safe shelter in the convent. I slept in the shelter as did two children who were boarding with us having, I believe, lost their mother. The two children were related to Mgr Carmelo Bonnici. We spent most of our waking hours praying for deliverance from the evils of war.

I was then ordered to take up nursing duties at St Francis Hospital, a school which had been converted into an emergency hospital in Birkirkara. During air-raids we dared not leave the inmates' bedside to take cover and daily risked our lives.

In 1943 when the typhoid epidemic broke out, reportedly caused by the contamination of drinking water by sewage, I was transferred to St Luke's to look after victims of the disease which carried off a large number of people.

One may mention here that children residing in the Ta' Cini and Ta' Bugeja institutes were transferred to Verdala Palace. The nuns, to whom these children were entrusted, faced many difficulties; for example they did not have a proper shelter and during air-raids had to take cover, along with the children, in the basement of the palace. When an air-raid warning sounded during the night, we had to wake up the poor children and lead them, half asleep, into the basement. Living in the vicinity of the palace was a Rumanian refugee family among whom was a fourteen year old girl who used to come running to us whenever she heard the siren wail so that she could be with our children. One day as she was running towards the palace she was killed by a bomb. Her body was carried into the palace and wrapped up in blankets until the ambulance came round. It was quite some time before the mother became aware of her daughter's fate; she thought that her daughter was, as usual, staying with us. When the news was broken to her, the poor woman could not contain her grief and wept uncontrollably for many hours.

In another incident, while Sister Rosa Borda was busily attending to inmates of the Mental Hospital at Attard, a bomb landed and exploded in the ward killing her on the spot. We wept for our departed sister who died while performing her duty.

The badly damaged church of St. Augustine, Valletta.

(Courtesy P. Spiteri).

In 1952, I left the community and joined the Augustinian cloistered nuns in Valletta.

Canon *VINCENZ AZZOPARDI*

I was ordained priest five years before war broke out in 1940 and I was living with my family in Valletta. My duties included teaching at St Aloysius College in Birkirkara. Soon after the first air-raids we moved to Sliema where we had a summer house, but when HMS *Terror* began to draw the enemy's fire, we packed up and went as refugees to Birkirkara. Fr Gwann Calleja, a close friend and a fellow teacher at St Aloysius', offered to share his house with us.

At Birkirkara, there was more than enough work to keep me busy: I was teaching at the College and doing pastoral work in the parish. Among my various duties I was often invited to bless shelters and military establishments. I remember once being asked to Ta' Giorni battery to perform one such ceremony during which officers and men confessed their sins and received Holy Communion. The following day, the battery received a direct hit; eight Maltese gunners perished in that action.

One day I went up to our house in Valletta to get some books. An air-raid warning stopped me in my tracks and I took cover in the crypt under-

Fr. Joseph Borg, OSA, HCF

lying the Church of St Augustine. It was a particularly heavy attack and many of the people sheltering there panicked.

I do not think that the refugees from the towns could be said to have exercised a bad influence on the local villagers. The people were like one big family; that is probably one of the few good things you could say about the war. When Italy surrendered we returned to our home in Old Bakery Street, Valletta. Doors and windows were badly damaged and the roof was in a bad state, but we decided to move in regardless.

Fr JOSEPH BORG OSA, HCF

In 1939, ten years after my ordination, I requested permission from the Archbishop to enrol in the Armed Forces as a military chaplain. The Archbishop readily gave his consent and introduced me to Fr Robinson SJ who invited me to celebrate Mass for the Irish Fusiliers, then stationed at Għajn Tuffieħa. Every Sunday morning an Austin two-seater would be waiting for me at the door of our priory in Valletta to take me to the camp; after the service the same car would take me back to Valletta. Later on I also officiated for Maltese soldiers stationed at Fort Campbell near Selmun.

In 1940, with Malta finding itself in the front line, the infantry regiments were strengthened; in addition to the existing 1/KOMR, two new battalions were formed, the 2/KOMR and the 3/KOMR. I was then offered a commission which I accepted after consulting my superiors. I was commissioned on the 13th of August 1941 and now as a member of the regular forces, I was in uniform with the rank of captain and billeted with the regulars. My regiment was the 3/KOMR with headquarters at Qrendi but I was also chaplain to all the men in the Southern Brigade dispersed over a wide area in the South of Malta stretching from Qrendi to Għar Dalam., In addition to the Maltese regiments, this Brigade comprised, among others, the Hampshires in Gudia and the Dorsets in Siġġiewi.

I was constantly on the move and though petrol was very

scarce, the Commanding Officer of the Southern Brigade, Brigadier de la Bere, issued me with five gallons of petrol per week. To take me round, I could also rely on "Censu tal-Bonu" and his pony trap. Mercifully, none of the men in the regiments to which I was attached was involved in any fatal incidents, at least as far as I can remember, even though we were stationed around Luqa airfield. But we passed through some hair-raising moments. While celebrating Mass for the Hampshires at the Xlejli Tower, Gudia, there was an air-raid warning, instantly followed by gunfire and earth-shaking explosions which were much too close for comfort. I confess to having been terror-stricken but on seeing that not one man in the congregation made the slightest move, I pulled myself together and went on with the Mass.

An incident which I remember clearly concerns the crew of a

TO THE

DIVINE HEART OF JESUS

IMMENSE IN GLORY

AS IN MIGHT

THE OFFICERS AND MEN

OF THE

3/ K.O.M.R.

CONSECRATE

THEMSELVES

THIS 24th DAY

OF

DECEMBER 1941.

Junkers which crashed in the vicinity of Wied iz-Zurrieq one night. The men managed to get out of the wreckage and hid in a cave nearby. An RAF man reported the incident and a detachment from the 3/KOMR manning a beach post marched to the cave. The Germans, of course, did not put up any resistance and gave themselves up. As they were being marched away, I could see that one of them was limping badly and obviously in great pain. One of the Maltese soldiers offered to help the man but the German scorned the offer. The prisoners were taken to battalion headquarters in Qrendi for routine interrogation. As can be imagined all this attracted a lot of villagers who flocked to see the Germans but not one hand was lifted against them.

One day the thought occurred to me that the Battalion should be consecrated to the Sacred Heart of Jesus. When I mentioned this idea to Colonel Mario Apap Bologna, he shot it down in no uncertain terms. "What?" he asked, "Are you proposing that we take all our men under one roof? And what if, with all these air-raids, we find ourselves responsible for a major tragedy?" I was not to be dissuaded so easily and proceeded to pile on the arguments until the colonel finally gave in and said, "Have it your way, then; but make sure you inform the Archbishop." At the time the Archbishop was convalescing at the Blue Sisters Hospital and when I outlined what I had in mind, he not only agreed but also promised, in the same breath, to be present for the ceremony. He suggested that I should celebrate Mass and he would assist me. The ceremony was in fact held on the 24th December 1941 in the parish church in Qrendi. All the men of the 3/KOMR were present. Some eighty men from the Hampshires also attended, riding to Qrendi from Gudia on their bicycles.

I still carry around, in my body, a souvenir from the war in the shape of a splinter which got embedded in my thigh. A large number of butterfly bombs had been released and one of these exploded some three or four metres away from where I stood; there was a cloud of smoke and an explosion, but that was all. When I tried to walk I felt a sudden pain; I looked at my trousers and saw a small bloodstained hole. I made my way to the First

Archbishop Michael Gonzi with group of German POW's. Fr Borg is seen second from left.

(Courtesy J. Borg).

Aid post and was seen to by Dr Ferrante. He explained that a splinter had lodged in the flesh but that there was no need to do anything about it. "It won't bother you!", he assured me, and true enough it's been there for fifty years without causing me any discomfort.

Chaplains enjoyed the esteem of all men from the highest officer to the latest recruit. When once I was introduced to the General Officer Commanding, he remarked, "The *padre* is the most important man in the Battalion". He was, of course, referring to the role we as chaplains played, a role in which spiritual advice was combined with counselling and the maintenance of morale. I must have spent countless hours comforting men who were worrying about their families or putting in a word for them with their officers. Sometimes I would stick my neck out to help them get permission to pay a flying visit to their families... then they would turn up a couple of hours after the agreed time and leave me to face the music!

One night, at about eleven, as I was resting in the Qrendi barracks, I was called to the sick-bed of a soldier in the Guarena

163

Palace where one of our companies was billeted; the man was in very bad shape from a severe inflammation of the tonsils. No transport was available and I had to walk the not inconsiderable distance. As I hurried past the dark field walls, I could see searchlight beams sweeping the sky. When I reached the man's bedside, I could see that his condition was critical; I gave him absolution and some minutes later, he was taken by ambulance to Mtarfa.

In addition to my normal duties I also found time to give religious instruction to a number of British soldiers, about seven I think, who wished to be received into the Roman Catholic Church before marrying Maltese girls. In one case, after marrying the girl and fathering a child, the British soldier deserted the

Foreword To all Catholic German Prisoners-of war in Malta	**Vorwort** Allen katholischen deutschen Kriegsgefangenen auf Malta.
The Archbishop of Freiburg - im - Breisgau, M g r. Groeber, in his Corpus Christi Pastoral this year wrote as follows: "Nor do I have any doubt that the Catholic priests in the c o u n t r i e s w h e r e German prisoners - of - war of their faith are held, will, in Christian charity, extend their pastoral love to them as well. ... Although	Der Erzbischof von Freiburg i. Br., M g r. G r o e b e r, schrieb in seinem apost. Briefe vom Fronleichnamsfest diesesJahres1945: „Ich zweifel nicht, dass die katholischenPriester aller Länder ihre Sorgfalt allendeutschen Kriegsgefangenen angedeihen lassen werden. — Obwohl wir verschiedene Sprachen sprechen

Prayer book printed locally for use by German prisoners of war in Malta.
(Courtesy J. Borg)

164

two and was never seen again. A totally different story was that of another soldier who became a fervent Catholic and brought up a model family, with one of his daughters joining a community of nuns.

After Italy's surrender, some two thousand German prisoners-of-war were transported to Malta; of these about eight hundred professed the Roman Catholic faith and having a working knowledge of the German language, I was appointed to serve as chaplain in the POW camps in Safi, Ta' Qali and St Andrew's. Some of the prisoners were accomplished craftsmen and they used to turn out large numbers of stone and wooden objects. During my term of office, I collected a number of prayers and hymns in German and had these printed in book form, with the Archbishop generously footing the bill.

When, later that year, the Archbishop travelled to Rome and had an audience with the Pope, he presented a copy of the booklet to the Pope in order, he told me, to show His Holiness that we in Malta were treating the German Catholics well. On his return to Malta, the Archbishop told me that the Pope, who had more than a passing knowledge of the German language, had taken a cursory look at the booklet and remarked briefly, "I'm sorry to have to say this but the title carries a mistake."

I was demobilised on the 28th March 1945. Before I left, in addition to be presented with the war medals, I was made an Honorary Chaplain to the Forces (HCF). When I look back at those days, I get a sense of satisfaction; I think I did my duty to the best of my ability and, I hope, my work was appreciated by the servicemen I came in contact with.

Mgr GERALD FRENDO

Months before the outbreak of hostilities, the Colonial Government prepared evacuation plans for the civilian population living in the harbour area. According to the evacuation plans announced in March 1939 residents of Cospicua were to seek shelter in Qormi, the people of Senglea were to go to Żebbuġ and

Siġġiewi, and those of Vittoriosa were to proceed to Lija, Attard and Balzan. But those plans were not followed when war did break out. The first bombings of the 11th June 1940 caused wide-

TIMES OF MALTA SATURDAY JUNE 15 1940

THE TREK FROM THE TOWNS

Measures to be taken in Reception Villages

His Excellency has already paid a tribute to the magnificent way in which those living in crowded areas near to Military objectives have behaved under most trying circumstances. Many of these people have now evacuated these areas and a host of new problems have arisen out of this removal, for the solution of which not only their own cooperation but also that of those living in the receiving areas, is essential.

It is only by the solution of these problems that the population can be stabilized, so that the essential shelter, health and food distribution problems may be tackled in the places to which their instincts have led the people to go. And this stabilization of the population is so essential that unless it is achieved and maintained by the good will of all concerned, the trials and sufferings of the people may well become worse than they were in their own homes.

The Italians want to demoralize the people. The people must realize that, that is their game, and organize to defeat such tactics and at the same time to help themselves.

In almost all of the reception villages there already exists a District Committee which should assume the powers of an emergency committee consisting of inhabitants of the village, and one or more refugees. Where no District Committee already exists, one should be formed immediately. This Committee will advise and assist in the practical application of the general schemes for amelioration which will be started throughout the Islands.

the strengthening and organization of shelters as will give them confidence to stay in their new homes, as the safest place in which they can be. Any further mass movement of the population, beyond levelling out under official supervision any areas which are now already impossibly overcrowded, will play right into the hands of the enemy and only precipitate further hardships for themselves.

With this object, the Emergency Committee in each village, with such additional helpers as are necessary, will make house to house calls through the village to find out which houses in each convenient group of three or four houses has the best protection. Families of that group will elect a leader who will be responsible for the proper running of that group shelter and for seeing that all members of the group at home during a raid find their way there safely.

SHELTER FOR REFUGEES

The group, after the selection of their shelter, will be advised how best, by their own labour and any assistance which they can obtain, this group shelter can be strengthened and improved. A small emer-

GOVERNMENT'S ACTION IN DEALING WITH PROBLEM

THE GOVERNMENT HAS TAKEN IMMEDIATE ACTION IN DEALING WITH THE PROBLEM THAT HAS ARISEN WITH REGARD TO THE EXODUS OF PEOPLE FROM THE CITIES AND TOWNS TO THE VILLAGES, AND THE FOLLOWING IS REPRINTED FROM THE GOVERNMENT GAZETTE FOR THE INFORMATION OF THE PUBLIC:—

1. With the exception of Ħal Far, Kalafrana and Luqa there shall be established in each village in Malta lying to the West of a line running due North and South, through, but not including Ħamrun, and to the South of a line running due East and West through, but not including, Tarxien, a refugee settlement centre. The term "village" in these Regulations means a village within the areas so defined and also includes Marsaskala. The address of such centre shall be advertised in writing outside the Police Station in each such village.

2. Every refugee who enters any village shall immediately report at the Centre before seeking housing accommodation. This regulation shall not apply to any refugee who has already made an agreement for living accommodation before entering the village.

3. The Officer in charge at each such Centre may direct a refugee to any house where accommodation is available, or may, where there is in his opinion no sufficient accommodation in that village, direct a refugee to leave the village.

4. Where a refugee does not obey such an order to leave a village, the officer in charge of the Centre may call upon any police officer to remove, and such ...

sufficient accommodation, and shall proceed thither as directed. Where any refugee refuses to make any election, the police officer may, if necessary, by the use of reasonable force, require the refugee to proceed to any village where there is, in his opinion, accommodation for him.

8. With the approval of the Government there may be appointed in any village, a Protection Officer, and such Officer may, where in any place there is in his opinion sufficient shelter against air attack, requisition, if there is convenient public land or building available and the use of the most suitable and available private land or building or of any private land or building or portion of a building for the construction or adaptation as an air raid shelter, may require any person in possession of suitable implements to lend them for the purpose of such construction.

Where he is unable on request to those living near such land or building to obtain any, or any sufficient voluntary labour for the construction or adaptation of such shelter, he may require all or any of the able-bodied males between the ages of sixteen and fifty, living within a space of a mile radius of such land, to work at the construction of such shelter according to his directions.

The *Times of Malta*, on the problems created by the mass exodus of people from the towns and cities in the Harbour area.

spread panic and confusion and the scene of multitudes of refugees streaming into the streets of Qormi from the Three Cities on that day has left an indelible memory in my mind. They carried mattresses, stoves, pots, kettles and bundles as they trudged aimlessly on, not knowing where they were to spend the night. The local Protection Officer enlisted the help of the parish priest to get the refugees organised and to find accommodation for them. The first places to be requisitioned for the purpose were the chapels, the parish centres and the warehouses in which *festa* decorations and equipment were usually stored. I am proud to say that many of my fellow villagers opened their doors to the refugees and gave them lodging.

During the first air-raid, I was assisting the priest officiating at a funeral - I was not as yet ordained priest - and the cortege had just set off from the church on its way to the cemetery. We all took cover in the Church of St Francis which was opened for the purpose and stayed huddled there until the all-clear sounded.

I was in my last year of studies in the Faculty of Theology which had transferred its seat from Valletta to St Joseph's Institute in Hamrun and I used to walk from Qormi to Hamrun for lectures and back. In 1941 we had our final examinations

Cardinal Spellman, Archbishop Caruana, Lord Gort and Bishop Gonzi.

which were held in the crypt of St Dominic's Church in Rabat. When the day of the ordination ceremony drew near, problems began to crop up. The Archbishop, Dom Maurus Caruana, was a sick man and his duties, like ordinations and confirmations, were being performed by the Bishop of Gozo, Mgr Gonzi. The constant air attacks and other problems made it extremely difficult for Mgr Gonzi to cross over to Malta and the ceremony was postponed time and time again. Finally the five of us who were to be ordained were asked whether we were prepared to make the trip to Gozo to have the ordination there. We agreed at once and on the 20th September we were ordained priests in the Gozo Cathedral.

As a newly ordained priest, I had a hectic time. For example, as often as not, I started hearing confessions at half past four in the morning and finished at around eleven, sitting for more than six hours in the confessional. The number of marriages increased sharply. There was no unemployment and wages improved so that workers could easily earn, say, eight shillings (40c) a day. Church ceremonies were, more or less, conducted normally with the exception, of course, of external festivities. At Qormi, one could say that we had even more ceremonies than before the war because the refugees tried to celebrate, in some way, their own feast-days. For example we celebrated the feast of the Immaculate Conception, for which occasion the Cospicua canons attended as a body. We did the same when the feasts of St Lawrence and of Our Lady of Victories came round.

Besides my pastoral work at Qormi, I had other commitments. For example I delivered sermons in Hamrun, Żebbuġ and occasionally Safi, going to those places usually by managing to get a lift on a military truck or a horse-drawn cart. Once I had to go, together with three altar boys, to Attard to officiate at some ceremony and I had arranged with a truck driver that he would pick us up at a certain place. We waited in vain and finally decided to go to the driver's house. We were met at the doorstep by his wife who explained that someone had planted a stolen case of sardines on the truck, and the police had as a result arrested him.

Part of the school at Qormi was converted into a centre for handicapped persons and old folk. The unit was managed by Dr Maria Condachi and had as its spiritual director Fr (later Mgr) Mikiel Azzopardi. The latter persuaded some nuns who were employed by the Department of Education to help in the running of the unit. One day a heavily laden RAF bomber developed engine trouble and before crashing into a small quarry destroyed a house killing both parents. The children survived; one of the boys was adopted by Fr Azzopardi and the other by Dr Condachi.

The 10th of February 1942 was a tragic day for the people of Qormi. On that day I felt unwell and had to stay at home. In one of the day's raids bombs were dropped on the village. When the all-clear sounded, a seminary student knocked urgently on the door. "The parish priest would like you to go at once; some people have been killed," he said. I dressed quickly and left. One tragic scene after another met my eyes, as I went round the devastated houses with their dead.

I cannot say that I ever went hungry during the war. Qormi managed pretty well in that respect. Many of the villagers worked as stevedores in the harbour area in those days. A ship with a cargo of grain foundered in the harbour and my brother, like many others, twice brought home a sack salvaged from its holds. Of course those who like my brother worked in the harbour always managed, somehow, to obtain extra provisions. One should also remember that many villagers had a plot or field in which to grow various products to supplement the meagre rations.

A certain degree of laxity in moral behaviour crept in during the war years but I do not agree with those who attribute such laxity to the influx of the Cottonera refugees. I would rather tend to attribute the lowering of moral standards to the inevitable promiscuity when too many people are crowded too closely together. Whatever the case, one thing stands out clearly: the readiness with which the people of Qormi welcomed into their midst the unfortunate refugees. I do not deny that there were occasions when quarrels and even fights broke out between the two sections of the population, but generally speaking the two lived in harmony, so much so that to this day you still find ex-refugees who regularly visit Qormi.

Can. Paul Galea, archpriest of Vittoriosa.

(Courtesy P. Galea)

Mgr PAWL GALEA

Before the war I was assistant parish priest at Vittoriosa, but when the war broke out and the parishioners left in a mass exodus I moved to Zabbar and for about a month was involved in the pastoral care of that village. When at the end of that month my family moved up to Rabat I joined them and served in the parish church of St Paul. One day, Fr Anton Buhagiar, the parish priest asked me whether I would be willing to go back to Vittoriosa as curate of the parish. I said that I would and on the 4th of October 1940, the archpriest, Fr (later Mgr) Gużeppi Farrugia handed over to me the spiritual leadership of the town. By that time daily life had almost returned to normal with a fairly large number of refugees returning to their home town. Then came the 16th of

January 1941 which abruptly and terrifyingly changed all this; I refer of course to the fierce attacks on the aircraft carrier *Illustrious.*

It was, I remember, a Thursday. At about half past two in the afternoon an air-raid warning sent people scurrying to take cover. Unlike many others who rushed into the church, I hurried into one of the bell-towers which, I had been told by architect Barbara - then in charge of the construction of shelters - was much more solidly built than the church and was therefore much more likely to stand up to bombing. Sheltering with me in the bell-tower were the sacristan Prutazju Casha and the son of the other sacristan, Wenzu Degabriele. It was not long before the roar of the raiders' engines, the intensive gunfire and the earth-shaking explosions made us realise that this was no ordinary air-raid. At one point an exceptionally powerful explosion shook the bell-tower and a blast of air ripped through the building. This was abruptly followed by a lull and we emerged into the daylight. We saw that Senglea had borne the brunt of that attack, but before we could look more closely a second wave of bombers sent us scrambling back to the safety of the bell-tower. Looking back for an instant I caught sight of some people who had just stepped ashore from the ferry boat running to take cover in the sacristy. Poor men, they did not know that they were entering their graves... Seconds later a tremendous explosion rocked the bell-tower. When the all clear sounded we emerged into a scene of devastation; where before stood the sacristy was now one huge mound of fallen masonry. We tried to gain access into the sacristy through the church but the doorway between the two was blocked with debris. A girl's voice was pleading weakly, "Help me, Dun Pawl! Help me!" Beside the girl, half buried among the rubble, was a man. The two were soon pulled out; the man expired soon after arriving at the hospital but the girl lived to tell the tale. A few metres away we came across a baby who was tenderly picked up; she, too, survived. As for the rest, some forty in all, there was nothing we could do. The only other person to come out alive was a woman who however died in hospital later.

On the following day, I went up to Mdina to report to

Archbishop Caruana who happened to be discussing some matter with Mgr Gonzi, then Bishop of Gozo. Three days later, that is on the following Sunday, St Dominic's Priory was destroyed. I therefore made my way to Mdina a second time to submit another report. At the conclusion of the interview the Archbishop invited me to spend a couple of days in the palace to recuperate, at the end of which period he suggested that I return to Vittoriosa "like the captain who does not abandon his post when the ship is sinking" as he put it. I understood that to be an order and I could not but obey, so back to Vittoriosa I went. I did not have a roof of my own to sleep under. By arrangement with the authorities, I was given a room at the police station, which conveniently had a chapel attached to it, and in this chapel I used to celebrate Mass

The chapel at Vittoriosa Police Station.
(Courtesy P. Galea)

and to administer the Sacraments. Labourers from the Public Works Department put up a hut for me in the Ditch (dry moat) which I made use of for the same purpose. At the request of the Archbishop, the Lieutenant Governor authorised the issue of daily rations for me so that I could have my meals with the staff of the Health Department, that is Dr Ramiro Cauchi, Dr Antonio Paris, Mr Lorenzo Vassallo and Mr Lorry Boffa.

In the meantime a large number of people from Cospicua, Vittoriosa and Kalkara began to congregate in the Ditch. Many lived there; others spent the day in their houses but passed the night in cubicles dug out of the solid rock at the foot of the bastions. At this time my appointment was that of an assistant parish priest. On the 9th of December 1941 the competition for the post of Archpriest was published and I submitted my application to the examining board. A few days later I was informed that I was successful and given the appointment of Archpriest.

Inside a private shelter at the Vittoriosa Ditch.

(Photo N. Genovese)

In Vittoriosa pastoral work was never interrupted during the war years. Christenings, marriages and funerals were held routinely and the cemetery of St Lawrence came back into use for interments instead of the Addolorata. I was the only priest left in

The Ditch at Vittoriosa where hundreds made their home during the war.

(Courtesy N. Genovese)

Vittoriosa but one day a week I was relieved by Rev Guzepp Mizzi Agius from the Cospicua parish; on such occasions I took the opportunity to spend the day with my mother in Rabat. Cospicua and Senglea had their spiritual needs met too. The former was served by Curate Rev Anton Camilleri and Rev Guzepp Cassar while Senglea was never without its archpriest, the Rev

An aerial view of blitzed Vittoriosa. The church of St. Lawrence minus its dome can be seen at bottom left.

(Courtesy L. Zahra).

Manwel Brincat who was assisted by Rev Gian Karl Burlo`. The last named frequently officiated for the military forces in the area and on his way to Fort Ricasoli or Fort Leonardo would often call on me.

I celebrated Mass daily. Church feasts, however, passed uncelebrated. Once, during Lent as I conducted spiritual exercises for the congregation assembled in the Ditch, there was an air-raid warning and minutes later the ground under our feet shuddered and a blast of air whipped past; a bomb had landed on the Kalkara parish church reducing it to a pile of ruins. We had a similar experience when Mgr Gonzi was administering Confirmation to children who were assembled in the Ditch and the service was interrupted by an air-raid.

When the war receded from our shores in mid-1943 we began

to celebrate feasts in the Church of St Lawrence, which was still standing - minus its dome, some side altars and, of course, the sacristy. Looking back on those times I cannot help feeling a sense of achievement at having managed to serve my parishioners in those difficult days. At the same time I feel that I am lucky to be alive still when I could easily have been among those poor souls who died, buried under the ruins of the sacristy on that first day of the German blitz...

Fr PAWL GALEA OP

Before the Italian declaration of war, Dr Albert Laferla, then Director of Education, called on us at the Rabat priory and asked us to be ready to accept into our priory refugees from the harbour area should the need arise. As a result of that visit, we made arrangements so that two sides of the cloister could be used for that eventuality. In those two long corridors, the Public Works Department constructed a large number of timber cubicles which were, in fact, later to be occupied by refugees from Cottonera.

I was an Air Raid Warden and as such had undertaken a First Aid course on the strength of which I performed the duties of nurse in our community for the best part of fifteen years. For many years I worked hand in hand with Dr GużeppiBugeja who gave his services as general practitioner to our community. At about the same time as Dr Laferla's call, we had a visit from Dr Victor Testaferrata Bonici who gave us lectures about safety measures and about ways and means of providing help to those in need. One of my duties was to find accommodation for refugees from the area around the harbours.

In spite of the heavy air attacks, I rarely ventured into the shelters; I could not stand the feeling of being confined in such a restricted area. Instead I would watch the action over the harbour through the window of my cell in the priory. It was through that window that I saw a bomber release the bomb that killed one of the Mallia Pulvirenti sisters in the family home close to where the Verdala Hotel stands to-day. I rushed out of the priory to give assistance. From the same vantage point I watched the E-Boats' attack and, six months earlier, the *Illustrious* blitz.

At one point in time, the Luqa parish priest asked for friars from our community to help in the pastoral work of that parish; I was one of the four friars to whom the task was assigned. With one of the other friars I used to spend two weeks at a time in that parish; it was extremely rare for us to have a raid-free night. During the time I spent in Luqa I had to overcome my aversion to shelters! From the shelter I would hear the officer giving the order to open fire when an enemy raider was caught in a search-light beam.

I lost a great friend of mine by enemy action. Magistrate Bartoli lived in a house in St Dominic Square opposite the priory and on that fatal day he was about to leave his house to take cover in a shelter when a bomb exploded nearby, riddling his body with splinters. He was rushed to Ta' Bugeja Hospital but his life could not be saved.

An anti-aircraft battery was sited near Tal-Virtu` chapel, two or three hundred metres away from the priory. I taught philosophy at the time at the priory and I can say that I never missed giving a lecture because of an air-raid. I think I can safely say that life in the priory carried on normally during the war.

Sister *KATERINA LAUTIER*

I had been a cloistered nun for fourteen years when I began to hear rumours that a war was in the offing. When war did in fact break out and air-raids followed, we had to take cover in the cellars of the convent as we did not have proper shelters. To keep up our morale during air-raids we recited prayer after prayer, but we could not conceal our anxiety and often wished that our spiritual director was present so that he would give us absolution if our lives were in peril. Sister Clementina was an exception; she adamantly refused to take cover and even chided us for taking such precautions. She often forgot to put out the lights when there was an air-raid warning with the inevitable result of having a constable knocking furiously on the monastery door and shouting for someone to extinguish all lights forthwith.

For the first eleven months of the war we remained at our nunnery in Valletta as the prospect of leaving it was, for us, as frightening as the bombing. However when on the 30th of April 1941 a bomb landed in the garden causing some damage we were ordered by the Archbishop to move out of the monastery and take up residence in Gozo. Six days later, carrying as many of our belongings as we could, we boarded a bus which took us to the Marina; as we drove through the streets of Valletta, we could not help being struck by the sight of the destruction and havoc caused by enemy action. No sooner did we board the Gozo ferry than an air-raid warning sounded. Fortunately most of us were so overpowered by the shock of leaving the monastery that we did not realise the gravity of the situation. On arriving at Mġarr, we found a bus waiting to take us to the Bishop's palace in Victoria. The Bishop welcomed us with open arms and filled us with courage and hope, and then we proceeded to Marija Buhagiar's "Palazz" at Ta' Ċenċ. The local villagers greeted us warmly and brought us all sorts of things" - beds, mattresses, pillows... The "Palazz" building had seen better days and was now sadly dilapidated and for some time past had been used for keeping livestock but any discomfort was certainly not to be blamed on the generous villagers.

There were no proper rock-cut shelters in the vicinity and during air-raids we sometimes climbed to the roof to watch air-raids in progress over Malta. From our vantage point we could see smoke billowing skywards in the far distance and our hearts sank as we remembered our families we had left behind. There was at least one occasion when bombs fell over Sannat and killed a number of the inhabitants. On that occasion a sister who was standing in the balcony was hurled inside by the blast.

In spite of the continuous enemy activity, my mother and father who had left their home in Cospicua to settle as refugees in Hamrun, occasionally crossed over to Gozo to see me. My brother never made the trip because he was wounded while on duty at St Angelo and spent a long time in the military hospital at

Mtarfa; even when he was discharged, I think he was too scared to face the long haul to Ta' Ċenċ.

Our stay at Ta' Ċenċ came to an end in January 1944 when we made our way back to the monastery in Valletta. Our hearts were filled with joy as we crossed the doorstep and found ourselves once more inside our beloved home. That evening we chanted the *Te Deum* and to this day we recall that happy event every year by intoning that same great hymn of thanksgiving after Mass.

Mgr GUŻEPPI MINUTI

I was ordained priest a few weeks before Italy's declaration of war. On the 11th of June I was due to say Mass at Vittoriosa but when the bombing started I decided to stay in Cospicua. Confusion reigned and many people were seized by panic and rushed around aimlessly. Many dashed into the parish church to take cover. The priest who was to celebrate the nine o'clock Mass did not turn up and I took over. Midway through the Mass an air-raid warning sounded and people began to scream in terror.

On that very same day the whole family, with the exception of my father, packed up a few belongings and hired a *karozzin* to take us to Żejtun where some relatives lived. My father was at his workplace in the Dockyard and we left a message for him saying that we had gone off to Żejtun. We were not the only ones to take the road to Żejtun; along the road we overtook hundreds of refugees from the Cottonera going the same way - a veritable exodus. Not all of them had a roof waiting for them and there must have been at least a hundred refugees standing in front of St Gregory's Church without a place to go to. The sacristan opened the doors of that church and the poor refugees trooped in with their few belongings. They spread out their bedding on the floor and tried to sleep. Their misery was indescribable and Canon De Domenico and myself collected some money with which we bought loaves for them.

Those were busy days for me. In addition to my normal duties, administering the Sacraments in the parish church, I was appointed chaplain to Bishop Emanuel Galea and conducted services in the rural chapel of Hal Tmin, on the road to St Thomas Bay. On Sundays I accompanied Father Ferriggi OFM, an Army chaplain who looked after the spiritual needs of the garrison manning Fort St Nicholas which lay halfway between Żejtun and Delimara. On occasion, I rendered services in Fort St Peter and Fort San Giacomo. Fr Ferriggi would call for me at Żejtun on his motorcycle or the pony trap. Several times we were caught in an air-raid as we stood in the fort and I once celebrated Mass with a steel helmet on my head while the gunners participated from their posts on the guns.

Among the many incidents which have left an indelible mark in my memory, the one which stands out is that which took place on the 2nd May 1942. It being a Saturday morning a large number of people were, as usual, standing around and talking in the church square. At about ten or eleven an enemy raider flying overhead dropped a quantity of anti-personnel bombs which exploded on impact showering splinters in all directions and killing some people. I was at home at the time and when I was told about the incident I rushed out. Sprawled on the ground were some bodies but what caught my eye were some bloodstained footprints leading into the church. I followed the prints and inside the building came across a young man whose body had been riddled by splinters and who had apparently limped into the church. I administered the last Sacraments to the lad who, I subsequently learnt, was called Buonvicino.

I practically never took cover in a shelter; more likely I would run up to the roof and watch the action from there. I witnessed the attack on the *Illustrious*, when the area around Cottonera and the Dockyard was covered by a thick pall of smoke into which *Stukas* dived at a steep angle, dropping their deadly load before they climbed out of the smoke. Late that evening, when he returned from the Dockyard my father told us that whole blocks of buildings in Senglea had been razed to the ground and that a large number of people, among them Canon Theuma, had perished under the debris.

I was not as badly hit by the food shortage as most refugees; I dined as a rule with Bishop Galea and somehow the nuns who looked after us always managed to put some food on the table. At the height of the shortage, I hired a cart and with my mother and aunt took the road to Mġarr. We left Żejtun at four in the morning; by the time we reached our destination it was eleven. We looked up a farmer one of whose sons was studying at the Seminary under my tutorship and he supplied us with a bag of grain, for which he refused to take any money.

No external festivities were held during the war years but otherwise all liturgical ceremonies were celebrated in the churches in the normal way. When enemy activity began to abate, I remember once accompanying Bishop Galea to Qormi for the celebrations of the feast of St George. The pealing of church bells was still banned at the time but the procession through the streets of Qormi was allowed to proceed as in the pre-war years. The procession was about to wend its way into the church when the news ran like wildfire that the Allies had entered El Alamein. One of the parishioners decided to take the law into his hands and scrambling up one of the bell-towers proceeded to ring the bells. Bishop Galea did not like this at all and left the procession in a huff and hurried into the church. The bell-ringing went on...

In all we spent nine years at Żejtun, leaving that parish in 1949 when I was appointed to a canonry in the Collegiate Church of Cospicua, and therefore moved back to that town with the family. Our house had been destroyed by enemy action in 1941 and we had a new house built on the site.

Looking back at the war years I cannot help recalling with pride the unity and solidarity shown by the Maltese and the strength of their faith in God.

Fr JOSEPH ORR, SJ

With three other Maltese students I was studying philosophy in the Jesuit College in Catania when, in June 1940, the news broke that Italy had declared war against the Allies. We travelled to Bagheria near Palermo to seek the protection of our Prefect who was so convinced that it was only a matter of days before Malta would fall to the Italian forces that instead of taking steps to have us interned he placed us in the Jesuit mother house in Palermo. I remember the walls of the city plastered with posters screaming out in the words of Gabriele d'Annunzio that Malta was "*terra irredenta*". Pro-Fascist rallies were held every evening and I remember seeing some Maltese nationals taking part in such rallies.

When, after about a month, Malta had still not fallen to the Italians, the Commissioner of Police gave us instructions to pack up and to take the night train to L'Aquila to join other Maltese nationals in the internment camp situated in that mountainous region. After a brief stay we pleaded to be allowed to resume our philosophy studies and a month or so later our request was met and we travelled to Milan where we took up our studies once more. There were no shelters in Milan and when the British bombardment of the city began, the people took cover in basements reinforced with timber scantlings. Others preferred to seek open places like public parks and gardens.

After a year in Milan, we moved to Turin where the bombardment was even heavier; thousands of buildings were destroyed. Before the actual bombing, the Allied air forces used to shower leaflets giving advance notice about the places which were to be bombed so that workers could take cover in time. For some reason or other, the FIAT factory was never bombed; it seems that there was some sort of secret agreement.

The bombing was not the only hardship. Famine began to make itself felt. In September 1943, the Italian government under Marshal Badoglio surrendered and there was widespread desertion from the armed forces. The deserters left their weapons behind and these were soon in the Partisans' hands. Units of the German army occupied Turin and in one episode took forty hostages threatening to have them shot unless the Partisans laid down their arms. In the meantime one of us, Fr Salvinu Darmanin, was moved to a concentration camp in Silesia. The

Police Commissioner, an anti-Fascist, suggested that we leave Turin and go to Rome which had been declared an "open city". There were eight of us in all and we decided to take up the proposal.

With the railway system thrown into chaos by the relentless bombardment, it took us five whole days before we arrived at a small township on the outskirts of the capital. We stopped there for a day. In the evening German soldiers put us on a bus, pockmarked with shrapnel, which conveyed us to Rome. We headed for the Jesuit College in the vicinity of the railway station. The day before our arrival, the San Lorenzo quarter in Rome had been bombed in a heavy raid which left thousands of dead. Germans swarmed the streets of Rome and food shortages were making life very difficult.

The civil war raging between the Partisans on one side and

Mgr Hugh O'Flaherty ("Scarlet Pimpernel").

Fascists and Germans on the other caused hundreds of men who were on the Germans' wanted list to seek refuge in Jesuit homes which enjoyed extra-territorial status. Some of the refugees were not averse to donning clerical garb to evade the attention of the German soldiers, and we felt safer carrying our identity cards. There was one episode which I remember vividly. I was strolling in the company of a Hungarian fellow student in the neighbourhood of Piazza Barberini when I heard the spluttering of machine-gun fire. A policeman told us to move on because the Partisans had shot some German soldiers. That same day the German command in Rome received instructions from Hitler that for each German soldier killed, ten Italians were to be executed. In fact 330 Italians from the San Vittorio prison were transported to the Ardeatine Caves and murdered in cold blood.

At about this time I was asked by Vatican Radio authorities to read messages sent by people in Rome who wanted to contact relatives in other parts of the world. My predecessor in this task was Brother Robert Pace, close friend and collaborator of Mgr O'Flaherty (the "Scarlet Pimpernel") and Mrs Chevalier.

We were ordained priests in July 1944 in a ceremony held in the Gesu` Church in Rome. Among those present for the ceremony I was overjoyed to see my brother Jimmy who served as chaplain to the Irish Fusiliers and the RMA. His flying visit to Rome was made possible by a friend of my father's, a British colonel. Three other Maltese were ordained in that ceremony: Fr Magro, Fr Pitre` and Fr Laferla.

I remember that when we were in Milan, some Maltese tried to approach us to persuade us to give up our passport and renounce our British citizenship. The Commissioner of Police, however, was decidedly anti-Fascist and did everything in his power to prevent them from meeting us.

During the war years we never knew what the situation in Malta was like. We did listen in to the news on the Italian Radio, of course, but we soon realised that what we heard was propaganda not facts. Our relatives in Malta were equally in the dark about us because the letters which we tried to send across through the Red Cross agency never made it to their destination. To sum up the war experience, I would say that though we suffered hunger and bombardment, we were not treated badly by the Italians especially those in the north where we came across several anti-Fascists who respected and helped us. In Turin, for instance, we had Italian friends who tuned in regularly to the BBC and relayed the news to us.

Mgr LORENZO SPITERI

I was appointed parish priest of Mqabba in 1936 and in that capacity I was involved in the preparation of plans for dealing with civilian matters in the event of war breaking out. Parish priests met regularly to be given instructions by government offi-

TIFKIRA GHAZIZA

TA'

GIUSEPPI ELLUL

MILL-IMQABBA

GHAJXIEN TAL-FAMILJA

LI

MIBKI MIN NIESU

U MIN SHABU TAD-DIPARTIMENT

MIET

ID-DISGRAZJAT FL-ETÀ TA 36 SENA

MILQUT MILL-EWWEL BOMBA

LI INTEFGHET FUQ ART TWELIDNA

11 TA GIUNJU 1940

Joseph Ellul from Mqabba who was killed, "aged 36 by the first bomb dropped over our country."

(Courtesy C. Ellul)

185

cials and when the Special Constabulary came into being, we were appointed Air Raid Wardens.

On the 10th of June 1940, as I was listening to the radio with a friend of mine, GużeppiEllul, we heard Mussolini declare war on Britain. We were struck dumb. On the following morning at about seven we had the first air-raid. From the church roof I watched as the Italian planes released their bomb-loads. I turned to my companion, a priest, and suggested we give each other absolution in case of sudden death. My friend made light of my proposal and said, "Let's not panic; this is the time when everyone has to play his part." On that first day, Gużeppi Ellul was to lose his life as he was on his way to report for duty; instead of getting off at Blata l-Bajda as usual, he decided to stop at Porte des Bombes where he was killed by one of the first bombs to be dropped over Malta.

Many people were on the verge of panicking on that day and hurried to the confessionals. Priests, I think, were as terrified as their flock but we tried not to show it and began to calm down the people, at the same time urging them to keep up their spirits. In spite of the pre-war planning, we were caught unprepared. All we had was a steel helmet and a gas mask and we had been told to take cover under tables or in cellars in the case of bombing. The proximity of the airfield was bound to make Mqabba suffer the ravages of war and as a consequence few refugees elected to make of Mqabba their second home. The airfield provided work for many of the villagers who were mainly employed in filling up bomb craters to keep the runways operational. At every air-raid warning the labourers would scurry into the village to take some sort of cover.

On the 19th of April 1942 during one such air-raid as the labourers flocked into the church square they were attacked by some German planes. The bombs dropped on that day caused severe damage to the church, wrecking the dome and the apse, and demolished several houses including mine; many people were killed or injured. I remember emerging from the shelter and seeing the havoc caused by the raiders. Three women lay dead in a large crater in the square and wounded persons sprawled on the

The heavily damaged Mqabba church.
(Courtesy K. Ghigo).

ground. In another tragic episode labourers returning home on a lorry were killed when a bomb blew up the vehicle.

With the parish church in ruins religious services were transferred to the chapel of St Basil and I tried to find some place to live in. All my belongings were lost; I did not have as much as a handkerchief left. At first I found accommodation with a family and later moved to a room in the house used for religious instruction which also began to serve as the parish office. In spite of the frequent air-raids, life went on more or less normally: religious ceremonies were held regularly, children played happily in the village square, farmers tilled their fields and workers laboured in the quarries. Few members of the congregation would leave the church during air-raids because they were steadfast in their faith. Such conduct on the part of my parishioners filled me with courage and hope.

Mqabba was like a second home to a large number of servicemen from several countries - Britain, Canada, Mauritius... Surprisingly we never had a mixed marriage in the parish and the young women of the village behaved in the most exemplary fashion. The only two girls who were married to servicemen in the parish came from other villages. Occasionally, instead of joining their mates in a wineshop officers or soldiers would come to have a word with me and we would have a chat on various matters - the war, their families... I often took the opportunity to remind them to keep in touch with their families. Incidentally, many years after the war, one of them, a Scotsman, called on me and among other things told me he was astounded at the changes which had taken place in Malta since those days.

In 1942 with the threat of invasion hanging on our heads, the bird-hunters of the village organised themselves into a "regiment" and every evening would station themselves, with steel helmet and shotgun, at the barbed wire barriers placed in every road leading into the village. The officer-in-charge was a priest from the village, Rev Mikiel Zammit. These hunters took their work very seriously and ever so often the "regiment" would parade in the village square; the spectators however found the performance less than awe-inspiring if not actually bordering on the comic.

In the war years parish priests were involved in many civil duties besides their normal pastoral work. The authorities, no less than the common people, looked upon the parish priest as the leader of the community. For instance when a Regional Protection Officer was to be appointed it was to me that the authorities turned for advice and public notices were brought to the attention of the villagers by parish priests.

As I said before the war seemed to make the people more steadfast in their faith and it was their trust in God that kept high their morale as bombs rained down and food supplies ran short. I can still see in my mind's eye the hungry mothers carrying their young in the middle of the night to the safety of the shelters with the children weeping in their inability to understand. The hardship endured by those mothers must have been enormous.

On the credit side you could say that the people were united and ready to help those in need; there was no foolish bickering between members of the different *partiti*. But there were also some negative aspects. Before the war, Mqabba was like a convent; children respected and obeyed their parents and their teachers, and the men and women respected the authorities both civil and ecclesiastical. All shops used to close down when some function was being held in the church, and on Sunday afternoons people crowded into the church to listen to the explanation of the catechism. All this went by the board as a direct result of the war and in their place we have now got the usages which were introduced into the villages by the refugees.

Fr *PAWL SPITERI, OSA*

I was appointed Prior of the Rabat Augustinian friars in 1938 and was holding that post when Italy declared war in 1940. The first air-raids drove the inhabitants of the towns and villages around the harbours to the safer villages in the countryside including Rabat. Following instructions from the authorities, our priory opened its doors to the refugees to provide a second home to these victims of the war. The corridors on the ground floor became classrooms for the children of the refugees with Mr Gużeppi Agius acting as the teacher in charge.

Eventually accommodation was found for the children elsewhere and silence reigned once more in the corridors - at least until that day in January 1941 on which the *Illustrious* became the target of wave after wave of German raiders. Thousands of refugees who had returned to their homes when people began to get used to the relatively light bombing of the Italians, took to the road once again and Rabat, for the second time, experienced a sudden and massive influx of refugees. By the end of that January, the priory had taken in over 300 male refugees, of whom a considerable proportion were old and sick.

As one can imagine, the crowding of so many men in a confined space could not fail to lead to problems - problems of hygiene and interpersonal relations. To make matters worse instead of being grateful to us some of these men seized every opportunity to find fault with every imaginable thing, passing snide remarks about the friars. With the men's indifference to matters of cleanliness, the place began to look filthy and we had to call in the welfare officer to help us solve the problem. The officer called up the men and gave them a stern warning and I am happy to say the situation improved considerably from that day onwards.

Incidentally in addition to receiving refugees, we also kept in store many objects which had been salvaged from the Church of St Lawrence in Vittoriosa which was badly damaged in the *Illustrious* blitz; among those objects were the pedestal of the statue of the patron saint and the artistic wooden staircase leading to the pulpit.

At one point the population of Rabat was in the region of 45,000 and therefore the clergy had their hands full administering to the spiritual needs of the inhabitants. One must also keep in mind that in times of war people tend to turn more readily to spiritual comfort and churches were often packed. The friars of our community were understandably pleased to observe that all our religious functions drew unprecedented attendances. As the director of the St Monica Guild I took the opportunity to launch a course for parents and their adolescent sons and daughters and the topic I selected for discussion was marriage. I invited experts to give lectures on the various aspects. When courses were later organised for the clergy, students and members of the professions, the response was so great that we had to make use of the Church of St Paul and the chapel of St Sebastian besides our own church. All this goes to show that pastoral work was not affected adversely by the war.

The tragic events of the 12th June 1942, a Friday, remain

Bro. Norbert Vella OSA
(Courtesy J. Mifsud)

engraved in my memory to this day. On that day at about quarter to ten in the night, there was an air-raid warning. The friars had minutes before left the refectory and were about to retire after a rather hectic day but instead of going to their rooms they proceeded, at a somewhat leisurely pace, to take cover. All of a sudden, a tremendous explosion shook the building followed instantaneously by the noise of shattering glass. Stones, pieces of iron and bits of wood flew in all directions. A heavy calibre bomb had landed on the house next to our refectory and kitchen.

When we were all gathered together we realised that Brother Norbert Vella, one of our students, was missing. Brother Norbert was only twenty; being very sick, he used to remain in his cell during air-raids. Many of the friars, fearing the worst, hurried to his room and found the youth sprawled on the floor in a pool of blood. He was still alive and after receiving the last Sacraments, was rushed on a stretcher to Santu Spirtu Hospital. By the time we reached the hospital, other casualties of the explosion, with splinter injuries, were being already attended to. It was a har-

†

TIFCHIRA GHAZIZA

TA

Fra NORBERTU M. VELLA
O.E.S.A.

STUDENT AGOSTINIAN
LI MIET B'MEUTA CHIEFRA
FIL-LEILA 13 TA GIUNJU 1942.
O GESÙ
CONSOLATUR TAL IMNICTIN
FARRAG IL KALB IMNICTA
T'OMMU, MISSIERU, TA HUTU
U TA L'ORNI AGOSTINIAN
LI TANT CHIEN IHOEB.

Gesù ħanin ghatieh il-mistrieħ ta' dejjem.
(Ind. 300 jum)

Gesù, Marija, Gużeppi.
(Ind. 7 snin u 7 qważ.)

Bro. Norbert Vella who "suffered a cruel death" on 13 June 1942".

(Courtesy J. Mifsud)

rowing scene. People were moaning and in a state of shock but the one who appeared to be most seriously hurt was our Brother Norbert. That night at three in the morning he breathed his last surrounded and assisted by all the friars in the community.

The funeral service was held on the following day. His body was carried into our church and High Mass was celebrated as is traditionally done when one of the friars departs this life. As prior of the community and master of the students, I led the service.

Brother Norbert was the only member of the Augustinian Province in Malta to die as a result of enemy action, but I should also mention another student, Brother Manwel Cutajar from Cospicua, who fell victim to the typhoid epidemic which raged for some months during the war. I was also struck down and at one point it was touch and go for me and I received the last Sacraments; after a while, things took a turn for the better and after some three months in hospital I was discharged in October 1941. The following year, other friars caught the disease and at one time six members of the community were at Santu Spirtu Hospital and two others in the emergency hospital in Birkirkara.

VI. Dockyard Workers

SPIRU AGIUS

I worked as a seaman on the tug-boat *Hellespont* which was mainly engaged in the movement of seacraft in the harbours. We naturally were in the thick of the action although generally speaking during air raids we used to take cover in the shelters. Of course when we happened to be afloat in a bombing attack there was nothing we could do except trust to luck and good fortune.

When war broke out the family moved from Vittoriosa, where we lived, to Rabat. However that was only for a brief period because we soon moved back to the harbour area this time taking up residence in Senglea where we lived until the 16th of January 1941 that is the memorable day of the *Illustrious* attack in the course of which our house like hundreds of others in Senglea was reduced to a mound of rubble. Because of the nature of my duties I used to sleep at the Dockyard and it was quite some time before I knew where my wife was. Some five days later one of the Dockyard apprentices told me that my wife was living as a refugee at the Birkirkara school. I sent her a message saying that I was not prepared to live with all that crowd in the school and asked her to try to find a small place or even a room which we could rent. A few days later she came down to the Dockyard and told me that she had managed to get a room with an old woman who lived alone and who was willing to rent the room to us on very reasonable terms.

M.V. *Moor* which sank after striking a mine on 8 April 1941.

(NWMA Collection)

A few months later, on the 8th of April 1941, just before five in the afternoon, HMS *Moor* struck a mine and went down with 29 of her company of thirty men. As compensation for their loss the families of those who had gone down were given ten and a half pence (4c2) per day which caused us seamen on the tugboats to go on strike in protest at this niggardly behaviour on the part of the naval authorities. That very same day the officer in charge suspended us strikers for three months and those of us who had only recently joined the Dockyard force were summarily sacked. Finding myself unemployed, I tried my hand at digging shelters, a job which was in great demand at the time. However when the Dockyard authorities got to know that I had found a job, I was barred from working as I was considered to be one of the ringleaders. When the chargeman attempted to intercede on my behalf he was told to shut up or he, too, would be fired on the spot. I then found a temporary job at Hal Far. During our suspension the tug-boats were manned by regular Maltese sailors from Fort St Angelo, with a sprinkling of British seamen.

When the term of suspension had run its course, I was re-employed on the tug-boats and when the Santa Marija convoy steamed into harbour we were detailed to take the *Ohio* on tow to Ricasoli. Other ships which made up the convoy included the *Pampas*, the *Brisbane Star* and the *Talabot*. The *Pampas*, a fuel tanker, tied up at Ras Hanzir Wharf. I remember that a fire broke out below deck on the *Pampas* and a worker from Cospicua perished. On that occasion as we were coming into the Grand Harbour with the *Ohio* on tow people were lining the walls, waving and cheering but I was so intent on the work in hand that I scarcely noticed them.

Looking back, I think that the food shortage was the worst part of the war. I remember I used to walk all the way to some relatives in Żejtun to get a few slices of bread to supplement the meagre rations. Once my wife came down to the Dockyard from Birkirkara to bring some food to me; she left the food with the police officer at the gate and this one gave the lunch parcel to someone else by mistake. I had to fast that day!

MANWEL BONNICI

I used to work aboard the Dockyard launches, ferrying workers to and from ships and occasionally towing lighters. Many were the occasions when we were caught in an air raid halfway across the harbour. Once we almost ran into serious trouble when we were ferrying some naval cadets from the Customs House Steps to their ship, HMS *Vindictive*. When an air raid warning sounded, the coxswain turned the boat round to get to the Dockyard where the nearest shelters were. The cadets did not like this at all and became boisterous and menacing. As soon as we were alongside the wharf some of the cadets tried to manhandle us and made as if they meant to hijack the launch. A few of them came down into the engine room where I was and you can imagine how terrified I was. By this time our superiors had been informed about the incident. We were later to know that before this incident when on shore leave in Valletta the cadets had been beaten up in a street fight and they were trying to get their back on us.

Because of the nature of our work we used to be on duty round the clock. There was never an idle moment in the harbour; ships of all shapes and sizes were constantly steaming into or out of harbour. When the Santa Marija convoy entered harbour, we were there to do our bit.

As long as we were not on board, air raids did not really bother us at all. There were plenty of shelters at the Dockyard with a hundred feet or so of solid rock over our heads. In fact it was these shelters which saved the lives of hundreds of Dockyard workers; when you think of the tremendous bombardment it is surprising how few lives were lost. When I was on the night shift I could always sleep in one of the shelters there with an easy mind.

The severe food shortage hit me hard until I found a benefactor who was in charge of the Victory Kitchen. Thanks to him I regularly contrived to get a double portion or even three portions. Sometimes if I was lucky I would also cadge some food on board one of the ships. Barter was the order of the day in those difficult times: cigarettes against foodstuffs... a loaf of bread... a tin of corned beef. Chronic smokers would give anything for a cigarette; they would go hungry rather than do without a smoke. Some people used to make a lot of money selling cigarettes near Dockyard Gate: these would as likely as not be home-made with dried medlar leaves, then a popular substitute for tobacco.

EDDIE CASSAR

In 1940 I worked as a plumber at the Dockyard. With nine other mates in the same trade, I was told to report for duty at Kalafrana to work on aircraft engines. I spent five years in that job of which three and a half years were spent at Muscat's

Garage at Gzira. One of our main tasks, then classified as top secret, at Muscat's was on routine maintenance work on Spitfires. Sometimes I was instructed to report for duty at Ta' Qali or Hal Far or Luqa.

On the 7th of May 1942 a number of delayed action bombs were dropped on and around Muscat's Garage. One of the bombs killed an RAF man and wounded a corporal. I was bowled over by the blast but was otherwise unhurt. I do not think I shall ever forget that day! At that time I was living at Paola and when I was on duty at Ta' Qali, I used to cycle there and back. There were days when my brother Joe who was in the Army borrowed my bicycle which meant that I had to walk all the way to Ta' Qali which took about an hour and a half. Once I was returning home in the company of a friend of mine. We had scarcely got out of the Ta' Qali grounds and reached the small wayside chapel when there was an air raid. Looking up we could see *Junkers 88* flying in towards us and dropping bombs. We threw ourselves flat on the ground, terrified and fearing the worst. When we eventually got home it was pitch dark. Later we learned that Ta' Qali had been the main target and the damage to the Air Force base was crippling.

On another occasion on our way home just as we were passing the Mriehel Technical School, we saw a pilot floating down under his parachute and we ran towards him as soon as he touched the ground. As soon as he saw us running towards him the German pilot drew out his gun and pointed it at us. Almost immediately an Army officer with two soldiers arrived from the nearby anti-aircraft battery. The pilot thereupon threw down his gun and gave himself up.

The first months of the war saw my family split up. My mother was an ARP matron and had to spend the night at the ARP centre at Tarxien along with some eight other women. Before the war she had completed a first aid course and she had the distinction of tending the first German pilot to bale out over Malta; she was a very capable woman, disciplined and gutsy. My father lived in Rabat with the Pullicino family, my brother was an Army conscript and I was attached to the Air Force, living with my aunt at Paola. On the 18th January 1942, I got married.

While the wedding Mass was being said, there was an air raid

The Superintendent, matron (Mrs Cassar) and NCO's at the ARP Centre, Tarxien.
(Courtesy E. Cassar)

which lasted through the entire ceremony. After the ceremony we went to Blackman's studio at Hamrun, for the traditional wedding photo, driving there in a carriage drawn by four horses. On the way back, the coachman took off his bowler hat and tail-coat, removed the decorative white feathers from the horses' heads, put away the gilded harness and whipped up the horses as if he was playing a part in some western. At the Marsa Cross road, there was another air raid warning and our coachman drove furiously to the Boom Defence site where there was a tunnel under which we, and the horses, could take shelter. On catching sight of the wedding group several British and Maltese servicemen struck up with a hearty rendering of "Here comes the bride". When the all clear sounded we resumed our trip to Paola where a very modest reception had been prepared for us. We were some fifteen people in all, mostly relatives, with two English corporals who were friends of mine.

Three weeks into my marriage, I had one of the worst experiences of my life. While I was busy on a job at Mùscat's Garage at Gzira, the Squadron Leader drew me aside and told me that several bombs had been dropped on Paola and asked me whether I would like to have some time off so that I could join my wife there. I got on my bicycle and pedalled with all my might. When I arrived, I found that the village was completely surrounded by the military who were stopping people from entering the place. Somehow I managed to evade the soldiers and made my way to my home. The house was razed to the ground and there was no sign of anybody. I hurried to Paola Square and there, too, the

Inside Muscat's Garage, Gzira

(NWMA Collection)

scene that met me was one of devastation. An aerial torpedo had landed in the square and the roofing covering the underground reservoir had collapsed. I was about to run down into the shelter in the square where my wife usually took refuge but at the entrance a woman told me that my wife was not in that shelter. I panicked and ran back to where my house used to stand and started screaming out my wife's name; I imagined her lying buried under the rubble and myself a widower after just three weeks of married life... A man who ran a small salami shop nearby pulled me up and said that he had seen my wife go down into another shelter. I hurried there and found her covered from head to toe in dust and plaster with bruises all over her legs but mercifully alive. She had escaped death by the skin of her teeth.

JOSEPH FALZON

I married a few months before the war started and was living happily at Senglea. Rumours were floating around that Italy would be joining the war on the side of Germany and my mother and I decided that it would be wise to rent a small place at Birkirkara to which we could go if the situation got worse. So, on the day the war started, we hired a horse-drawn cab, put a few essential belongings and made our way to Birkirkara, leaving all our furniture behind. We heard later that at Senglea several houses which had been deserted by fleeing refugees were being broken into and pilferage was rife. We therefore rented another room at Birkirkara and moved all our furniture there. Soon after, my wife and I went to live at Rabat with my mother-in-law who had a large house.

At the time I was employed as an engine-fitter, and later a chargeman, at the Dockyard. There was a lot of work to be done and I was on duty most Sundays. On Sundays public transport was not available due to fuel-saving regulations in force at the time and I therefore used to take the bus to Birkirkara on Saturday evening and spend the night at my mother's so that in the morning I would find it easier to make my way to the

Dockyard. From Birkirkara I would walk to the Valletta Customs House steps where a boat would be waiting to ferry me across the harbour to the Dockyard. Then on the Sunday evening I would walk all the way to Rabat. Sometimes as I, and other Dockyard workers, were on our way we would be caught in an air raid and we would try to find some shelter. One evening as we were about to go past the Ta' Qali junction a policeman stopped us because, he said, there was an unexploded bomb right in the middle of the road. He suggested we turn back, walk towards Żebbuġ and then take the Rabat road but of course being dead tired I did not fancy taking such a roundabout way. I therefore muttered a few prayers and kept going to Rabat. There indeed was the bomb and I hurried past it as fast as my legs could carry me.

The Dockyard, of course, was a prime target for enemy bombers but ample precautions had been taken and there were enough rock hewn shelters for everybody so that danger to life and limb was minimal. But some workmen were reckless and seemed to relish taking risks. I remember one incident when dur-

H.M.S. *Breconshire*

(*Courtesy J. Borg Bonello*)

ing an air raid a few workers decided to stay out and sat on some steps near the dispensary. Berthed at the wharf in the vicinity was HMS *Lance* which on this occasion appeared to be the main target of that attack. One of the bombs burst a few yards away from the workmen, one of whom happened to be a close friend of mine at whose wedding ceremony I had been the witness. I went to see him in hospital and he told me that he was feeling a bit dizzy but was otherwise unhurt. That very night he died, as did the other workers.

At that time I was a chargeman of divers and you can imagine that our job was very risky. One of the incidents which I remember vividly concerns the *Breconshire*, a fleet auxiliary ship which normally berthed at Sa Maison wharf where these days you can see the Gozo ferry boat. After a series of bombings this ship caught fire and was towed out of the harbour to Marsaxlokk Bay where she was beached. She settled on her side and we, as divers, were given the hazardous task of salvaging the cargo consisting mainly of munitions. A platoon from the Royal Engineers was on hand to transport the crates packed with shells and other explosive material.

When we tied up alongside the *Breconshire*, I went down with one of my men as it was the normal procedure to have two divers working in pairs. I saw what looked like a bomb and went up to report this to Captain Sloan of the RE's. I was assured that what I had seen was a parachute flare and I therefore submerged again to put a cradle round it so it could be hoisted. I confess I was really scared while I was doing that job!

On a number of occasions we were attacked by German aircraft while we were plying between the harbours or diving. Once there was a raid as I was diving, naturally without my being aware of the fact at the time. On surfacing I was horrified to learn that while I was below one of the men manning the air pump which supplied us with oxygen panicked and was about to leave his post when he was stopped in the nick of time by a Dockyard Police inspector. The latter marched up to the man and brandished his revolver, saying, "If you do not return this instant to your post, I'll shoot. Don't you realise that with your action you are putting a man's life in jeopardy?"

But perhaps the incident which stands out most vividly in my memory is when I was working on a boiler in the engine room of the aircraft carrier HMS *Vulnerable* which was anchored in Kalkara Creek opposite the Royal Naval Hospital at Bighi. Oil had leaked out in such quantities that even though I was carrying a 2000 watt lamp I could not see a thing. I had to feel my way around in those murky depths and from time to time my hands would grasp the corpses of seamen who had died there. To complicate matters further as I started to go up, my life-line and air-pipe got tangled up in something and I could proceed no further. I began to say my prayers in great earnest and at last broke free.

I can recollect one other narrow escape. We had just completed our night shift and were about to leave the Dockyard by the Senglea Gate when we saw the harbour launch about to cast off. We waved our arms so that they would wait for us, which they did. Those few minutes of waiting were providential for they saved our lives and the lives of all on board the launch; a short interval after casting off a bomb fell some yards ahead of us.

I think it would be fair to say that the vast majority of Dockyard employees worked hard and gave their contribution to the war effort. But there were exceptions, of course. Some were so scared that they suffered mental breakdowns or went sick, and we had to shoulder their duties. It may be relevant at this point to remind the reader that when one considers the dangers and hardships, we were very poorly paid for our services. In fact my wages as a fitter were 44 shillings (Lm 2.20) a week with overtime being paid at time-and-a-half. Ironically, when the war started our wages were reduced by three shillings (15c) a week in the interests of economy, as we were told. There was no sick leave: no work, no pay. We workers were still without a strong and well-organised trade union. Yet, in spite of all that, I still have a soft spot for the British who, I think, appreciated the workers' effort.

On the 21st April 1944 I received a letter from Sir David Campbell, the Lieutenant Governor, congratulating me on being awarded the Governor's citation on "the exceptionally meritorious and devoted service which led to your name being recorded in the *Malta Government Gazette* No 9169 of the 1st February 1944".

GORG FAVA

In June 1940, when the first bombs were being dropped by Italian bombers, I was an apprentice and on certain days I had to attend lessons at the Dockyard School. When the first air attack came just before seven o'clock in the morning, I was at home studying as I was advised to keep away from the Dockyard area on that day. As soon as that first air raid was over I went out to see what was going on. Qormi was all agog and there was excitement in the air. The news soon came that bombs had been dropped in the vicinity of the dockyard and that a number of people had been killed. The first wave of refugees from the harbour area began to arrive at about noon in horse-drawn carts, vans and lorries; some were in rags, others were carrying sacks. None of them seemed to have any idea as to where they were going and some were pleading with the locals to put them up. Many Qormi residents received the refugees with open arms and provided them with a room.

Among the many memories of the war, one stands out clearly: the bombing of the *Illustrious*. On that memorable day I was on a job in the motor repair shop which stood near the Corradino tunnel on Parlatorio Wharf which nowadays is the site of the Red China Dock. The *Illustrious* was lying at anchor a few yards away from the tunnel in which we were sheltering. Some of us went to the entrance of the tunnel to have a look and were terrified to see a formation of German planes flying towards us. Hardly had we got back to the safety of the shelter when we heard a series of tremendous explosions which made the ground under our feet shudder and shake. A large number of British sailors who were sharing the shelter with us were from the *Illustrious* and their faces showed fear; no doubt they had been through appalling experiences in previous attacks on the aircraft carrier. On coming out of the shelter when the all clear sounded, our eyes fell on scenes of fearful destruction: mounds of rubble, twisted beams and shattered iron work were lying all round.

Another incident which I think I will never forget was when some smoke- screen canisters caught fire in a tunnel where some

Dockyard workers were stationed. At one point, a friend of mine, Remig Sacco by name, asked me to go along with him so that he could check whether his brother who was normally in that tunnel had come to harm. As we entered the tunnel we saw some six corpses lying on the ground; one of the bodies was that of Sacco's brother. Remig, poor man, was in such a state that at first he did not recognise his own brother. That was a scene that will haunt me for ever…

There was also the day when some bombs fell on Qormi very close to the school. On that day I had decided to stay at home so that I could prepare myself for the City and Guilds examination. I had heard the drone of enemy aircraft but had never imagined that bombs were about to be dropped on Qormi. Suddenly I felt the ground shake under me and I rushed out of the house; smoke was billowing up from buildings in our immediate neighbourhood. When the all clear was given, I hurried towards the buildings which had been hit. I was shaking with apprehension because my fiancee` lived in that part of the village. On the way

TIMES OF MALTA WEDNESDAY JUNE 12 1940

EIGHT AIR RAIDS OVER MALTA
Our First Day Of Active War

TROOPS SING "GOD SAVE THE KING" AS THEY MAN THE GUNS

Italy declared war on Great Britain and France at midnight on the 10th of June. By seven o'clock Malta time on the eleventh June, Mussolini's air raiders were bombing Malta.

So much for the vaunted assertions that Mussolini would never bomb us.

On the outbreak of war with Italy all personnel who were not at their posts were recalled to duty, and no time was lost in manning the defences which are at a high pitch of efficiency.

On that day, His Excellency the Governor, General Dobbie, received a telegram from the Chief of Staff:

"Wish you and all under your command every good luck in whatever lies ahead".

General Dobbie replied:

"Many thanks for your telegram which is much appreciated. All here are in good heart and ready for all eventualities."

A day of almost incessant air raids and air raid warnings has not altered this neither will the continual repetition of the tactics used yesterday make any difference in Maltese and English morale.

First Warning

The first air raid warning was sounded at 6.50 a.m. yesterday

morning and anti-aircraft batteries opened fire against two formations of seven and three hostile aircrafts making ten in all. As they directed their guns against the enemy, Maltese and English gunners sang "God Save the King" and then blazed away.

These formations approached the Grand Harbour, Valletta, from the south-east, flying over Kalafrana and Hal Far. A number of bombs were dropped on Hal Far aerodrome, with an accuracy that suggested that this terrain was not unfamiliar to the attackers who no doubt had often flown the Italian commercial planes to Malta, but they did little damage. Further bombs were dropped between Fort Benghaisa and Birzebbuga, but these, likewise, did little damage. The all clear was sounded about half an hour after the alarm was sounded.

But almost immediately a second raid commenced. The machines fol-

lowed the same course at the outset, and then made for Korradino and Portes des Bombes, Pietà' Creek, Sa Maison and the new hospital.

Meanwhile one machine carried out a low flying attack on Fort St. Elmo.

Porte des Bombes

At Porte des Bombes a crater was made in the road a few feet across which suggested that the size of the bombs being dropped was medium and their weight about 250 lbs.

The Government Water and Electricity shed was damaged by two bombs falling between it and the bastion wall. One of these bombs blew in an iron door and this killed two Maltese workmen.

The building itself stood up to this bombardment with striking success, only the very far end of the structure being somewhat cracked. Workmen were busy clearing away debris and digging tunnels into the face of the neighbouring rock. Mr. Mortimer was with them and said how splendidly everyone behaved during the actual raid.

Hospital Hit

Other bombs hit the new hospital and destroyed a house near by, while yet other wrecked a house at Msida killing a man and his wife.

The total civilian casualties reported yesterday was five killed and several wounded with shrapnel. This does not allow for what many have

---

TO LET

UNFURNISHED HOUSE 22a, Sda Tigne', Sliema. With all modern conveniences. Apply Capt. A. Caruana 12, Sda. Reale, Valletta.

FOR SALE OR HIRE

UNIQUE OPPORTUNITY. Furniture and bedsteads for sale or hire Apply 163, Sda. S. Lucia, Valletta.

W. S. ROBINSON'S Piano Rooms. Best English pianos for sale or hire reasonable prices. Entrance through Collis & Williams, Chemists, Sda. Reale Valletta.

ORPHEUM THEATRE   Gzir
TODAY and TOMORROW
STANLEY LUPINO and CLAIRE LUCE
"OVER SHE GOES"
with MAX BAER and GINA MALO
(Children are Admitted)
Telephone: Sliema 1

CAPITOL THEATRE   Vallet
TO-DAY
Ralph Bellamy and Josephine Hutchinson
"THE CRIME OF DR HALLET"
with Barbara Read and William Gargan
(Children are not Admitted)
PRICES OF ADMISSION: 1/3, 1/4 & 2
Telephone: Valletta 1

MANOEL THEATRE   Valle
TODAY
PATHE' GAZETTE
STUART ERWIN in

OUR CROSSWORD No. 877

I came across another terrible scene: some men were dragging out the lifeless body of one of my friends. The blast from the explosion had shrunk the body almost beyond recognition. After the raid I made a resolution that I would seek shelter at the first sign of an attack, a resolution that I observed dutifully… for three weeks. In fact I used to spend nights in the company of a few friends watching parachute flares floating down. It was a spectacle of sorts until the explosions followed and rocked the ground under our feet.

Although there was a war on, I used to bike regularly with a couple of friends to Żejtun where we had private lessons from a Mr Spiteri who taught at the Dockyard School. Those private lessons turned out to be a good investment: I passed the examination and was awarded the certificate. I will finish with a comment about the social impact which the refugees had on the people of Qormi; I believe that the refugees were instrumental in bringing about changes in the way of life of the locals but I am not so sure that all those changes were for the better.

MANWEL GATT

Very soon after the first air raids, trucks were sent to Vittoriosa to provide transport for refugees. We were told that we were being taken to Qormi and within a few hours my family found itself in a room in a cattle farm at Qormi which was previously used as a store for fodder and straw. I need hardly say that the place was crawling with rats and mice and I very often could not sleep because of my aversion to such creatures. I would sit by the window watching these pests climbing along the vine trellis with the dogs barking their heads off at them. From that farm we were re-located in another building in the same locality and with the same problem - rats. We could not get used to those conditions and were eager to go back to our Vittoriosa home. In December 1940, the three of us, my mother, my sister and myself moved back to Vittoriosa as did a lot of other refugees, among them my married sister and her family. For a whole month we lived in relative tranquillity until the 16th January of the following year when the situation changed dramatically.

On that eventful day before leaving the house to go to work as a blacksmith at the Dockyard, I warned my mother that should there be any air raids during the day she was not to leave the house; with its unusually thick stone walls, the house itself was as safe as any shelter. At about two in the afternoon, the sirens started wailing. Some friends and I, as was our habit, did not bother to take cover. When we went down into a shelter it was usually so that we could have some fun at the expense of the occupants. We were still young and foolish in those days! Suddenly we became aware that the soldiers who were manning the anti-aircraft guns on the bastions near the Senglea clocktower were frantically signalling to us to dive into a shelter; they shouted that hundreds of aircraft were approaching but we chose to ignore their advice. In a couple of minutes the first wave of dive bombers had released their deadly load. After a brief interval the second wave flew in, raining bombs over a wide area covering Senglea, Vittoriosa, Cospicua and the Corradino heights, and churning up the water around the *Illustrious*. It was a terrifying spectacle but my companions and I kept watching as if hypnotised until the last German plane had left.

I then returned home. The door and the windows were wide open. "Mother! Mother!" I yelled but there was no answer. I rushed up to the rooftop and saw that what used to be the vestry of the Church of St Lawrence was now a pile of rubble. I rushed down again and hurried towards that place. In the large crowd which had assembled, I caught sight of my married sister sobbing uncontrollably. She mumbled that our mother was buried under that rubble. I grabbed my sister and her son by the arm and hurried them to the dry moat which was honeycombed with shelters and made them promise that they would not budge from there until I came back. Luckily on that day my other sister had gone to Qormi to visit some acquaintances; if she had not done so she would almost certainly have been with my mother.

I went back and stood with a lot of other people, including Fr Paul Galea, the parish priest, watching servicemen and ARP per-

Marija Gatt, one of the many victims of the *Illustrious* blitz.
(Courtesy E. Gatt)

sonnel going about the rescue operations. Through the rubble came the muffled moans of those who were still alive, saved by the stone arches which had remained standing. One of the people buried under the fallen masonry was a certain Lorenza who had just given birth to a baby. The baby was dead when extricated from under the debris but the mother was still breathing; she however was to die on the way to hospital. I stayed there through the bitterly cold and wet night until my sixty-year-old mother was brought up lifeless in the early morning. That was a cruel, tragic, unforgettable night.

The whole story emerged later. At first, my mother had stayed

The war victims memorial at Vittoriosa.

(Photo N. Genovese)

in the house as I had told her; then, when the second wave came she had been so terrified of being alone that she had panicked and rushed out to take shelter in the vestry as so many others were doing. In that one incident, some sixty persons perished. Some of the victims were not Vittoriosa residents; they had been on the harbour ferry when the siren sounded and as soon as the boat tied up at the St Lawrence Quay, they had rushed into the first place they could find which happened to be the vestry.

After this tragic episode one woman, Nina, nicknamed "the wine-seller", who had known us at Qormi and who had heard about our tragic loss, invited us to go and live with her and so we went back to Qormi.

There were several other incidents in which I was directly involved.

One of these concerned the *Bonaventure* which entered harbour during an air raid and therefore there were no men around to tie her up to the quay. A few friends and myself, all foolhardy young men, emerged from the shelter and volunteered to do the work. Some *Stukas* started dive-bombing the ship and she answered back with her anti-aircraft guns and all the while we were trying to make her fast to the quay. No sooner was the ship made fast than the seamen on board, with the exception of those manning the guns, rushed down the gangway and into the nearest shelter. We, of course, did likewise. Another incident I remember clearly was when HMS *Penelope* was dry-docked in No. 4 or No. 5 Dock. The Germans had so riddled her with shrapnel holes that she was nicknamed the *Pepperpot.* When she was floated out of the dock, she tied up alongside the boathouse and the workmen from that section stopped up the holes with wooden plugs. With the *Penelope* out of the dock the Germans kept pressing their attacks on the dock and caused a lot of damage. At nightfall the *Penelope* steamed out of the harbour, giving the German raiders the slip.

As one would expect the Dockyard was the main target of the bombing raids but the number of casualties among workers was surprisingly low thanks to the large number of bomb-proof and easily accessible rock-cut shelters that abounded in the area.

H.M.S. *Penelope*, nicknamed "Pepperpot"

Among the few casualties, two were close friends of mine. These two, along with other young workers, used to enjoy a game of football in the break. One day while they were kicking a ball around there was an air-raid and the men took shelter in one of the latrines; unfortunately the place received a direct hit and my two friends were among the victims. Incidentally I may here add that the morale of the Dockyard employees was always high during the war and work was only interrupted during air-raids. As soon as the all clear sounded, everybody would troop back to work and take up the job where they had left off.

There were occasions when workers could not do any useful work at the Dockyard because the place they worked in was put out of action as a result of the bombing. In such cases the workers concerned would be detailed to carry out tasks elsewhere. For example for a period of time I was attached to the Department of Demolition and Clearance; others were sent to the airfields to fill up the bomb craters in the runways. I was assigned to a working party detailed to clear away the rubble from the flour mills buildings. Our job was to recover the sacks of flour from under the debris and then to transport them to a warehouse in Żebbuġ. The leader of the working party was a tough guy from Hamrun called "iż-Żuż". From time to time this man would take up a flour sack, rip it open with his flick-knife and say, "This is for sharing among us; I don't want to see any spillage or that will put an end to it". I remember the trepidation with which I would take my share, packed into a pillow-case, from Marsa to Qormi, expecting all the time to be stopped by C.I.D. policemen or, equally worrying, to have the flour snatched away by delinquents. At the time, of course, you could be stopped by the police to have any stuff you happened to be carrying inspected. You could see starvation staring you in the face all around and the pangs of hunger were a familiar feeling for me. I often used to give my bread ration to my sister's children. Sometimes I would feel so ravenous that I would cut the thick leaves of the prickly pear plant, remove the spikes and boil the rest along with the leaves of some edible weeds. That would often be my mid-day meal and at night I often went to bed hungry. As far as I am concerned, the food shortage was the greatest hardship of the war.

WATTY GATT

My father was employed as a dockmaster and as he had to be on call round the clock we lived in a house within the precincts of the Yard. I was employed as an assistant estimator on the Dockyard establishment.

On the 10th June 1940 I was working the night shift and at around six in the evening my father told me that he had heard rumours that Mussolini was expected to declare war against the Allies before the day was out. He also warned me to be prepared for the possibility that Italian forces might bomb Malta or use paratroops to invade the Island during the night. In those early days there were certainly not enough safe shelters to accommodate the Dockyard labour force which was then in the region of 14,000 men and when the *Duce* boasted that the aircraft of the Italian Air Force would soon be darkening the skies, tension among Dockyard workers understandably ran high. As a precaution the Dockyard had been partitioned off into a number of sections separated by barbed wire under the control of the Army which included volunteers who manned the newly formed *Dockyard Defence Battery* equipped with the latest version of the Bofors anti-aircraft gun.. In the late evening of the same day the Manager, Constructive Department instructed my father to flood Dock No. 2 which was occupied by HMS *Terror*. The Manager emphasised that the flooding operation had to be carried out in the dark without the use of electricity; the men had to resort to the use of candles! The *Terror* was under orders to remain in the dock for the next forty eight hours and to be at the ready with her powerful anti-aircraft guns should Italian raiders decide to pay a visit.

A few minutes before seven in the morning of the eleventh the sirens began to wail, not to signal the start of the working day, but to announce the first air-raid over Malta. At first the workers did not quite understand what was going on until the first shots were heard and everyone hurried to seek some form of shelter. I remember that first bombing attack quite clearly.

Equally clear is my recollection of the *Illustrious* blitz which took place on the 16th January of the following year. For me the attack on the *Illustrious* came as no surprise as I had heard "Lord Haw Haw" (William Joyce) boast on the radio that a convoy which was on its way to Malta was about to be annihilated and singled out as a special target the *Illustrious*. As the convoy was steaming off the Island of Pantelleria, aircraft of the *Luftwaffe*, which had only recently established a base in Sicily, attacked the convoy mercilessly concentrating their bombing mainly on the aircraft carrier which was repeatedly hit and suffered considerable damage including the destruction of some of her planes. In spite of this, the aircraft carrier limped into Grand Harbour under her own steam, carrying 126 dead and a large number of wounded. Other ships of the convoy also made it into harbour.

The attack on H.M.S *Illustrious;* painting by Joseph Galea.

William Joyce, ("Lord Haw Haw") who was hanged for treason in 1946.

The German air force seemed to have sworn to send the *Illustrious* to the bottom and the attack was resumed with renewed and increased ferocity when she tied up at Parlatorio Wharf. At enormous risks to their lives Dockyard workers worked round the clock to carry out essential repairs to propellers and rudder and to parts of the hull. I was one of five draughtsmen detailed to go on board to survey the damage but we could only do this in the intervals between air raids as all men, except those manning her anti-aircraft guns, had to leave the carrier and seek shelter during raids.

The blitz on the *Illustrious* was a nightmarish scene. *Stukas* screamed as they dive-bombed the carrier, releasing their bombs just before pulling out of their steep dives while anti-aircraft guns around the harbour kept up a dense and ear-splitting "box barrage". Remarkably enough, in spite of the concentrated bombing kept up by wave after wave of German bombers, the *Illustrious* was only hit once and was able to leave the harbour under her own power a week later. If the *Illustrious* can be said to have suffered relatively minor damage, the same cannot be said of the Three Cities. Whole blocks of buildings were razed to the ground and several of the residents were killed or injured. Senglea was the worst hit and the devastation caused to that densely built-up town was appalling.

During the war I was also official photographer to the Dockyard and I carried the responsibility of surveying the damage caused by every bomb falling within the Dockyard perimeter. Sometimes during air raids, if we had a task in hand, we would remain in the dark-room rather than take cover. On one occasion, when the alert sounded, we decided to leave our post and get into the shelter. That was a lucky decision because on that day the dark-room happened to be at the receiving end of a direct hit.

Throughout the war period, the morale of Dockyard workers remained high and they performed their duty to the best of their ability. The soldiers manning the Dockyard Defence Battery were positively heroic in their actions. One of the gun emplacements of this battery was right on top of the bastion, in the shadow of the great clock tower. One of my cousins was stationed there and I remember between one raid and another the men would play the accordion. The only time these men seemed to be depressed was when they were given orders not to fire their guns during the night as it was feared that the gunflashes would light up the surroundings and help enemy raiders locate their targets.

I used to listen in regularly to the wireless and rarely missed the news. One of the stations I used to tune in to was Vatican Radio, through which Maltese nationals residing in the city sent messages to their relatives and friends in Malta. I was in the habit of taking down some of these messages and then passing them on to the relatives in Malta. One of the messages I noted once was that from a friend of my sister's who happened to be on a bursary in Italy and had to spend the war years in Italy.

Our residence was in the Macina, and in the shelter we often encountered Admiral McKenzie and his family who occasionally gave us the latest update of the news from the fronts. I remember the Admiral telling us during an air raid that a sea-borne attack on the defences of Malta was expected any day. The predicted event materialised in July 1941 when *E-boats* attacked the harbours in July 1941. The defenders were obviously prepared for the raiders and the harbour batteries were on the alert. I know for certain that with British agents constantly toing and froing between Malta and Sicily, the British Intelligence personnel were fully aware of every military movement in neighbouring Sicily. It transpired later that British agents could even be found on board Italian sea-craft, occasionally sporting Italian military uniforms.

I lived at the Dockyard with my parents until 1944 when I married and set up house at Attard.

JOSEPH GENOVESE

I heard the siren giving warning of the first air raid at a few minutes before seven in the morning of the 11th June as I was going through Bormla Gate (now walled up) on my way to report for duty at the Dockyard where I was employed as an apprentice. On that day a large number of bombs were dropped hitting, among other places, the Boathouse at Cospicua and Porte des Bombes at Floriana. A few days later we apprentices were told by the Admiralty not to report for duty and that we were to consider ourselves as being on leave with pay until further notice. Three months later, in September, we were instructed to return to work.

There was a regular bus service for Dockyard workers between Rabat, where I lived with my family, and Cospicua. However when shortages of most commodities, including fuel, began to be felt the Rabat bus terminus was moved down to the shrine of Our Lady of Victories at the bottom of the hill, a measure which was meant to save on petrol.

I spent some of my time on duty at the Kalafrana plant, one of the outstations of the Dockyard. Every morning I used to sign in at the Dockyard, collect some papers and go with them to my instructor at Kalafrana. At that time, the *Breconshire* was lying on her side on a reef at St George's Bay, having been run aground for salvage purposes. At the torpedo depot at Kalafrana we had a rock-cut shelter excavated under the road leading to the seaplane base; one day a bomb exploded on the roadside bursting a six-inch water main. This led to flooding in the shelter in which we were taking cover. Both entrances to the shelter had been blocked by the debris and it looked as if we were going to end up drowned. Fortunately RAF personnel stationed nearby rushed to the scene and managed to clear one of the entrances. By that time the water had reached to just above our knees and you can imagine our relief as we emerged from the shelter... only to find that there was an air-raid on and bombs were dropping all around. That was perhaps the most terrifying experience in my life during the war.

I only sought shelter under ground when I happened to be at the Dockyard or at Kalafrana. Otherwise I could never bring myself to go underground. In the darkness of the night I used to watch, fascinated, the aerial battles taking place over the harbour area and Luqa airfield. The searchlights playing across the black sky and the flares turning night into day would hold me spellbound as I watched from the Saqqajja near the Saura Institute. Of course my friends and I were breaking the curfew regulations in force at the time and we had to keep a constant lookout for police or Special Constables. Whenever any of these "spoilsports" came along we would make a run for it; we were in our late teens then and no policeman had a hope of catching us!

The searchlights ... turned night into day.

(NWMA Collection)

I would say that the worst incidents at Rabat occurred when enemy raiders dropped "butterfly" anti-personnel bombs. These used to be housed in a large canister which would burst open on its way down and shower the bombs over a large area. On another occasion the Hotel Point de Vue received a direct hit and a number of RAF pilots who were billeted there were killed or wounded. Other bombs dropped over Rabat also left their victims.

The food shortage did not worry me too much because although my brothers and I were non-smokers, we had our ration of cigarettes which we could readily barter for bread. At the time the statutory price of a loaf of bread was four pence (less than two cents) but on the black market you would have to fork out between three and ten shillings (15c to 50c) for it.

OSCAR PULIS

In 1940 I was employed as an Admiralty clerk and I used to live at Cospicua. When the first raiders flew in on the 11th June at a few minutes before seven in the morning, I was getting ready to go to the office. A few seconds after the air-raid warning sounded, it seemed as if all hell was let loose: explosions followed one another in quick succession, guns were firing all around us and the ground under our feet shuddered intermittently. People rushed out of their homes, not understanding what was going on and there was a general panic. My father was a Special Constable and happened to be hearing Mass at St Paul's Church in Cospicua. In the excitement he rushed out leaving behind him his steel helmet and the white armband with *SC* stamped on it. As soon as the all-clear went I left home and signed in at the office as usual but my colleagues who lived at some distance did not turn up until much later and a few failed to turn up.

On that very day, my father and mother left our house at Cospicua and made their way to Birkirkara to find some kind of lodging there, while I stayed in my home town as I had an appointment with a friend later on in the day. On leaving the office I went to my friend's house which was situated about half way between the St Thomas and St Helen gates. The eighth and last air-raid for that first day of the war came late in the evening and bombs dropped over Cospicua killed a number of people. In that raid, we were taking shelter in a small shed in a garden and had to support the makeshift roof with our hands during the bombardment! We spent the night in the open air but there were no further air-raids. On the following day my friend's family moved to Żejtun and when I left the office I made my way there and spent the night with them. On the third day I decided to go to my parents at Birkirkara which was packed with refugees from Cottonera. In the evening, most of the refugees kept up their usual habit of promenading, an activity which was very soon taken up by the locals.

The fiercest raids that I remember were those of the 16th of January 1941 when the *Illustrious* was made the target of a concentrated blitz. Like all Dockyard employees, I was sure that when the Luftwaffe established a base in Sicily, we were going to be in for some heavy bombardments. In fact, at around two or half past two in the afternoon of that day, the sirens began to wail and we immediately left our desks and took shelter. Seconds later, hell broke loose. Guns were firing away and bombs were exploding in quick succession, shaking the earth under our feet. The cacophony was such that our stone-deaf head of department, a certain Mr Munro, exclaimed as he placed the palm of his hand against the rock face, "What's the matter? I can feel them." A few days after that bombardment, Mr Munro made arrangements for those of us who worked in the Cash Office to move from the Dockyard to the Carmelite Priory in the old capital, Mdina. We were given the use of the cloister and we could therefore perform our duties without constant interruption; the clerks who handled the cash were accommodated in one of the palaces in the main street of the same town. We were not to move back to the Dockyard before August 1944.

Another wartime incident which comes to mind goes back to the time when I was engaged to a girl from Mosta. I was, as you can imagine, a frequent visitor to that village and I often spent hours talking with my fiancee's father who was a sanitary inspector. Once when I was in his company two bombs fell within yards of each other and blocked both entrances of a shelter in which several people had taken cover. The death toll was high and among the victims was a man who lived next door to my fiancee's family; the man was stationed at Fort Mosta and on that fateful day happened to be on leave. His wife suffered some injuries too and when the dead body of her husband was being carried past her, she muttered, "Poor man!". She had not even recognised him through her blood covered eyes. During that raid my fiancee's father and myself had been taking cover in another shelter and when the raid was over, we went to give a hand to the rescuers.

I can also recall the great pilgrimage which wended its way from Birkirkara to Cospicua in November 1944. You may remember that during the war precautions were taken to move invaluable objects from the threatened areas to safer sites; accordingly, the statue of the Immaculate Conception as well as the main altarpiece were transferred from the parish church at Cospicua to that of St Helen's at Birkirkara. When the bombing began to devastate the Dockyard area, the Chapter of the Parish Church vowed that should the church come through the war unscathed, the statue and the altarpiece would return to their

⊠

The people of Cospicua dispersed throughout the whole island by the cruelties of war celebrating for the first time the feast of

THE IMMACULATE CONCEPTION

in the Parish Church of Birkirkara humbly pray

OUR LADY

QUEEN OF PEACE

to spread her maternal mantle

over

MALTA

and to grant

The British Empire

a

Victorious Peace.

- --+- --

Serie C G

8/XII, 1941.

The penitential pilgrimage with the statue of the Immaculate Conception which took place on 19 November 1944.

proper place in solemn procession. When war activity began to peter out, a committee was set up with the object of organising that pilgrimage which, it was decided, was to be held on the 19th of the month. After High Mass in which the Birkirkara and Cospicua Chapters officiated, the statue and the altarpiece were carried out of St Helen's and conveyed in procession through Fleur-de-Lys, Hamrun, Marsa and Paola, arriving at Cospicua at around half past nine. The ringing of bells and the playing of bands welcomed the procession as it picked its way through the rubble which had once been Cospicua to the church which was still standing.

It was a wonderful spectacle, a manifestation of faith and joy, tinged with sadness at the memory of those people of Cospicua who did not survive the bombardment.

Open spaces appeared where buildings once stood.

WALTER ZAHRA

The Naval Armament Depot in which I worked as an Admiralty clerk had a branch at Alexandria and on the 19th May 1940, I left Malta in the company of a colleague of mine, Lorry Bonanno, and sailed to Egypt on the merchantman *Colon* arriving at Port Said on Empire Day, that is, the 24th May. From Port Said we travelled to Benha station where we caught the train to Alexandria. No sooner had we walked out of the station at Alexandria than we found waiting patiently for us our friend Robbie Siracusa with a military car in attendance and we were soon comfortably set up in the hotel room which had been booked for us in advance

At that time I was married with a two-and-a-half year old son. Before I left Malta, I promised my wife that as soon as I settled down in Egypt I would make arrangements for her and our son to join me. I soon applied formally to my superiors for the required transport. In mid-August one of my colleagues was sent to Ismailia, a town which is halfway down the Suez Canal. In the first days of September I was summoned up by my principal officer and told that I was in line for promotion. "But," he added, "you know that we now have a station at Ismailia and I would very much like you to go to that town to give a helping hand to Mr Fisher. Quite understandably you've made a request to have your family brought over. Ismailia is a small, clean and quiet town, almost European in character and should be an ideal place to settle your family in." On the 8th of September I found myself in Ismailia.

Italy's declaration of war and the consequent bombing which was taking place in Malta worried me not a little and I was anxious to see my wife and son close to me and away from danger. In fact my wife and my son, Rene`, embarked on the *Colon* at Marsaxlokk on the same day as a convoy escorted by, among others, the aircraft carrier HMS *Illustrious* was steaming towards Malta. Probably the enemy concentrated on attacking the convoy and the *Colon* was left to continue on her way without harassment, arriving at Port Said after an uneventful four day voyage. I had prepared a flat in Ismailia; our neighbours were Greek families who welcomed and helped us. When my wife had time on her hands, she used to come to my office and bring along some embroidery work or knitting. I look back on those two and a half years as among the happiest of my life even though there was the occasional bombing attack as if to remind us that there was a war on. The enemy tended to rely more on dropping magnetic mines in the Canal in a bid to prevent ships carrying munitions from using the waterway. During those infrequent raids the only shelter we could count on was under a bed or a table.

I think we had only one really serious attack in those years.

That was a night of terror for us, crouched as we were under a table, expecting every minute to be buried under the ruins of our own roof. The main targets of the attack seemed to have been the railway station and the telephone exchange and we were spared the worst. Several buildings were demolished and there were casualties among the residents but the railway station came through unscathed.

Lt Trevor Meadows reported missing over Holland.

(Courtesy A. Meadows)

I had another first-hand experience of an aerial attack the day I paid a visit to a family friend, Trevor Meadows, an RAF pilot. An air-raid alarm sounded while we were having a chat over a drink in the canteen, and we looked for one of the slit trenches which afforded a measure of protection. As we stepped out, Meadows turned to me and said, "Look, there's a bomb crater over there; let's get in there. The same spot is never hit twice!" As we ran towards the crater, enemy planes were already hovering over us and I answered, "We'll never make it that far; let's crawl into this trench here." Luckily we did just that. As we made our way back to the canteen when the all clear was sounded, we learnt that contrary to Trevor's beliefs a bomb had landed in that crater killing some Arab labourers who were employed at the airfield. During our stay in Ismailia the Allies were retreating before Rommel's divisions but I was so engrossed in my work that I was never really aware of the desperate situation.

In the meantime, most of the British and Maltese employees were moving from Alexandria to Ismailia and my hands were full with the task of making provisions for their accommodation and local transport. The principal school was requisitioned for the Commander-in-Chief of the Fleet and his staff who had to fall back to Ismailia. The subsequent Allied victory at El Alamein, of course, changed all that and turned the tide of war in North Africa.

Towards the end of 1942 my wife broke the news that she was expecting our second child. With a bit of help from my head of department I got a transfer to Port Said where there was a private maternity hospital staffed by French sisters. At the time there was in Port Said a thriving Maltese community some members of which occupied influential posts including that of British consul. In spite of the normal situation at Port Said, I cannot say that we were happy; our thoughts were often on Malta where conditions were very bad and there were serious shortages of practically every commodity. We tried to feel that we were doing something about it by sending food parcels from time to time. We were lucky to have a friend like Meadows who was often engaged in flying VIP's to and from Malta and who was only too ready to deliver the occasional parcel for us.

I will mention one incident which almost caused a panic in Port Said. When Nazi forces invaded Greece, some Greek ships were detained in various harbours in Egypt by the British authorities. Among these was a cruiser whose captain demanded the immediate release of his ship; when his demands were refused he threatened to bombard the town, a threat which was taken seriously as there wasn't a single British man-of-war in harbour at that point in time. While negotiations between the captain and the British authorities were in progress, a British party went on board in the night, disarmed the guns and disabled the navigation instruments. This was an incident with a happy ending but you can imagine how we were biting our finger nails during the negotiations.

During our stay in Egypt we made three trips to Cairo where we could see - and touch - the awe-inspiring remains of the Pharaohs. With my identity card attesting to my British officer status, many doors were literally opened for me and I had no difficulty in gaining access to the treasures of the National Museum which was then closed to the public. As 1944 was drawing to a close, my father suffered a heart attack and I was determined that I should see him before he died, something which I had not been able to do in the case of my dear mother. I therefore put in a request for repatriation with the result that in the first weeks of 1945 my family and I stepped ashore, back in our motherland, to join our relatives.

King's Own Malta Regiment

OUR ALLIES THE COLONIES

(Courtesy J. Borg Bonello)

VII. Other Workers

BEATRICE ABELA

A few months after the war broke out, I got a job as a typist with the Services. My first posting, towards the end of 1940, was in the Ordnance Department. There were eight of us girl typists in the Department. I was in the "Spare Parts" section while some of the others did routine office work like typing and correspon-

M.V. *Talabot* ablaze off Pinto Wharf.

dence. The Ordnance offices were mostly chambers cut into the solid rock under the Floriana walls on the Pinto Stores foreshore. To report for duty I had to walk down to the Manoel Island bridge which was then the nearest bus stop, catch a bus to Floriana and then walk down Crucifix Hill.

I have many memories of the war. One of the most vivid is the attack on the *Talabot* which happened to be moored at the wharf where the Ordnance offices were. The *Talabot* was carrying a cargo of munitions and when she was hit, the Ordnance offices were quickly evacuated. We were put on board a launch which took us round to Marsamxett Harbour so that we could catch the ferry to Sliema. People were saying that if the *Talabot*'s cargo were to explode, the whole of Floriana would be devastated. However things turned out differently; the *Talabot* was scuttled at her moorings and the danger was averted.

Another day which I recall from time to time is when with some other typists I went up to Valletta to buy a wedding present for one of the girls in the typing pool. We had gone as far as the War Memorial when an air-raid warning sounded and we took cover in a slit trench nearby. In the next few minutes it seemed like all hell was let loose: bombs were crashing down and exploding everywhere, making the ground shudder time and time again. As you can imagine we were so terrified that we could not even articulate a prayer but just crouched there as if petrified. When the "raiders passed" sounded we did not dare go on with our errand but decided to get back to the office.

I remember another episode: I was sitting at my desk typing something or other to the dictation of a serviceman who was standing beside me. A bomb landed nearby and exploded and the next instant the serviceman disappeared from sight, hurled out by the blast. The first thought that came to my mind then was that he was playing some kind of joke!

One need hardly say that lots of things changed during the war but for girls like me I do not think that life was monotonous - there were servicemen aplenty! Most of the young women I knew could not complain of a shortage of dates, even if there was a shortage of everything else. Dances were held regularly with the

A caterpillar shelter opposite the Phoenicia Hotel, Floriana.

occasional party thrown in, usually in one of the Services clubs. At the height of the war, I remember going to a New Year's Eve dance at the Union Club in Valletta; luckily there was not a single air-raid warning that night. Dances were also held routinely at the British Institute in Valletta; these were called "tea dances" presumably because they were held between 3.00 p.m. and seven in the evening. The dances were very well patronised by British and local servicemen and, I need hardly add, by young women. I have very happy memories of those days. When the dance was over we would rush out to catch the last bus from Valletta or to cross to Sliema in a *dghajsa* (harbour boat).

During those years I met Watson, an observer on an RAF plane. His plane had the misfortune to be badly damaged during a dogfight with a German aircraft and the pilot was wounded and could not control the plane. Although injured, too, Watson took the pilot's place and somehow managed to land the crippled plane. I went up to the military hospital at Mtarfa to see him and found him with his face completely covered with bandages except for the eyes. I believe that action earned him some sort of decoration. I still have in my possession the wing which he wore on his uniform - over his heart... He was transferred to a hospital in England and I never saw him again.

You would probably conclude that a lot of Maltese girls married British servicemen but that was not the case; there were a number of obstacles in the way, as for example the differing religious denominations. There were other difficulties besides. For instance, many of us had the sort of upbringing which would make us think twice before marrying an unknown foreigner, even though he might be a high ranking officer. In spite of these problems there were a few marriages of this sort; I can think of at least two of my friends who married British servicemen during the war.

A few weeks before the arrival of the Santa Marija convoy I went through the most trying experiences of my life. The word was going round that Malta was on the verge of surrendering to the enemy. The possibility of that coming to pass was, to me, much more anxiety provoking than the bombing and the food shortage. My family was known to be staunchly pro-British and I dared not imagine the treatment we would be getting from the Germans and the Italians.

I firmly believe that the Maltese office-girls were thoroughly respected by the British and their contribution to the war effort was keenly appreciated. Some of the British servicemen became personal friends and were often invited to meet our families.

VICTOR CURMI

When the war broke out I was an eighteen year old lad helping my father run three grog-shops in Strait Street, Valletta. I was exempted from compulsory war service. With all those servicemen around you can easily imagine that my father's business flourished especially when the Fleet was in harbour; we were, in fact, much busier than in peace time. During air-raids it was "business as usual" for us and we kept our shops open even though at times we were scared. I remember once one of those raids which lasted for hours and hours and our customers, as well as myself, began to feel rather relaxed. I was outside, standing at the corner, when I saw a string of bombs dropping down. Two other young men and myself rushed off to take cover in the shelter which stood near the Palace. Before I managed to get inside bombs began to burst in several places and I was hurled by the blast down the steps leading down into the shelter. That was the raid in which the Casino Maltese and the Regent Cinema were destroyed with great loss of life; many of those killed were servicemen who were watching a film. The prior of the Carmelite friary down the street was also killed on that occasion.

In the first few days of the war my family went as refugees to a farmhouse in Birkirkara but very soon we were back in Valletta, but instead of living in our house we lived in a shelter which we had dug out under the Marsamxett bastions.

Like many people who had shops in those days we were never really starving. Somehow or other we always managed to get hold of tins of preserved food and bully beef; cooking was normally done outside over the *kenur*, the old-fashioned stone stove. Cigarettes and tobacco were rationed and one could only buy beer, whisky and brandy on the black market. We also used to sell wine which seemed to go down quite well with the sailors.

My father played the mandolin, one of my brothers had an accordion and the other a violin and with two other musicians we used to go round the streets of Valletta singing and making merry. Sailors and other servicemen would often join in and people enjoyed the free entertainment.

There is one raid at least which I will remember for as long as I live. I was standing somewhere near the Cafe` Premier, which incidentally never closed during the war, when I saw a *Spitfire* and a German fighter engaged in a dog-fight. The German raider was hit and I saw it plummeting down. It crashed just behind the La Valette Band Club. This was one of the very first actions in which the newly-arrived *Spitfire* squadron had been engaged.

PAWLINA CUTAJAR

I lived with my family in Cospicua and taught in a small school run by nuns in nearby Vittoriosa. When the war broke out, the family including myself moved to a large house in Qormi where my married sister and her husband had taken up residence. Besides ourselves there were a few other refugee families living in that house, each family packed into a room. We did not like that crowded place at all and when we found alternative accommodation in another house we moved at once. The woman who owned the house let us have the first floor while she lived downstairs. Before I started teaching I had spent some time living as a nun in a convent and I had become quite good at sewing; this skill I put to good use during our stay in Qormi.

When Victory Kitchens were set up I got a job as a supervisor and my sister was employed as an assistant. My main task was to

At the Victory Kitchen.

(NWMA Collection)

keep track of foodstuffs. From time to time the books were inspected by officials from the central office who went through the registers with a fine tooth comb. But in spite of every precaution pilferage was rampant and abuses like presenting forged coupons were common. We pretended not to see through such tricks because we were afraid of reprisals should we lodge reports.

One of the employees at the Victory Kitchen, a habitual pilferer, was caught red-handed and arrested. Before he was due to appear in court, my cousin, Fr Rikard Attard, went personally to Mr Axisa, a close friend of his and then occupying the post of Police Commissioner and begged him to stop all proceedings against the man. Mrs Rosie Debono, who was the Deputy Director of Victory Kitchens also interceded on behalf of the arrested man and eventually the case was dropped, but not before the man was dismissed from his post.

There were several Victory Kitchens in Qormi. From time to time people complained about the quality of food we were providing and once we had a proper riot on our hands when we served liver which had turned green. Rumour had it that we mixed goat's meat with the day's meal occasionally; I have never found out if those rumours were true. As far as I was concerned I never touched meat. The woman we were living with ran a bakery and so we managed to get an extra loaf now and then. For just over two years, I kept my job with the Victory Kitchens at a monthly salary of eight pounds. There was not much to spend one's money on in those days; it was not only food that was scarce but practically everything including clothes and shoes.

GREZZJU FALZON

The digging of public shelters in this part of the Island was in the hands of Captain Serafin Xuereb, the well-known contractor, and I was employed with the firm as a foreman in charge of all the miners in Qrendi and Mqabba, a total of some twenty-four men. Normally the digging of a shelter was started at both ends with three men at either end. Of these six, four would be employed in the actual digging while the other two would carry the excavated rock to the surface. It was my responsibility to decide on the depth and direction of the digging and also of course to keep a record of the work done by each labourer. The working day was usually from seven in the morning to five in the afternoon. One has to remember that in those days there were no mechanical aids available - everything had to be done by hand so that a normal shelter would take up to six months to complete, depending of course on the dimensions and depth. Later on we began to use dynamite on a very small scale as otherwise damage would be done to buildings in the vicinity. I was exempted from conscription because my work was considered to be essential to the war effort.

As a rule, miners were paid from eight to twelve shillings (40c to 60c) a day; others who worked privately, as for example, excavating cubicles in the public shelter always went for piece-work. Before shelters were available, people used to take cover in the churches during air-raids or in cellars reinforced with scantlings and planks. A number of bombs were dropped on Qrendi. One day on my way to see some work in progress, an air-raid sounded. I took cover in a small room in a field and then, when the all-clear was sounded I decided to turn back home. When I looked in front of me I saw that the dome on the parish church had disappeared; it had received a direct hit during the raid. As I walked on, I saw on the ground before me a sack. I lifted one end of the sack and there, beneath, was the disfigured body of a woman shrunk by the blast of the exploding bomb. The woman's sister was also killed. The two of them had been fetching some fodder for their cattle. A number of other people had also perished in the same attack.

The local farmers tilled their fields as before; in fact the farm produce was fetching higher prices than ever before - in many instances four times higher than before the war. In one particular year, the entire wheat harvest was bought by the government at four or five times the normal price. We had some fields and therefore we were never short of food. My father had also taken the precaution of hoarding necessities in large quantities.

Towards the end of the war, precisely on the 30th May 1943, I got married to Scolastica whose parents ran a grocery and a wine-shop. During the war their grocery business was practically at a standstill but trade in the wine-shop flourished as the villagers regularly came there to slake their thirst in the evening.

JOE FARRUGIA CASSANO

In September 1940 I found employment as a clerk with the British Services. The Germans were establishing a foothold in Southern Europe and the British took immediate steps to strengthen the defences of the Island. Heavy and light anti-aircraft batteries sprang up all over the Island especially around strategic places. From our offices located in the Attard area, we looked after two batteries, that of San Blas and the one at Busbesija in the vicinity of Ta' Qali airfield. Each of those batteries was armed with four 3.7 inch guns and was provided with accommodation, kitchens and toilet facilities for its men. Ta' Qali housed the fighter squadrons and as such was often the target of enemy raiders; about a dozen gun emplacements were built round the perimeter and armed with Bofors guns. I remember the guns were named after English towns beginning with the letter *T*: *Truro*, *Torquay*, *Tonby*, etc.

Our chief clerk happened to be a rather nervous person and whenever an air-raid sounded he got extremely edgy. I remember whenever he had to do the rounds of the work in progress he regularly gave instructions to his driver to keep the engine running; as soon as he caught sight of the red flag being run up he would jump into the car and tell his driver to drive as fast as possible to Mtarfa. One day as I accompanied him on one of these tours bombs fell on the building which we had left a few minutes before. A horse belonging to one of the labourers had its head blown off.

One Friday I was accompanying Captain Lee of the Royal Engineers to pay the wages to labourers at their place of work;

after stopping at various places - Attard, the Rabat road, the Ta'
Qali perimeter, Buqana and so on - we proceeded to Busbesija to
hand out the pay packets to the labourers. At one point we saw a
number of German fighters coming in at a low altitude from the
direction of Mellieha. As we stopped and ran out of the car to
take shelter in a rural room, three of the fighters opened up with
their machine-guns but we were unharmed although the car got
two bullets. I count that as one of my lucky days.

A number of large sheds intended to serve as a depot for the
RAOC were being built at Attard in the vicinity of the Mental
Hospital (now Mt. Carmel Hospital) just before the war started
and in their incomplete state had been turned into billets for the
Buffs, the well-known infantry regiment. For a period of time,
this site was not attacked by the Germans because they were
under the impression that it was a prisoner-of-war camp. One of
the regimental officers, the quartermaster, did not form part of
the gun-crews and therefore used to come to take cover in one of
the shelters annexed to our offices when heavy air-raids were in
progress. I remember him telling us, on a memorable Thursday
afternoon, that a heavy bombing attack was in the offing as some
five hundred enemy aircraft were preparing for take-off from various airfields in Sicily. That turned out to be the opening action
of what became known later as the *Illustrious* blitz. I witnessed
the entire awesome spectacle from a vantage point at Attard and
I can say that I never saw, before or after that day, so many
bombers in action in one raid.

Some time later the same officer urged us to take cover immediately as the target of an imminent raid was the Buffs camp. The
order was for "everyone including the regimental mascot" to
clear out of the camp and take shelter. When we emerged from
the shelter at the end of the raid, we saw that most of the buildings had been reduced to mounds of rubble.

Most of the people in the shelter used to be terrified when they
heard the whistling of falling bombs and I used to try to calm them
down by saying that the bomb travels faster than the sound and
therefore when they heard the whistling the bomb would have
already exploded and the fact that you could hear it could only mean

that you were safe. I never followed that up by saying that that did not necessarily mean that the next bomb would miss you...

LOUIS E. GALEA

When in June 1940 war broke out my marriage was in its first weeks and my wife and I were living with my in-laws in Valletta as our house was not yet ready for occupation. My father-in-law, Colonel Gatt, was the Commanding Officer at Fort St Elmo and you can imagine the shock which my wife and I had when we learnt that in the very first raid of the war, bombs had been dropped on the Fort and that a number of men had been killed and others wounded. You can also imagine our relief when our anx-

Fort St Elmo monument to the memory of the six gunners killed on the first day of the war.

(NWMA Collection)

239

ious enquiries revealed that my father-in-law was unscathed. Shortly afterwards we went to live with my brother-in-law who had his residence in Attard, a much safer place than Valletta.

I was then a clerk with Barclays Bank, a post I had held since 1932; the bank had two branches in those days, one in Valletta and the other in Sliema. Barclays were bankers to the Services, the British authorities and the Maltese government and also to many Maltese business firms. The Bank's first measure on the outbreak of hostilities was to change its working hours: instead of being open to the public until four in the afternoon, we began to close at noon, finish off the day's work and then leave the office. Valletta was not the best place to spend long hours in during the war!

Gradually people started getting used to living in wartime and life started slowly getting back to normal. My wife and I therefore decided to move from Attard to take up residence in our own house at Sliema. In the meantime our first child was on the way. On the 16th of January 1941, the day of the *Illustrious* attack, we were in Valletta visiting my in-laws and during the apocalyptic action, my wife was so terrified that she miscarried. After that trauma she spent some six weeks in bed unable to go down inside a shelter during the bombing and my mother-in-law came to live with us to look after her. When my wife recovered we went to live in a beautiful villa in Rabat; the only drawback was that I had quite some distance to go to the office. At that time buses did not go all the way to Rabat but stopped about halfway between that town and Attard and instead of taking you to Valletta, the bus would drop you at Porte des Bombes, so that you had to walk for a considerable distance at either end. Our Head Office was in Kingsway, and we often had to pick our way through the rubble heaped in that street.

I remember the day when the Casino Maltese received a direct hit and other bombs fell on Strait Street; I was in the Bank's strong room at that instant and I could feel the whole place shuddering and rocking as if the building was going to collapse on our heads. Sometimes an air raid warning would sound as we were busy working on our ledgers; we rarely left our place on such occasions in spite of being given instructions to proceed to the bank vaults during air raids. However there were some tasks which one could do in the shelter as, for instance, the computation of interest rates.

Several incidents in which I was personally involved stand out in my memory. There was the time when on alighting from the bus at the bottom of the road leading up to Rabat, we saw a squadron of German raiders heading in the direction of Ta' Qali airfield. As the bombers released their deadly loads we threw ourselves flat into the roadside ditch and with heart in mouth waited for the explosions. The bombs fell some distance away and none of us was hurt but we were terribly shaken. Another

Queen's Square,
Valletta.

time I was seated in a stationary bus at the Gzira terminus when I caught sight of five Italian bombers heading towards HMS *Centurion* and releasing their bomb-load. The other few passengers and myself were out of the bus in next to no time, spread-eagled on the ground. The bombs fell into the sea some fifty yards away from us.

We had a hard time during the war, especially when the enemy attacked at night and those with babies and young children had to carry them down into the shelter. However there was one redeeming feature in all this: the solidarity among people without distinction to their social class. The people were really united in those dark days, a situation which unfortunately came to an end when political division reared its ugly head.

CARMEL J. MALLIA

In 1939, with war clouds on the horizon, people read the ominous signs and began to leave their homes in the harbour area to move to places like Żebbuġ, Birkirkara, Qormi and Gozo which were regarded as being safer should war break out. I was then newly married and living at Paola, but instead of following the general trend, I moved to - of all places - Cospicua where I had managed to find a nice house with a large garden. On the 10th of June while I was pottering about in the garden, my wife came running and blurted out that Mussolini had just declared war against Britain. Although I cannot say that the news was wholly unexpected, I was struck dumb. Early next morning we could hear the sound of gunfire which we took at first to be some kind of military manoeuvres but soon after realised that the shooting was in earnest. Throughout that day, at the first warning of each air-raid, we would take cover under the stairs; then we settled the baby in the pram, made up a few bundles with necessities and walked to Zabbar where my wife's uncle had a house with an underlying cellar. At that time, of course, it was believed that a cellar provided adequate protection from bombing.

My wife and I were not the only people to leave Cospicua for

Zabbar. On the night of the 11th June, a stick of bombs practically wiped out Bull Street in Cospicua and we saw a long procession of panic-stricken people, some covered with dust, moving into Zabbar, all recounting their terrifying experiences and saying that a large number of persons were still buried under the debris. My sister, who was married to a police inspector, had spent a few years as a headmistress in a school in Gozo, and she and her husband were toying with the idea of going as refugees to take up residence in that Island. I got in touch with her and told her that my wife and myself were thinking of taking the same step. Before doing that, however, we moved to a relative's house in lower Merchants Street in Valletta.

Although an Evacuation Commission had been set up before the war to prepare for such an eventuality, panic and fear took hold of the population at the first bombing attacks. As things

Times of Malta on Malta's first day of the war.

turned out we did not move to Gozo but instead moved first to Fleur de Lys and then to Rabat where a colleague of mine at the Public Works Department, took us into his house. It seemed that we were destined to be forever on the move because after a time we went to live in the Tigne` area of Sliema. People in those days were encouraged to borrow picks from Government stores so that they could dig their own shelters and I took up the idea and started to excavate a cubicle in the public shelter. Before finishing the job, we decided to go up to Rabat again as Tigne` was dangerously close to the submarine base.

As an employee in the Public Works Department, my job was to co-ordinate the day-to-day work of my Department and that of COSUP (Office for the Co-ordination of Supplies), a job which was considered to be sufficiently essential for me to be exempted from compulsory military service. Much of the work of the PWD was contributing to the war effort, especially the excavation of underground shelters. The Department's civil engineers and draughtsmen used to go round houses and indicate to the occupiers the safest place in which they could take cover during raids. Labourers were then sent to the houses to reinforce with scantlings and planks the selected areas. At about the same time, so-called "elephant shelters" were being constructed along the main country roads; these shelters consisted of slit trenches roofed over with tree trunks and branches. Incidentally most of the tree trunks used in this work came from the cargo holds of the Italian steamer *Polinice* which was seized in the Grand Harbour when war broke out. The *Polinice* was sunk by Italian bombers, but was later re-floated and her name changed to *Reborn*. The elephant shelters were intended for people who might be crossing from one village to another and who might be caught in an air-raid; they provided adequate cover from flying splinters and, psychologically, they served a very useful purpose. This type of shelter was the brain-child of the then Director of Public Works, Professor J L Gatt.

The Department was also heavily engaged in the excavation of rock-cut public shelters in the towns and villages of Malta and Gozo, an initiative which had started in 1939. It was a massive project by any standards, employing tens of engineers and thousands of labourers.

Another project in which the PWD was closely involved was the conversion of a number of buses into ambulances. A demolition and clearance unit was based at Porte des Bombes and the old railway station at Birkirkara; the old station became the headquarters for the PWD when its offices in Valletta were wiped out in the bombardment

Certain incidents which I personally witnessed are indelibly stuck in my memory, as for instance the *Illustrious* blitz which I followed from the rooftop of the Palace Tower; that was a sight the likes of which I had never seen before or since. Once, when

Battle over Malta; painting
by Denis Burnham.
(Imperial War Museum)

on duty at Birkirkara, I saw a flight of *JU 88*'s approaching from the direction of Mosta. The anti-aircraft batteries in the area soon engaged the bombers in a dense barrage and one of the raiders was hit. Within seconds four of the crew baled out of whom three were saved by their parachutes, landing safely but the fourth man's parachute got caught on the tail of the aircraft and the unlucky airman was killed when the plane crashed and exploded. Once as I was walking with my son near Dingli there was an air-raid and some German fighters were flying at rooftop level; one of the fighters had apparently been hit and the pilot began to machine-gun everything in sight. That was another terrifying experience...

Most of our furniture was destroyed by enemy action. One of the few articles which survived, and which I still have, was an umbrella-stand which had been designed for me by Alberto Laferla, an architect who worked for the PWD. Mr Laferla died

Alberto Laferla, A&CE
(Courtesy A. Soler)

when the internees' camp at St Agatha received a direct hit during an air-raid.

As a rule I used public transport to make the daily trips between Rabat and Birkirkara, but even so I had to walk a lot because buses used to stop at the bottom of the Rabat hill, presumably to save on scarce fuel. I bought a bicycle for thirteen pounds, paid in instalments, and began to use it for going to work.

During the war one did things which we would consider absurd these days. For example I remember once tying an empty petrol can to the handlebars and cycling all the way to Sliema to try and persuade the Regional Protection Officer to provide me with an extra ration of kerosene. I still feel peeved that after going to all that trouble I returned home empty-handed.....

PAWLU MUSCAT

I farmed some land between Ghajn Tuffieha and St Paul's Bay; I had enough water for irrigation and I regularly took my crops to the Birkirkara market. I was married with two children.

Soon after the war broke out, the village where I lived began to see a large number of refugees streaming in with their few possessions. The refugees were from many parts of the Island and my father shared his house with a few of these. The local school had been requisitioned by the military and none of the refugees could be housed there. Some soldiers lived in tents pitched in the fields and sometimes they used to trample on the crops, though probably this was done unintentionally. Troops and villagers got on very well together. I got a job with the military at Mtarfa, mainly carrying various things on my horse-drawn cart. But one day the foreman told me that the horse was too old for that sort of work and I began to use my shoulders instead.

I remember once as I was taking some crops to the market being caught in an air-raid and seeing a dogfight between two Italian planes and an Air Force fighter. One of the Italian planes was hit and the pilot parachuted safely down, only to be met on the ground by a crowd of peasants armed with shotguns. It was lucky for the pilot that the parish priest, Fr Edgar Salomone was on the scene too and stopped the crowd from lynching the poor man.

Mġarr received few bombs during the war. We were never short of food because we always had something growing in our fields; we could also barter vegetables for other necessities. I always tried to help others and I never resorted to selling the produce on the black market, as did many farmers in those days. At one time, we were only permitted to sell our crops to the government; we had to take the crops to the place indicated and then we would receive a cheque later on.

Once I made up my mind to take some grain for milling privately instead of passing it on to the government. When it was dark, I went to the local miller without telling anybody and we agreed that I would call for the flour a couple of days later, again

Mġarr woman wearing the traditional faldetta (ghonella) with her son wearing gas mask.

(Courtesy A. Deguara)

when it was dark. It seems that someone got wind of my intention and lodged a report with the police. The police were soon at the miller's and seized the flour. Besides myself other farmers, about twelve in number, had done the same and so the amount of flour seized was considerable. We were hauled up to court and handed down a fine of about three hundred pounds; however the parish priest, Fr Edgar, spoke on our behalf to the Governor and we finally got away with a fine of some ten pounds.

I confess that that was not the first time I tried to get around the law. I had never experienced any trouble before that because I always took the precaution of handing some of the stuff to an influential person who saw to it that I would not receive any unwelcome attention from the police. That sort of arrangement was quite common during the war...

JOHNNY NAVARRO

I was married a few weeks before Italy's declaration of war. My wife went as a refugee to live with her relatives in Gozo and I went to live with my brother in Valletta as my house in Sliema had been badly damaged in an air-raid. We spent most nights in the old railway tunnel which became one of Valletta's main shelters.

I have several memories of the war. One of the most vivid is when the Opera House was hit and I saw lots of backdrops and theatrical costumes blazing away fiercely. I also remember the raid during which the parish church of St Publius and the Capuchin Friary in Floriana were badly damaged and many people were killed and injured. Then there was the time I decided to pay a visit to my wife in Gozo, taking one of the Gozo boats which did the trip from Marsa. As usual there were two boats making the trip, leaving within a few minutes of each other; I was on the second boat. The first boat had only got as far as the Customs House when it struck a mine; we in the second boat could not do anything at all for the unfortunate passengers and crew and we continued on our way.

The heavily damaged church of St Publius, Floriana

Later in the war I was transferred to Gozo where I was placed in charge of the stores of food. Every evening I used to make the rounds with a police sergeant and a constable to check the numbers of sacks of the various commodities like rice, sugar and flour. There was always the sack or two gone missing and this was officially attributed to the work of rodents.

Compared to Malta, Gozo was spared the heavy and continuous bombardment but a few bombs were dropped. I will just

Military parade
marching past the
Royal Opera House,
Valletta.
(Photo W.J. Jones)

mention the day that bombs fell on Sannat, the village in which
my wife's relatives lived. The bombs devastated a whole street
and left a large number of casualties. The family, now with
myself included, moved to Rabat where we continued to live till
the end of the war when we returned to our house in Sliema,
which until then we had only lived in for six weeks.

The Opera House in ruins

EMANUEL SPITERI

I was employed as a teacher in the primary school in Ghaxaq, the village in which I lived and where I first saw the light of day. When the war started and the Protection Offices came into being, I was exempted from teaching and took up duties as Assistant Protection Officer. My immediate superior was Dr Matteo Zammit, a lawyer, who left after some time leading to my promotion to Protection Officer in April 1941.

My duties as Protection Officer included all matters relating to rationing, refugees, vacant premises and the reporting of war damage. At first, when my area consisted only of Ghaxaq, I had to work on my own but later when I took in Gudia, I was provided with an assistant and two clerks. The distribution of the food ration was carried out by sixteen grocers in the two villages; each grocer had a number of registered families, each with its own ration book showing the kind and amount of foodstuffs allotted to the family. The ration was distributed once a fortnight with the grocer marking the book as appropriate. In our files we carried the necessary records such as the details of the families registered with every grocer, constantly updating such records when births or deaths occurred. Whenever a family moved to another locality, it was our duty to send the relevant information to the Protection Officer of that locality. I was particularly careful to ensure that the ration was distributed in good time and in the manner indicated so as to forestall complaints. Most of the refugees who settled in Gudia and Ghaxaq came from the Cottonera district. By the time I had taken Gudia under my wing, the refugees had already fitted in, generally finding accommodation with the local families or renting houses. The Band Club at Ghaxaq and a requisitioned house were roped in to accommodate a number of refugees. Some garages were also requisitioned to serve as stores for the Food and Commerce Control Department (FCCO). Before public shelters became available, I used to go round the houses with the civil engineer to advise people on the safest place in the house in case of air attack and, when eventually public shelters became available, we readily gave permission to people who wished to excavate a cubicle inside the shelter for their own private use. We issued strict orders that no person was to obstruct the access to the shelter by loitering on the stairs.

Indigent families were given some sort of social assistance, usually in the form of money tokens which could only be exchanged for foodstuffs at the grocer's where they were registered. The grocer would then cash the token at the Protection Office. Occasionally bundles of clothes were distributed to these families in need.

Very few painful experiences persist in my memory. Of these I remember an air-raid during which I was taking cover in a shelter and for some reason or other, before the "raiders passed" was given I went out and was about to cross the road when a bomb exploded some distance away and I was hurled against a field wall by the blast. On another occasion, I was in my Gudia office and disregarding an air-raid warning, kept working at my papers; a bomb exploded some distance from the office, causing my desk and whatever happened to be on it to rattle and shake. Some people were killed in that raid.

The Protection Office was wound up in March 1945, giving way to the newly set up Housing Department with a Housing Commissioner at its head. I was appointed Assistant Housing Commissioner. Protection Officers became Housing Officers. In August 1947, I handed in my resignation to take up my former post in the Department of Education. The new Director was Mr Brennan who appointed me headteacher.

KARMENU VASSALLO

I joined the Police Corps as a constable in 1940, a few months before the outbreak of the war. There were six of us and we were attached to the Water Police section based at the Valletta marina. During the war we were often detailed to go on board ships in harbour, sometimes while an air-raid was on. I was eventually transferred to the Defence Security Officer (DSO) unit with duties in Valletta and Floriana.

I did a spell of duty at the Marsascala police station at a time when this seaside village was practically doubling up as a military camp. During the day, I used to be the only policeman in the station and soldiers were coming in all the time, asking to use the telephone or for other trivial matters. One of my duties was to sound the hand-operated siren whenever the message came over the telephone that an air-raid was in the offing. The reception on one occasion was very poor and I did not get the message; the air-raid warning was therefore not sounded and I found myself charged with dereliction of duties. It was some time before my explanation was accepted and the charge withdrawn.

It was shortly after that experience that I was transferred to the DSO. This section controlled a number of houses in Sliema in which were lodged a number of persons engaged in espionage for the British; there were, among them, Italians, French, German and Jews. Cooking was never one of my strong points but on occasion I had to cook up something or other for them. Luckily there was a proper cook on the premises and I could take instructions from him.

There must have been some thirty odd members of the Police Force detailed to perform duties in those houses. I remember two Italian brothers, who were constantly toing and froing between Malta and Italy on secret missions. Before leaving they would don the uniform of an Italian colonel and leave on a launch driven by a certain Captain Grech, a man of short stature and great courage. Each mission generally took four days. One day they failed to return and we later heard that they had been taken captive and executed somewhere near Trieste. One of the two brothers went by the name of Victor, an assumed name as likely as not. The two brothers were once walking along the Sliema front and were seen by some Maltese passers-by to wave a handkerchief at a low-flying Italian fighter. The Maltese were about to manhandle the two Italians and were only prevented from doing so by my shouting "Leave them alone! Leave them alone!" When the Commanding Officer paid us a visit a few days later, he drew me aside and said, "Well done! Those two are more British than we are". All the Maltese constables who were on duty at that place were treated very well and had an allowance of four pounds a month on top of the regular salary which was then six pounds a month. I think we were chosen for those delicate duties because we were fully trusted. My father was a staunch Strickland supporter and was as pro-British as they come.

Balzunetta, the red light district in Floriana, was the scene of frequent brawls between English and Irish troops. The bars in the area were regularly packed with servicemen drinking beer or, when that beverage was unobtainable, cheap wine. Business was never lacking in those parts! Some British servicemen attached to the DSO were in the habit of frequenting the bars in Strait Street, flashing gold sovereigns which they offered for sale. The sovereigns were in reality meant for payments to persons engaged in espionage work.

I was offered a promotion to the rank of sergeant on condition that I travelled to Algiers to provide security cover at the residences of spies based in that town. I did not accept the offer and remained in Malta as an ordinary constable. However I remember at least five Maltese - three men and two women - who volunteered for an overseas posting and who were attached to the Allied headquarters in Tunis.

DAVID VELLA

As a young man of seventeen, I helped my father run the OK Bar in Birkirkara. Then I joined the Air Ministry as a civilian employee, and with my bartending background soon found myself posted to Casa Leone in Sliema, then serving as a hostel for officers. From there I was transferred to the Imperial Hotel and after that to the Melita Hotel; these two provided accommodation for the air crews. A number of Maltese girls were employed at the Imperial. My duties were those of a head waiter, overseeing the serving of food and making sure that nobody took more than his portion for the day. The airmen regularly flew sorties over Italian territory and the sea around Malta and when they returned from a particularly successful mission, there would be celebrations without end. But sometimes one or more planes failed to return safely to base and on learning that a particular airman was reported missing, the Maltese girls would take his blanket to make coats for themselves. I am ashamed to say that there were times when I, too, made off with blankets to pass on to members of my family. A routine job for us was to provide each airman with a thermos flask filled with hot tea before leaving on a mission; this they would promptly empty and re-fill with whisky.

Food was always readily available in the officers' mess and I can say that I never went hungry; I even managed to take home some food for the family. The girls on the staff often asked me for food; sometimes I would lock the pantry door but leave the key in place and tell the girls not to take away too much food.

Once one of the officers discovered that some provisions were missing and ordered a search to be made. The missing stores were found hidden in the women's toilets. That was the last time that I dared "forget" the key in place!

One day, when off duty, I was asked by my father to pay a visit to his mother, that is, my grandma who lived in Rabat. I was soon off on my bike but as I was passing by the mental hospital (now called Mount Carmel Hospital) I met a friend and, ignoring an air raid warning, stopped for a couple of minutes to exchange a few words with him. He told me that he was on his way to the cinema and we parted. He had scarcely taken a dozen steps when I heard the whine of a falling bomb, followed by a tremendous explosion. I was hurled into the roadside ditch by the blast but though badly shaken, was otherwise unhurt. I scrambled out to look for my companion and soon found him stretched on the ground, lifeless.

There was another incident which I will never forget. A heavy calibre bomb fell in the vicinity of the parish church of St Helen at Birkirkara but failed to explode. The police soon cordoned off the area and stood by to stop people going past the barriers. I was on my way to see my aunt when an explosion rocked the buildings around; the bomb was armed with a delayed action mechanism and had gone off. When I got to the scene of the explosion my eyes fell on a horrifying sight: badly mutilated bodies were scattered all over the place. I learned later that on insisting to be allowed to go through the cordon, some workmen were allowed to do so by the policeman on duty and were within yards of the bomb when it went off. That was the worst tragedy to hit Birkirkara during the war. My aunt was standing on her doorstep, trying to open the front door at the instant of the explosion. She was struck by a splinter which lodged in her chest. As I arrived on the spot I saw her clutching her chest while two or three neighbours were holding her up. A priest who was passing by asked them to take her into the nearby chapel of St Roque and to pray for her recovery. My aunt, fully conscious, joined in the prayers and then suddenly passed away. She left four children.

In the war years, Birkirkara was bursting at the seams with a population almost doubled by the refugees. Practically every household in the town hosted refugees. We had an American sergeant living with us. Many pilots and servicemen stationed at Ta' Qali patronised my father's bar where there was always something available. My father bought flour and sugar on the black market and my mother produced doughnuts by the dozen. A sack of sugar could easily fetch sixty pounds. Throughout the war, whatever the conditions, my father somehow kept the bar going; ours was a large family - I had three brothers and six sisters - and it must have been hard going for my father to provide for us.

Air-raids were becoming less and less frequent and it seemed as if the war was drawing to an end when I received orders to report for draft service and undergo the usual medical examination. My request for a postponement of fifteen days before joining the Army was granted. During that period, the Royal Fleet Auxiliary vessel, *Cherry Leaf* entered harbour and I embarked as a seaman even though I did not have any documents. I hurried home, told my mother that I had found a job afloat, packed a suit and a couple of trousers into a pillow case and left. We landed in Tripoli a bare eight hours after it had fallen to the 8th Army. Wherever one looked, one saw devastation. I had managed to evade the draft only to get into this sticky situation. We were constantly harried by German bombers and one day German dive bombers attacked the ships lying in the harbour and before long several of the ships were in flames and rent by exploding ammunition. The sea itself seemed to be on fire. Tons of foodstuffs lying on the quay were destroyed.

From Tripoli we proceeded to Alexandria, a trip during which we were attacked eleven times. One of the ships in the convoy was torpedoed and caught fire, suffering a great many casualties. We spent some months in the Middle East, plying the waters between Jaffa and Cyprus, before returning to Alexandria where I got my discharge papers. I returned to Malta on the *Princess Katrina* after spending over a year at sea.

CENSU ZAHRA

It was just before seven in the morning that we had the first air-raid. At the time I was in the vestry of the parish church of Paola where for the last two years I was employed as a sexton. When the people in the congregation heard the sirens, panic broke out and the women who had come for the seven o'clock Mass hurried home to their children. On that first day of the war, there were several air-raids in one of which a bomb fell on a house in Ditch Street killing a woman.

A few days later, I moved with my family to Siġġiewi and I used to bicycle to Paola practically every day. We spent nine weeks in Siġġiewi and then decided to go back to Paola where we lived through the war. Immediately after war broke out, thousands left their homes in the Cottonera area and set up house in Paola which overnight rose in population from six to twenty two thousand. We at the parish church were overwhelmed with the abrupt increase in pressure; for instance on one occasion we had nine christenings in all of which incidentally I carried out the role of godfather. Very soon however Paola was declared a danger area and within a matter of days Paola began to look like a ghost town with a population of just thirty five souls. All the priests who were attached to the parish joined the exodus with the exception of one, Father Bert Grech.

In the first months of the war, when Paola was practically deserted, there was only one resident in the whole of Tal-Borg Street, a certain Paul Camilleri, and he was feeling uneasy, being all alone. He asked me to share his house so that he would have somebody to exchange a few words with. One day, as I was having a chat with him at his doorstep, there was an air raid warning, and there being no public shelters as yet, I decided to take cover in one of the bell-towers. Incidentally, the few people who still resided in Paola used to take cover either in one of the bell-towers or in the Hypogeum until shelters became available. When I began to walk away, Paul said, "Are you scared?" to which I replied, "Hadn't you better come too?" He said he would be following me but would first fetch his pipe, tobacco and matches

Tal-Borg Street, Paola.

(Courtesy J. Buontempo)

Buildings razed to the ground in Paola Square.

(Courtesy J. Buontempo)

from inside. I had scarcely reached the entrance to the bell tower when an explosion rocked the building. On emerging into the street at the all clear, we saw a column of smoke rising from the Tal-Borg area. I hurried there and saw that many of the houses,

Carmelo Borg Pisani who was hanged in November 1942.

including Paul's, were in ruins and I began to call his name at the top of my voice. Suddenly I heard a muffled voice coming through the rubble, "I'm here...I'm here" and I ran to one of the nearby houses where some British soldiers were billeted and asked for help. In a matter of minutes, with their help and that of a few other men, Paul was hauled out from under the debris, badly shaken but otherwise unhurt.

An incident which had a very different ending occurred in 1942 when a heavy calibre bomb landed and exploded in Paola Square killing forty-two persons and injuring some hundred others. Many of those who lost their lives were taking cover in a shelter when the explosion ripped off an iron gate which crushed those sheltering inside. Others were buried alive under the rubble of their homes. That was one of the worst tragedies of the war.

There was a particularly unusual incident which happened when the invasion of Sicily was in progress. The parish priest, Father Frangisk Xuereb, asked me to be at hand that night because a wedding was due to be held at eleven; I was to be one of the witnesses, the other being a student from the Seminary. The groom was an Army deserter and the ceremony had to be conducted clandestinely. Immediately after the ceremony, the man hurried to Marsa and boarded a steamer bound for Italy; unfortunately the stowaway hid between two boilers and as the ship raised steam, the poor man was scalded to death.

I remember every detail of that day in 1942 on which Borg Pisani was hanged. On the day fixed for the execution, in my role as sexton, I had to be on attendance at the Church of St Ubaldesca. Following a long-standing tradition, three quarters of an hour before the execution of the condemned man, members of the Archconfraternity of the Rosary walked in procession from the Corradino prison to the church to attend the so called " Good passage" Mass and then, immediately after the sentence had been carried out, held a Requiem Mass for the repose of the soul of the departed. From the belfry, which I climbed to ring the knell, I saw the members of the confraternity accompanying the corpse to the prison graveyard as the black flag was run up the prison flagpole.

In the darkest days of the war, no shops were open for business in Paola. Ration was distributed from a small store close to the Hypogeum to the few families still living in these parts. One detail which may be of some interest is that the parish church was entitled to a ration of sugar for the priest who delivered the sermon and who was always given a cup of coffee at the conclusion of his duties. This ration was classified as a "special allowance" which meant that I had to collect it once a month from the depot in Marsa. A ration of oil was also issued to the church for the altar lamps. One day the Marsa depot received a direct hit and the parish priest was informed that the oil and sugar ration was to be collected from the store in Paola.

VIII. Legal and Medical

Dr TONI BONNICI

As a medical student I had my lodgings in a house at St Venera. During the war years university examinations used to be held at Rabat and on such occasions I had to walk all the way to Rabat in the company of a few other students with whom I shared the house at St Venera. There were times when we would be caught in an air-raid as we made our way to or from Rabat and then we would have to dive into the nearest roadside ditch as a precaution against the machine-gun bursts which German fighter pilots often resorted to when they caught sight of any people on the road. Luckily none of us was ever injured in such incidents. Perhaps the closest shave I ever had during the war was during the first attack by the Luftwaffe. On that day, in January 1941, I went to our house in Floriana next to the Salvation Army headquarters to get some food and clothes. On arriving there I saw that the front door was standing ajar but on entering I was surprised to find that there was nobody at home. I felt sure that my parents had gone, as usual, to the public shelter in Crucifix Hill and I made my way there to meet them. As I walked along a German *Junker 88* dived and released its bomb load which landed and exploded in the water. Terrified I tried to run but tripped over something and fell. On getting up I found that I was wet through, drenched with the wave and spray caused by the explosion.

Looking back now I am surprised at the high morale of the local population during the bombing; I remember young boys hurling stones at low-flying aircraft. When, as a medical student I had to perform some duties at the hospital, I was equally impressed by the fact that during air-raids doctors and nurses never once abandoned their patients. In January 1943 I graduated in medicine and set up my practice in the Sliema and Birkirkara areas but concurrently I worked in Government hospitals.

Dr JOSEPH BUGEJA

Several months before June 1940 I was a member of a committee which had as its terms of reference the planning of provisions for refugees in case Malta, especially the harbour area, was attacked. In such an event it was expected that thousands of people living in and around the Cottonera would leave their homes to seek refuge in safer localities such as, among others, Rabat. One of our first decisions was to earmark the Government school as a reception centre for refugees should the need arise.

As a medical doctor, I started giving lectures on First Aid, home nursing and the treatment of patients suffering from gas poisoning. On the 10th of June, that is the day on which Italy declared war, I was giving one of these lectures when the news broke. On the following morning the harbour area experienced the first bombing attacks and the first refugees from the Cottonera started arriving at Rabat. These were immediately put up at the Government school as planned. After a few days all the available space in the school had been taken up but still the refugees kept coming and something had to be done to house them. Other places were soon requisitioned for the purpose: St Paul's College, St Dominic's Priory, Villa Messina, Depiro House at Mdina and Chadwick House (now *Il-Veduta Restaurant*). The number of refugees was so large that in one hall in the school, we had to put no fewer than ninety persons.

Thousands of refugees found accommodation in private homes which the Rabat residents were willing to share. My father's house was very large - it had some sixteen rooms - and he took in a number of refugees of whom some were related to us and some were total strangers. After the first wave of refugees there was a lull which lasted until the *Illustrious* blitz when a second wave came.

It is hardly necessary to say that wherever there is overcrowding, problems of hygiene are bound to arise. I therefore made it a point to circulate among the refugees whenever I found the time to talk about health matters, how to recognise certain symptoms and how to proceed in the presence of such symptoms. I used to stress very strongly the need to report to the health authorities certain symptoms at once; doing this, I used to emphasise, was not the same as snooping but a case of safeguarding their own health and that of others. Dr Emanuel Agius, the Health Department pathologist, kept me supplied with diphtheria and typhoid inoculations which I used regularly with refugees. Giving inoculations to those thousands was a mammoth task and my assistants and I worked overtime. We also had a small infirmary where we could keep any patients showing symptoms of infectious diseases; this was situated behind St Paul's College and consisted of four rooms equipped as necessary with the help of a number of people among whom were Judge Montanaro Gauci, the Area Protection Officer and Mrs de Trafford. The latter gave us beds and blankets brought over from the Hotel Phoenicia. Through the services of the archpriest of Rabat, two Ursuline sisters and another two Sisters of Charity were assigned to assist the patients. Seriously ill patients were, of course, conveyed to the hospital. My appointment at the time was that of District Medical Officer, a post I had been given a week after the Italian declaration of war,

One of my assistants was a certain Miss Cortis, a hygienist, whose task it was to pay visits to refugee homes and to report on the state of health of the inmates. Another assistant, Emanuel Tonna, an apothecary assistant, helped in preparing medicines.

One of my duties was to look after the health of some seventy internees housed in the St Agatha institute; these were visited twice weekly. Of all my duties, this was perhaps the most delicate and problematic. To me the internees were no different from any other group and the aspect of political allegiance was, as far as I was concerned, totally irrelevant. I felt that I had to fulfil to the best of my abilities my responsibilities both to the authorities and to the inmates. Problems arose from time to time; for instance some of the internees would in defiance of regulations refuse to go down into the shelters during air-raids. Their excuse was usually that they were sick and could not move from their room. The camp authorities would then ask me to subject them to a medical examination. Time and time again I tried to persuade these internees to stop that practice as I was not prepared to certify that they were sick if in fact they were fully capable of moving about and reminded them that I too had my professional responsibilities. Some time later the St Agatha Camp received a direct hit and I hurried there in the company of another doctor from the ARP section. Almost completely buried under the rub-

The Rabat ARP Group together with volunteers. Dr Bugeja is seen squatting first on right.

(Courtesy J. Bugeja)

266

ble was the lifeless body of one of the internees; another internee died in the same incident. Both belonged to that group which had always refused to go into the shelters.

Here I would like to say that I set up three First Aid centres in the Rabat area, all three in monastic buildings: St Augustine's, St Dominic's and St Agatha's. Each of the three centres was fully provided with all that was likely to be needed in emergencies. In addition to the centres there was also the public clinic (locally known as *il-Berġa*) which was the main First Aid centre. To run these centres we had several qualified and experienced persons such as Dr Paul Aquilina and Dr Peppi Paris (then a medical student), as well as a number of pharmacists and nurses. We had an ambulance at our disposal so that we could cope with emergencies and to transport serious cases to the Ta' Bugeja Hospital.

Although Rabat was supposedly a "reception area" for civilian refugees, bombs were sometimes dropped on that village and a number of civilians were killed and others injured by shrapnel. I remember the time when hundreds of anti-personnel bombs were

Doctors and Superintendents, ARP (1942).

showered on and around Rabat resulting in death and injury. A time-bomb once fell in front of our house while we were in our shelter in the garden; mercifully it was defused and removed by men from the bomb disposal unit and practically caused no damage at all. In our shelter I had a Rediffusion set installed so that at the first announcement of "raiders passed" I would be able to hurry to attend to any casualties. As a rule I rarely moved out of Rabat unless there was an absolute need for me to do so.

My family was never really short of foodstuffs. My profession was my life and I used to treat patients as if they were members of my own family. When in my capacity as a private doctor I charged fees, these were at best nominal and my patients would sometimes repay my little kindnesses with some article of food. I remember once being called to see a patient at Mtahleb and as I made my way back to Rabat I was stopped by some soldiers, as was the practice in those days, for my car to be searched for unauthorised foodstuffs. I was carrying three or four pumpkins but I was allowed to proceed without any action being taken against me. I think it is only fair to say here that whatever I got in the way of food was always shared with others; that was the way in which I had been brought up.

My employment as emergency DMO was terminated on the 8th January 1944, after having received a month before a letter from the then Chief Government Medical Officer, Professor A V Bernard, which read as follows: "It is regretted that in view of the present situation it is no longer necessary to utilise your services as emergency medical officer and they will be terminated as from the 8th proximo. I wish to thank you for the services you have rendered."

Dr GEORGE CAMILLERI

I graduated Doctor of Medicine in 1937 and began to practise as a general practitioner in the Cospicua area; I was then living with my mother and one of my brothers who was a NAAFI employee serving afloat. My other brother was a Dominican friar. I was engaged also in part-time work for the university where I was a Demonstrator in Anatomy.

We spent the first few days of the war in Cospicua but when bombs started falling around we went to live in our summer residence at Marsascala. In the meantime I had been engaged as an emergency doctor and posted to St Joseph School in Paola which had been requisitioned and converted into a hospital. A few months into the war rumours of an impending invasion started making the rounds and my mother decided to move to Rabat. However, she was not destined to stay in Rabat for long. One day while I was on duty at Ta' Bugeja Hospital a telephone call came through, saying that my mother had been taken ill. I hurried to her bedside and found her in a deep coma; two days later she was dead.

Promotion in my posting at Ta' Bugeja Hospital was rapid. I was first promoted to senior resident medical officer, and then, when the incumbent superintendent died I was appointed emergency superintendent in his stead. This hospital was reserved for surgical cases while the emergency hospital housed in St Francis School at Birkirkara treated medical cases. In addition to carrying out routine surgery, the hospital received all those who had been injured through enemy action. Our busiest day was when both the entrance and the exit of a shelter in Mosta simultaneously received direct hits. Besides the many people killed, some eighty others were badly injured, several of them with extensive burns; all these were brought into our hospital seriously stretching our resources. The dead were also carried in for identification purposes, but some of the bodies were so badly mutilated that they were almost impossible to identify. As the superintendent, it was my duty to issue death certificates and to enable us to identify the dead we often had to cross-question those who were injured in the same incident.

At first we did not have a proper shelter attached to the hospital but eventually a large one was excavated. When an air-raid sounded walking cases used to make their own way down into the shelter; those who were confined to their beds naturally had to stay put. Doctors and nurses used to stay with the latter through air-raids. Occasionally I went up on the roof to see the action; I am one of those people who feel less anxious if they can see what is going on. We felt fairly safe as we had a very large red cross painted on the roof which could easily be made out from an aircraft. It was on such an occasion that I witnessed the *Illustrious* blitz, which, if one could forget for an instant its deadly nature, made an awesome and unforgettable spectacle. The *Stukas* would fly in mathematically precise order and after diving vertically release their deadly cargo onto the target. After that they would flatten out and skim over the water of the Grand Harbour, regain height and disappear. The sky was covered with puffs of bursting anti-aircraft shells. I remember one *Stuka* being hit and with thick black smoke issuing from it, flying towards us almost scraping the rooftops before disappearing into the distance.

Prof. Peter Paul Debono
(Courtesy M. Ellis).

All doctors were expected to sleep in. Professor Peter Paul Debono used to sleep and lunch with us. In addition to the regular nurses, we had several others who had been employed on a temporary basis; these all pulled their weight and gave a significant contribution to the war effort. The staff included also a number of chaplains and sisters from the religious orders who, in their own way, worked very hard to lighten our load. One of the doctors was a good banjo player and when off duty used to entertain us.

Over and above the hardship caused by the bombing, we had other problems to keep us busy. The food shortage was partly met by the provision of some canned stuff though it was said that the only meat available was mutton; that did not bother us unduly. The fuel shortage caused us more worry. Power cuts were all too frequent and we solved that by getting hold of an old generator. One has to remember that antibiotics were not as yet available though we had adequate supplies of aspirin and medicines of the same sort. Although as the superintendent my duties were mostly of an administrative nature, I made it a point to lend a hand when things became a bit hectic; in such cases I would administer anaesthetic, treat injuries, stitch up cuts, and so on. The hospital was adequately equipped at least by the standards of those days; we regularly used the same needle over and over again for blood transfusions, a procedure which would be unthinkable nowadays.

At the beginning of the war I used to go out with a girl from Senglea; later on she moved with her family to Naxxar. On the 10th February 1941 we were married in the chapel attached to St Joseph Institute, almost next door to the hospital. For the occasion we wore our normal clothes and the ceremony itself was as simple as possible. Halfway through the wedding service there was an air-raid but that was not allowed to interrupt the ceremony. As husband and wife we took up residence in a house in one of the streets behind the hospital. Our first daughter was born in the Cini maternity hospital quite near to my place of work. I was so busy that I could not be present at the birth of our child; I rarely could take an hour off and when on one of these rare occasions I grabbed the opportunity to spend a few hours at home it almost cost me my life. While I was at home there was an air-raid warning and with my wife I went up on the roof to watch the proceedings. One of the planes veered off from the main formation and, as it flew towards us, released a stick of bombs. We hurried inside in terror and the next moment a series of explosions rocked the house. The bombs had landed about fifty metres up the street.

During the war I rarely missed listening in to the BBC news service. I was thrilled whenever Churchill delivered one of his speeches and his best known speech, "We'll fight them on the beaches.... on the squares...." is engraved in my memory. His words were, to me, a constant source of courage and inspiration.

During those years I saw every kind of injury and mutilation but I never became immune to man's suffering although it was all in the day's work. The worst experiences were cases where amputation had to be resorted to, not to mention the many dead of all ages. Once a woman from Tarxien was brought in; she had been trampled to death when the occupants of a shelter panicked.

Towards the end of the war, I successfully applied for the post of resident medical officer at the Gozo hospital.

On the 21st of April 1944 I received a letter over the signature of Lieutenant Governor D C Campbell which read: "I am directed by the Governor to convey to you His Excellency's appreciation of the exceptionally meritorious and dedicated service which led to your name being recorded in the *Malta Government Gazette* No 91699 of 1 February 1944."

Notary V M PELLEGRINI

In my work as a notary public, I shared two offices - one in Valletta and the other in Rabat - with a lawyer friend of mine. In the first few months of the war the Valletta office suffered structural damage and the two of us had therefore to carry on our work from the Rabat office. I was never short of clients since many of those who used to come to the Valletta office were now refugees in Rabat.

I am by nature claustrophobic and could never bring myself to enter a rock shelter during air-raids. There was one exception however; during a heavy raid while I was in the Law Courts at Valletta I stepped into the shelter annexed to the court building but within minutes I was seized by panic and had to rush out feeling very sick.

Rabat got off comparatively lightly and few bombs fell on the town; the number of deaths caused by enemy action was quite low compared to other localities. But from time to time I had to leave the town for several reasons. For instance official business often took me to Valletta where the Public Registry was and to Lija where court sittings were being held ever since the court buildings in Valletta had received a direct hit. Transport facilities were very limited and walking for miles was not always pleasant especially on hot summer days. One morning, during a court sitting presided over by Judge Schembri, I entered the chamber wearing shorts. I stood very close to the desk so that my unconventional dress would pass unobserved. I repeated the feat two or three times but then my unbecoming outfit was noticed, and after the sitting, Judge Schembri with raised eyebrows said to me, "Don't you think that that kind of informal dress is not acceptable in court?" I tried to explain that one could not really walk all those miles from Rabat in a formal suit, but I am afraid the learned judge would not be moved by my pleadings and I had to comply.

There were times when while drawing up some legal document the air raid warning would be heard but being at Rabat my clients and I felt safe enough to ignore the warning and to proceed with the business in hand. As I remarked before I practically never saw the inside of a shelter; on the contrary I got into the habit of leaving my office during air-raids and going to nearby Saqqajja Square, an excellent vantage point from which I could observe the action over the harbour area. Rabat was rarely the scene of any bombing incidents but I recall one such incident very clearly. Probably the heaviest bomb to fall in the Rabat area was one which landed in Museum Road just outside Howard Gardens, very close to where I lived. The bomb made an impressive crater and the damage was considerable; some people were killed and I can still see in my mind's eye a few corpses covered in white dust strewn on the ground. I was so shocked that for some time I could scarcely bring myself to touch any food.

I can also remember equally clearly the *Illustrious* blitz. I was in my office with some clients going through a promise of sale contract and the two parties had just put their signatures on the documents when the silence was shattered by the sound of powerful explosions and gun fire. Driven by intense curiosity we hurried to the Saqqajja and saw, over the harbour area, clouds of thick black smoke billowing up and the sky around dotted with the familiar white puffs of the anti-aircraft barrage. It was an extraordinary sight. These were the opening shots of the heaviest bombing attack sustained by Malta during the whole course of the war. At one point a squadron of fighters flew away from the harbour area and in our direction and in next to no time with machine guns blazing were directly on us. We were lucky to escape, unscathed, thanks to the high walls of Mdina under which we took cover.

There was an occasion when I was in a client's house to draw up a contract and while this was being done there was an air raid warning. The client, a rather timorous man, hurried us into his private shelter and the contract was signed there.

As far as I can say, there was no noticeable increase in the number of wills drawn up during the war period. There was possibly an increase in the property sales; presumably some owners were selling because they were afraid that money in hand was safer than houses. I have been told that a good deal of demolished, or damaged, property was often sold for absurdly low prices but that is only hearsay and I had no similar experiences.

Dr JOHN PULLICINO

I graduated in 1934 and set up my legal practice. Besides taking up civil cases I was also involved in providing legal aid to British and Maltese servicemen undergoing court-martial proceedings. It was in this latter role that I met the Lieutenant Governor, Sir Edward Jackson who was also performing duties as judge-advocate in courts-martial.

A few weeks before the outbreak of hostilities Sir Edward called me to his office and asked me whether I would be interested in a post, with the rank of captain, at the internees' camp in Malta but I did not feel attracted to that kind of work and I declined the offer. Among the many reasons for my answer was the fact that some of the internees were personal friends and that would inevitably have led to embarrassing situations which I was naturally anxious to avoid. Three days into the war, Sir Edward called me again this time asking me to take on the duties of Protection Officer for Rabat and Mdina, an offer which I was quite happy to accept. At the beginning this new post did not carry a salary and I therefore continued my legal practice concurrently with the new post. One of my cases concerned the defence of a Welsh soldier who was being tried charged with the murder of a fellow soldier. The accused and the victim, both in the South Wales Borderers, had quarrelled over a Maltese girl from Marsa and the accused shot the other. It so happened that the Advocate of the Poor was living in Gozo at the time and was so terrified of the bombing that he did not want to risk making the trip to Malta to take up the defence of the Welshman. The Crown Advocate therefore appointed me as the accused's counsel. The jury returned a verdict of guilty but since the verdict was not unanimous, the Court sentenced him to life imprisonment. Eventually the man was transferred to a prison in England and it was from there that he sent me a letter of thanks for saving him from the hangman's noose.

For the first few months of the war the Law Courts carried on their day-to-day work in the Valletta premises, but when in 1941 the building received a direct hit, the sittings were held at the Seminary in Floriana. Later on the Seminary was severely damaged by bombing and the courts moved to Lija. The courts never ceased functioning at any time. Of course there were cases where the presiding magistrate or judge might decide to transfer a sitting to an air raid shelter; such instances used to remind me of the

Judge Anthony J. Montanaro Gauci; portrait by Willie Apap.

early Christians carrying on their ceremonies in the darkness of the catacombs. Some judges would however ignore air raid warnings and carry on as if everything was normal. Judge Montanaro Gauci was like that; I remember a particular session being held at the Seminary when the deportation of internees was being considered by the court and this judge carried on in spite of a heavy bombing attack going on a couple of miles away.

I would like to say here that sometimes sittings of the magistrates' court were held in other localities. For example Magistrate Willie Soler held sessions at the Mdina Police Station while the police station at Birkirkara was used by another magistrate. At one point in time the Council of Government began to receive complaints that the general public was not being adequately served by the Protection Offices as the officers in charge were in some cases more often away from the office than not. The decision was therefore taken to have Protection Officers serve full-time and it was then that the post began to carry a salary. Incidentally many lawyers served as Protection Officers; probably the best-known of them was Sir Ugo Mifsud who ran the Lija office.

At the time I was married, with one son, and living with my father at his house in Mdina; my family had moved there from Sliema after a bomb had damaged our house.

The demolished Law Courts in Kingsway (Republic Street) Valletta.

The functions of the Protection Office were almost similar to that of a local council: there was the accommodation of refugees to be seen to, distribution of bread and other rationed foodstuffs to grocers and retailers and so on. The accommodation of refugees was a major headache for us and the problem bordered on the intractable in the immediate aftermath of the *Illustrious* blitz when a large number of families from Valletta and the Cottonera flocked to Rabat. We were forced to put them up in all sorts of places: in private homes, in schools, in chapels and convents, even in the crypt of the Carmelite Church. On several occasions I was called to arbitrate in quarrels arising in the air raid shelters especially as to the space allotted to each family. Feuds, quarrels and fights were quite usual in the communal shelters.

There is one charming incident which comes to mind when I recall the war years. Wistin Gatt, a tailor from Mdina, called at my house and asked me to obtain permission for him to go out during the curfew hours. His home consisted of one small room and he felt he could not bear to be cooped up for all those hours. The only persons authorised to break the curfew were issued with a special armband with the appropriate initials on it. I was in the mood to humour him and so I asked him to come to see me in my office on the morrow bringing with him a white band with a string at either end. When he turned up I said, "What is your full name?". "Agostino Gatt", he answered. "Fine", I said, "I will mark your initials, A.G., on the armband." From that day onwards, no one stopped him in the street as he walked about during the curfew; there were so many different armbands in those days that another one could hardly be noticed.

Another incident which certainly was devoid of any comic element could have cost me my life. During the war we had many souvenir hunters around; they collected bits of aircraft, cartridges, lengths of parachute fabric, bits of mica... In July 1942, during one particular attack in the Rabat area a large number of anti-personnel bombs were dropped, causing loss of life and injury. When the air raid was over one of the employees in the office came up to me and showed me an unexploded butterfly bomb. "See what I've got for you! I know you collect things like this", he said. I instantly saw the danger to him, to me and to my secretary and I was about to start telling him off but instinctively I must have realised that that would make him drop the bomb with consequences I could well imagine. So, as calmly as I could, I told him that he was carrying a bomb and that he had to, with as little movement as possible, place it in the farthest corner. We then trooped out of the office and I called the bomb disposal

278

squad. When members of the squad started pulling the bomb out with a length of string, the bomb dropped one step and exploded making a small crater in the pavement.

Some two months before that incident, at about three in the morning a bomb landed on the convent of the Benedictine sisters in Mdina and exploded. Though the convent was less than two hundred metres away from where we lived, the explosion did not wake me up and it was only after my brother, Philo, pulled me out of bed that I was aware of the explosion. I threw a raincoat over my pyjama, put a pair of shoes on and pulled my steel helmet over my head and rushed out of the house with my brother running alongside. The main door of the cloister was wide open and clouds of dust and smoke were streaming out. We rushed in. In the vestry, shaking with terror were several nuns, some sobbing, others praying and others looking paralysed with fear. One of the nuns told us that one of the sisters was dead; she had gone down into the crypt and the roof had collapsed under the weight of the falling masonry. In the meantime two other persons appeared on the scene, an ARP member and a pilot from the near-by Xara Palace, then used as an officers' billet. The four of us then carried the lifeless body of the unfortunate sister to the chapel.

The air attack was, meanwhile, still in progress and through the gaps in the roof we could see searchlight beams playing in the dark sky. Some of the sisters on hearing the sound of more aircraft became hysteric; my brother, Philo, an eminently practical man, calmed them down assuring them that no place was ever hit twice. This, somehow, seemed to help and calm was soon reigning.

Dr ARTURO VALENZIA

In 1934 I graduated Doctor of Laws and a year later began to practise my profession. In 1937 we moved house from Valletta to Attard where my brother Ercole had taken a house on lease. During the first months of the war Court sessions continued to be held in Valletta, and I had to go there practically every day until the court moved first to Floriana and then to Lija. As a rule I used to borrow my brother's car to make the trip to Valletta. One day I was driving into town with my wife when, as we were passing by Fra Diego Square in Hamrun there was an air-raid warning. My wife panicked, opened the car door and jumped out of the car before I had time to stop. Mercifully she was not seriously injured. My wife was so terrified of the bombing that we used to say that she made it to the shelter before the sirens had finished sounding the warning.

Lawyers were less often called upon during the war; court activity substantially diminished. Many lawyers had been called up for military service. Court proceedings were often interrupted by air-raids; sometimes we had as many as eight air-raids in a day. During the war years many petitions were lodged for exemptions from paying rent or ground-rent. There were many cases of petty crime, especially theft of foodstuffs from government or services stores, which were then punishable by stiff sentences. If you, as a lawyer, could get the accused a verdict of not guilty, you would probably be given a hundred pounds or so, which was a considerable sum of money in those days. The explanation behind such sums of money is quite simple: if the accused could stay out of prison he would easily "earn" that amount by committing more theft. Of course if your pleading was unsuccessful, there would be no fee at all.

Once during a court session in Valletta with Magistrate Dr Manwel Bartoli presiding, we heard a very unusual deafening noise; this turned out to be an Italian plane which had crashed into the courtyard of the Franciscan Priory less than a hundred metres away. (Incidentally Dr Bartoli was killed while at his home in Rabat when he was struck by a shrapnel.) I was appointed Registrar in the Gozo courts on the 6th January 1942. Twelve lawyers had applied for the post and I was selected because for some time previously I had exercised the profession of notary public. As a Registrar one would automatically be the Director of the Public Registry.

That appointment implied that I had to take up residence in

Gozo which meant that we had to transport our furniture to that Island. I remember that when the truck with our furniture on board went through the Fleur-de-Lys Arch, which was then still standing, the superstructure of our massive wardrobe got stuck on the arch and we had to leave that part of the wardrobe behind. On leaving Mosta, we had to stop because of an air-raid; it was during this raid that several people were killed in Mosta when the shelter in which they had taken cover received two direct hits, one at the entrance and the other at the emergency exit. We count that experience as one of our lucky days. Eventually we arrived at Marfa only to experience another air-raid. When the "raiders passed" signal was given the furniture was loaded on to a Gozo boat, we cast off and crossed over without any more mishaps.

One morning, I was returning to Gozo from a visit to Malta with my wife and son; on the same boat was Magistrate Serafin Vella. As I was about to say something to the latter, a *Messerschmitt* dived towards us; this was followed by two other *Messerschmitts* which went through the same manoeuvre without opening fire. There were some soldiers on board and I think we were lucky when we took the precaution of covering the soldiers with some sheets so that they would not be recognised. Of course we were terrified all the time.

In Gozo, life was pretty busy for me; some seven thousand Maltese went to live there during the war. Civil Status acts, usually in the region of a thousand, rose to four or five thousand and we found it difficult to cope with all that paperwork. The substantial influx of Maltese people led to much prosperity among the locals and many Gozitans became rich overnight. As far as war activity was concerned, Gozo suffered far fewer attacks than Malta, but somehow because it was unprotected I felt much more vulnerable in Gozo than in Malta.

Like many others I had done a course on the shooting ranges; this was meant to prepare us for an expected invasion by paratroops. At the end of the course I was issued with a rifle which I kept at home. A German plane crashed into a hillside between Rabat and Xewkija and two members of the crew were captured and taken to Rabat. I was in the company of the Commissioner and as soon as the two Germans saw us they asked, "Are you going to shoot us?" We quickly reassured them, "No; you are prisoners of war", and handed them over to the military.

As regards food, we never had any real shortage. You could always get a few potatoes and vegetables and I usually made it a point to take some food - a loaf of bread, a fish, a few vegetables - to my mother whenever I crossed over to Malta. God bless her, how she enjoyed having these little things! When food started getting scarce, I had to resort to the black market. There were a few Victory Kitchens in Gozo, too, but I only patronised them once. Which reminds me of an incident involving my brother Ercole: this brother of mine was a member of the Council of Government and one day he happened to be having a chat with Mr Cohen in the Palace. Both were aware that the stocks of food on the Island were practically exhausted and there was only sufficient food left for a few days and as they thought more and more about the situation, they got so depressed that they hit upon the idea of drowning their worries in alcohol. On the following morning the two of them were found lying on the ground, dead drunk. Soon after this incident, the Santa Marija convoy entered the Grand Harbour and Malta was saved.

My term of office as Registrar, Gozo Courts, came to an end on the 19th of September 1945.

Dr FORTUNATO ZAMMIT

On the 10th June 1940 we had the last session of our final examinations for the degree of Doctor of Medicine. In the evening, much relieved after the strain of examinations, I was having a walk with my fiancee (now my wife) at Floriana when I saw a cluster of people who seemed to be very excited about something. My curiosity was aroused and we moved nearer. On asking one of the people I was told that Mussolini had declared war. Thoroughly alarmed I escorted my fiancee to her home in Valletta and then made my way to Kalkara where I lived with my parents. At about ten that night there was a knock on the door and on opening the door I saw a police constable and a hospital nurse. I was told to go to Paola the following morning and report for duty as a medical doctor at St Joseph School which had been converted to an emergency hospital to cater for the Cottonera population and the Dockyard workers. In fact in the very first few days of the war we treated a small number of casualties in this hospital but it soon became evident that having the hospital so close to the harbour area was not such a good idea.

After a few weeks, with some other doctors, I was told to report for duty at St Aloysius College, Birkirkara, which had likewise been converted into a hospital for routine medical cases not including war casualties and surgical cases. Another hospital intended also for medical cases was located in St Francis School in Birkirkara. The Central Hospital in Floriana was reserved for X-rays and ophthalmic cases. Six months later, I got another

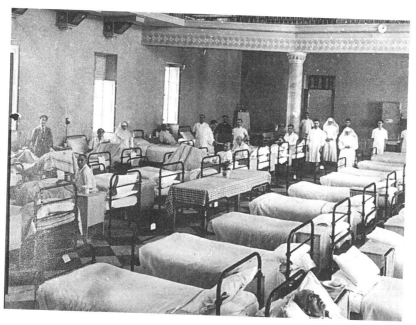

St. Aloysius College Hospital, Birkirkara.

(NWMA Collection)

move, this time to the Ta' Bugeja Hospital in Hamrun. My move coincided with the first attacks of the Luftwaffe and the hospital was soon inundated with cases. We worked overtime and nights and days were equally busy. The Chief Surgeon was Professor Peter Paul Debono who worked his heart out, night and day. He was not only an exceptionally talented surgeon but also a man of extraordinary energy and I remember he would sometimes ask me to have a break while he, much older than me, would carry on with the case in hand.

Our hardest day was when bombs fell on the two openings of a shelter at Mosta. Besides the many dead there were several badly burnt and badly injured persons; our resources were thoroughly stretched on that occasion. Another difficult day was when the Regent cinema in Valletta received a direct hit leaving many dead and a large number of severe casualties; we had to do a number of amputations.

As a hospital, Ta' Bugeja was well-equipped by the standards of the day, but sometimes equipment was rather primitive. For example to sterilise surgical instruments we used a *Primus* pressure stove and the only available X-ray unit was the personal property of Dr Henry Sacco and his brother, Paul, a pharmacist. The latter was entrusted with the operation of the unit. Such anomalies gave one the impression that the planning for war emergencies had been less than thorough.

Once during a night attack, we heard someone calling for help. With two nurses I hurried to a large house further down the street. As we got nearer a second bomb exploded in the vicinity and we took cover in a doorway, We were unhurt but the two nurses panicked and ran back to the hospital. I kept going on and on reaching the villa I stepped on some round object and nearly lost my balance. I was wearing my night slippers and the darkness was impenetrable. In one of the rooms of the villa a young woman was lying dead and in an adjoining room was her sister, also handicapped, with two nuns. All three were terrified, cowering under a table. I escorted the three of them to the hospital and immediately after put a telephone call through to the ARP section so that they could deal with the dead woman. I went back to the villa and met the ARP personnel who drew my attention to a large round object which was lying in the hall, the same object I had stepped on previously. That round object was a time-bomb and we rushed out. Some twenty minutes later a huge explosion rocked the buildings around us; the villa where, up to a short while before, lived a number of handicapped girls and their carers was reduced to a mound of rubble and twisted beams.

Another wartime experience which comes to mind was when, towards the closing stages of the war, a large number of anti-personnel devices were dropped and these were exploding like so many fire-crackers. I must say here that at the time I was still a young man and foolish enough not to take the necessary precautions. I walked on as if these were festa fireworks. When I was about to step into the hospital one bomb exploded a few metres away; a shrapnel went through my thigh missing the main artery by a hair's breadth. That laid me up for a couple of weeks and the scars are still visible to this day.

Towards the end of the war, when bombing attacks became less and less frequent, I moved to the Gozo hospital as a resident medical officer. I remember once seeing a lot of American seaplanes in Marsalforn harbour. They were carrying personnel to lay an air-strip in Gozo; that was the first time that I had ever seen a bull-dozer. Within the space of a week the Gourgion tower was pulled down, rubble walls were demolished and an air-strip was ready for the first planes to take off and provide air cover for the Allied invasion of Sicily. The air-strip was used only once or twice as far as I know.

Some weeks later, the air-strip was dug up, the field walls were re-built and everything reverted to its original state, except, of course, the tower which was never re-built.

(Courtesy J. Borg Bonello)

IX. Servicemen

CARMELO CALAFATO

On the day Italy declared war, I was living with my family at Msida. After the first bombing attacks, my father decided to take the family to Santa Venera where a friend of his, a farmer, had offered us accommodation. I was then employed as an apprentice with the firm of Gio Batta Delia, furniture dealers, reporting for duty at their warehouse at Ta' Xbiex. When we moved to Santa Venera, I gave up that job and became an agricultural labourer.

Seven months later I turned eighteen and was liable to be called up for national service any moment. My brother was enrolled in the British Army in the Royal Army Ordnance Corps (RAOC) and I volunteered to join the same regiment. When, during the initial interview, I told the recruiting officer that I was a joiner by trade, I was told that the corps was only interested in recruiting engine fitters. But when the officer saw that I was very keen to join, I was accepted provided that I would attend a crash course at the Ospizio, Floriana and at Mamo Brothers Workshop at Gzira. The RAOC was quartered at the Casemate Barracks. On the 3rd May 1941, barely two weeks after my joining up, during a night attack by the Luftwaffe, a mine landed in the open space between the barracks and the Central Hospital (now Police Headquarters). The buildings at the rear of the hospital were razed to the ground and although the barracks suffered no serious structural damage, windows and doors were blown in and all the contents of the barrack room in which I was billeted - iron bedsteads, lockers, rifle racks - were twisted and battered beyond repair.

Sharing the barrack room with us were some sappers from the Royal Engineers, of whom five were killed and several injured. Luck was with me on that night. A cloud of thick dust filled the barrack room and I felt as if I was choking. I staggered to the guard room, picking my way through the rubble, twisted iron and shattered furniture and when I got there I suddenly realised that I could not hear a thing. My ear-drums had almost burst and it was a full week before I could hear properly again. Ironically the English soldiers who perished had come to Floriana from bomb-riddled Luqa for a rest...

On the 8th of December, together with some other locally enlisted soldiers, I left Casemate Barracks to embark on the *Breconshire* which was berthed at Hay Wharf. A Squadron Leader from the R.A.F. met us on board and briefed us: we were detailed to keep under surveillance a batch of Luftwaffe pilots who had baled out over Malta. It was quite some time after we steamed out of Marsamxett Harbour that we learnt that we were bound for Alexandria. At break of day we were attacked by German raiders and I took up a vantage point in the bows to watch the proceedings - but not for long because the captain's voice came over the loud-hailer ordering me to take cover immediately. As we sailed into Alexandria harbour and prepared to berth at one of the quays, some workers crowded around, gesticulating and shouting. They were Maltese Dockyard workers who had been transferred to the Dockyard there. As soon as they saw us they started asking us about the situation in Malta about which they had been having worrying news. They wanted to know whether their home town or village had been badly bombed and whether many people were being killed. It was a pathetic scene which I am not ever likely to forget.

From Alexandria we were taken to the camp at Armija. The small Maltese group was split up and we were attached to different regiments stationed in the desert. When, about a month later I bumped into one of them, he told me that one of our group had

Carmelo Calafato in
Western Sahara.
(Courtesy C. Calafato)

been killed; he was not yet twenty. I spent my leave in Cairo
where I had a very pleasant surprise. I had long wanted to be in
the same regiment as my brother but all my attempts had failed.
You can imagine how delighted I was when, walking up the main
street, I came across two Maltese soldiers. One of them I recognised immediately as a certain Vella who had made the crossing
to Alexandria in a submarine ahead of me. When I greeted him
he asked, laughing, "Don't you know my friend here?" His companion and I looked each other in the eye for a second and fell
into each other's arms. He was, of course, my brother whom I
had not seen since 1938. Without more ado we made a bee-line
for the nearest bar and over drinks exchanged news. My brother,
naturally, asked a hundred questions about members of the family and the war news from Malta. He was in Cairo having travelled on duty from Kufra where he was attached to the Long
Range Desert Group, a platoon which worked behind enemy

lines. The nature of their work was such that they would never take any prisoners. But once they made an exception to that rule because one of their captives turned out to be a young lad of seventeen. My brother was given the task of escorting the youngster to the prisoner-of-war camp in Cairo. That was what brought us together! A couple of days later my brother returned to his post in the desert and I was not to see him again before the end of the war.

In June 1943 I found myself, with hundreds of other soldiers, on the west coast of the Red Sea. The place was a veritable hell and we spent most of the time on manoeuvres with none of us knowing where we would be going next. Some were saying that we would soon leave for India, others said the Balkans or Greece. What we did in the end was to land in Augusta in Sicily. We were technically part of the Eighth Army, but in Sicily our Division veered off to the west and joined up with the Americans advancing on Palermo. From Palermo we crossed to Salerno, and eventually entered Naples. Some time before Italy surrendered I wrote to my girl friend (now my wife) that I would be spending Christmas at home. In Naples I lost a close friend, a British soldier who committed suicide; we had been great pals since our days in Egypt.

We entered Rome on the 8th of June 1944 and the first thing I did was to pay a visit to the Vatican. As I was walking along, much to my surprise, I heard someone call out my name. It was the voice of a childhood friend of mine, George Borg from Santa Venera, who was in the Royal Air Force. George made me change my plans because he made me accompany him on a visit to Mrs Henriette Chevalier. This plucky Maltese lady was instrumental in assisting hundreds of Allied servicemen to escape, an activity which was not only hazardous to her but also to her family. Mrs Chevalier welcomed me with open arms and treated me as if I were her own son. I cannot help remarking here that the name of this formidable woman who risked her life and that of her family in the struggle against the forces of Nazism seems to have been forgotten in our country. Ironically it was the Italians who honoured in some way this heroic Maltese national in the RAI television film called *Scarletto e Nero*.

From Rome, our next stop was in the neighbourhood of Florence. There it was more of the same thing: hundreds of American soldiers camped in the woods between Siena and Leghorn. We were all curious to find out where we were going next. The most likely destination appeared to be France and that is precisely what happened. We landed at Marseilles and advanced along the Rhone valley until we crossed the frontier into Belgian territory where we joined up with the 30th Corps of the British Army. November and December saw us under great pressure not so much from the German forces as from the hundreds of *V1*'s and *V2*'s that rained down on the town of Antwerp. These missiles struck without any warning; death and destruction came unheralded. Our Company lost twenty-eight men killed in those attacks. From Belgium we swept through Holland and advanced into German territory.

As far as Europe was concerned the war came to an end on the 8th of May and now I was as sure as can be that I would be home for Christmas as I had promised my girl friend. But things turned out differently. I could get leave for practically any destination except Malta because as I was told by my Commanding Officer the means of transportation were not available as yet. Halfway through December transport problems eased up and I could travel from Germany to Calais where I took the train to Taranto. I had ample time to look around that port because for several weeks I could not find any transport to Malta. Finally I hit upon a Royal Navy LST which was about to leave for Malta and I persuaded the young officer-in-charge to give me passage to Malta. And that is how, after an absence of four eventful years, I stepped ashore in Malta on the 20th January of 1946, a date that will always remain in my memory.

LOUIS CAMILLERI

In 1928, as a young lad, I joined the NAAFI and eleven years later when World War II broke out I was serving on board HMS *Protector* which in addition to laying and maintaining defensive nets at the mouth of harbours was also involved in photography work for the Royal Navy. As she formed part of the Mediterranean Fleet, the home base was Malta. On the outbreak of hostilities we were despatched to Freetown on the West African coast and then ordered to proceed to Scotland so that we could join the convoys transporting troops to Norway in the Narvik campaign of 1940.

When the Allies were forced to retreat from Norway we made our way back to our base in the United Kingdom and from there the *Protector* received orders to steam to the Alexandria station. On the way we stopped for six hours in Malta. That was on the 6th of June 1940, just four days before Italy declared war. Those six hours gave me the opportunity to pay a flying visit to my family in Cospicua. That was the last time I was to see my mother alive for she died two months later that is on the 6th of August. On arriving at Alexandria, I was to have my first experience of aerial attacks when Italian planes dropped bombs on the town. The *Protector* was hit by shrapnel from a bomb exploding on the quay where we were tied up, causing the death of one of her company. Our next port of call was Suez, where we spent some time in dock for repairs, and from there sailed to Crete before that Island fell into German hands. Before 1940 was out I was promoted to canteen manager and transferred to the aircraft carrier HMS *Eagle*. We spent most of the time cruising in the Eastern Mediterranean until we received orders to proceed to the South Atlantic where German armed merchant cruisers and submarines were constantly menacing Allied shipping. It was during these operations that we heard on the BBC the news that Pearl Harbour had been attacked by the Japanese and that, as a result, the United States was drawn into the war.

After that stint in the Atlantic, the *Eagle* entered the dockyard at Liverpool for installing new apparatus which, if my memory serves me right, was intended to counter magnetic mines. When the *Ark Royal* was sunk, the *Eagle* was posted to the Mediterranean station with Gibraltar as the home base. That, for me, was the beginning of the "Malta experience". Malta was then passing through a harsh ordeal, with almost constant heavy bombing from the air. Together with the USS *Wasp*, the *Eagle* used to steam close enough to Malta so that Spitfires ferried over from the U.K. could fly off her deck to join the defending forces of that Island.

In August 1942, the *Eagle* joined the memorable convoy code-named *Pedestal* which in Malta is referred to as "the Santa Marija convoy". On that occasion a large number of naval craft and merchantmen of all sorts and sizes congregated off Gibraltar and set off eastwards. The first air attacks came when the convoy was three days out of harbour and when we were, I believe, more than

The "Santa Marija Convoy" en route to Malta; painting by John Hamilton.

(Imperial War Museum)

halfway to Malta. After some heavy aerial attacks, there was a lull, during which we were instructed to rest and get ready for more, and heavier, attacks which were expected to hit us in the early afternoon. During the lull, I would say at around one in the afternoon of the 11th August, I was sitting with a member of my staff, an Englishman, when we felt a shudder closely followed by a second. We thought it was a depth charge. My companion was about to move away when we realised that the carrier was listing heavily and would founder in a matter of minutes. The word soon went round: "Abandon ship. Every man to himself." I rushed to the nearest whaler and was about to clamber in when someone shouted that the boat was made fast and that I would stand a better chance if I plunged into the sea. So calmly and deliberately I slid along the side of the hull and found myself floating in the

The carrier was listing heavily and foundered in a matter of minutes; painting by W.Mc Dowell.

water. I have never been a good swimmer at all and I could just about keep my head above water and begin to say my prayers. After a short time, I found myself close to a Carley Float, which is a sort of life-raft made of cork and canvas and with ropes all round. A commander handed me his life-belt and I grabbed one of the ropes on the float. I remember there was another young seaman clutching a rope but he was dead; even though so many years have passed I can still see in my mind's eye that terrible scene. We learnt later that the *Eagle* had been hit by a salvo of four torpedoes fired by a German submarine. Some two hundred of the ship's company went down with her. We were picked up by the destroyer *Lookout* and her crew did their best to make us comfortable. In the meantime the *Lookout* resumed her task of escorting the convoy which was still being subjected to one air attack after another. At some point, the destroyer turned back and made her way to Gibraltar where the *Eagle* survivors were transferred to other ships, with myself getting a berth on the aircraft carrier *Victorious* bound for Scapa Flow in Scotland. From Scapa Flow, we returned to Rosyth for re-victualling.

For some time after that I was posted ashore performing duties as chief clerk and cashier eventually being transferred to Londonderry in Northern Ireland, from where I was flown to Algiers. I soon learnt that preparations were in hand for the Allied invasion of Sicily. In the summer of 1943 I paid a visit to Malta where I was struck by the ruin and destruction evident wherever I turned my eyes. During the Allied occupation of Sicily and southern Italy, I served in Naples supervising NAAFI establishments and planning new NAAFI facilities in the newly occupied territory, setting up branches in Taranto, Bari and Manfredonia and later on in Piombino, Leghorn and Genoa in the Northwest. For a period I had an office in the Italian Naval Academy in Leghorn, the base from which the NAAFI Naval Canteen Service North West Italy was run. In October 1945 I got my release from the Royal Navy and returned to Malta as a newly promoted district manager. My services in Italy were rewarded by a mention in despatches published in the *London Gazette* of the 11th of December, 1945.

SALVINU CAMILLERI

I started my career with the NAAFI in 1937 and served afloat from the very first day. When the Second World War broke out I was a canteen manager on board HMS *Graham*, which was on patrol duties round the coast of the British Isles. We did not have any particular base but were constantly on the move from one port to another: Dover, Portsmouth, Chatham, Plymouth... We saw action in the North Sea when the *Graham* was cruising with a destroyer flotilla which was attacked by two German cruisers. We were no match for their armament and when one of our destroyers was damaged we beat a hasty retreat. On another occasion we were attacked by enemy aircraft when cruising off Dover and two officers were killed when a bomb struck our bridge. One consolation for us was that our anti-aircraft guns brought down one of the attackers.

Probably my worst experience occurred when we were attacked while cruising in Norwegian waters. During the action I looked around and saw the AO sprawling on the deck near one of the guns; at the same time I was conscious of a burning sensation in my eyes and felt very groggy. I was carried to the sick bay where other wounded were being tended. I heard the steward say, "You're bleeding, you..." I didn't quite realise that I was badly injured by a bomb splinter. I was seen to and my eyes were bandaged. During all this our ship was under constant and heavy air attack and our guns were firing back without respite. Mercifully our ship managed to get through that action with relatively minor damage and our little fleet of some five or six ships eventually made port in Dover. Dead and wounded were landed and I soon found myself with several other wounded on the train to Coventry. I remember that train journey took some nine hours and when we arrived at Coventry it was already three in the afternoon. I was detained in hospital and was to spend the best part of a month there. In the meantime word had been sent to my wife that I was missing in action; shortly after that my wife was told that there had been a mistake somewhere along the line and that I was recovering in hospital. When my wound healed, I was stricken with tetanus which meant another couple of weeks in hospital.

On getting a clean bill of health I made my way to London and reported for duty. My supervisor informed me that my next tour of duty would be on board a battle cruiser but by that time I had had enough and told him that I would never go afloat again, at least not before the war was over. I was very anxious to go back home and see my wife. I was in a position to refuse because as a NAAFI employee I was considered to be a civilian. From London I went to Portsmouth and got a clerical job until I got myself a berth on a warship bound for Malta. On the voyage to Malta we were pounced upon by German U-boats but we were not hit.

The first thing I did on getting ashore was of course to go to Qormi where my wife and her family were living as refugees. We spent about a year there during which time we had an addition to our family in the shape of a daughter.

EMANUEL GALEA

I joined the Army in 1931 as a gunner in the 1st Coast Regiment, RMA; at first we were billeted in Fort St Elmo but later we were moved to other quarters such as Marsaxlokk and Żejtun. When Mussolini declared war I was stationed at Ta' Karax halfway between Żejtun and Ghaxaq; by then I had been promoted to sergeant. I was married with two children and the family home was in Hamrun. During the war years I had several narrow escapes.

Probably the closest shave was when I was stationed at Birżebbuġa manning a Bofors anti-aircraft gun. It was my day off and so I left as usual on my bicycle to go and spend the day and night with my family at Hamrun. On the following morning as I was setting off to return to my post a friend came up to me and said, "Leli, your Bofors is no more." I could not believe my ears at first but when the truth dawned upon me I pedalled as fast as I could to Birżebbuġa; there I found that the gun position had received a direct hit and three or four of my mates had been killed and several others wounded. Later when I was happily settled at the RAF Billet at Marsamxett, my commanding officer told me I would have to move again. I protested that I was being moved too often but orders were orders and I had to obey. A few days after I left, that gun position was hit and the men who had replaced us - Scotsmen of the Royal Artillery - were killed. The sergeant who took over from me was flung into the sea by the blast.

I was present during the heavy attacks on the *Breconshire* when that ship was beached in the harbour at Marsaxlokk. I was on duty at Fort St Lucian and a large number of *Junkers 87* and

Maltese gunners manning an anti aircraft gun.

(NWMA Collection).

88 were sighted at around seven in the evening. Their target was obviously the *Breconshire* and bombs were soon raining down around that ship but no hits were registered. I remember how, after the raiders left, large quantities of fish stunned or killed by the exploding bombs, rose to the surface providing us and the villagers from Marsaxlokk with an unexpected feast of delicious food. The Germans came back on the following day and this time they did not miss! The *Breconshire* was soon burning fore and aft and black smoke was billowing up in huge clouds. We received orders to leave our posts as the *Breconshire*'s cargo included ammunition besides grain and there was the possibility that she would blow up. On the morrow when we were ordered to return to our stations, we were in for a surprise! During our absence the villagers had cleared out the kitchen and made off with every pot and pan and plate in sight!

I recall another incident when I was stationed at Karwija in the neighbourhood of Mqabba where we had just taken over a battery from the R.A.'s. When a formation of German raiders flew over us we opened fire and immediately found ourselves the target of a stick of bombs which made havoc of our camp but mercifully caused no fatalities though some of our men were injured. When the raid was over, a couple of village girls stopped to have a chat with us and we were told that the British detachment which manned the battery before us had never been attacked because they never opened fire on German aircraft. We thought this was a made-up story because we always regarded the British soldier, no less than his Maltese counterpart, as being fearless when under attack. When we were under attack, I do not remember any of us showing signs of being scared. The nearest I can remember to a man losing his nerve under fire was once when one of our mates begged us to make the sign of the cross and say our prayers. Of course we had the services of a chaplain, a Dominican friar, who regularly celebrated mass and heard our confessions.

Possibly our bitterest experience was when ammunition for our guns was strictly rationed. We had strict orders not to fire below a certain elevation, for instance 15 degrees and even then we could only fire about eight rounds regardless of any circumstance. We were therefore exposed to attacks without the means of defending ourselves and hitting back.

During the war years my family life was totally disrupted.

When my wife gave birth to a daughter it was quite some time before I knew; my wife never knew where I was stationed at any given time and therefore could not send a message. She would often ask me when I was due to come home and the only answer I could give was, "when you see me there". Raids were so frequent that sometimes we had seven or eight raids in a day. The sight of enemy aircraft flying over us by the dozen made our hands itch with the urge to go into action and very often made us throw caution to the wind.

During a stint which I had at Fort Ricasoli we were strafed and bombed by a formation of *Stukas* which dived almost vertically before releasing their load and would then fly so low that you could say they were just skimming the surface and of course we could not fire at that angle as we would hit the Valletta bastions across the harbour.

The food shortage never really affected us; we had our rations of biscuits, bacon, jam and bully beef. Besides I used to engage in barter with farmers, getting fresh vegetables in return for preserved food and in the summer, when grapes were ready for harvesting, we used to scramble over field walls to slake our taste with grapes.

The men in my company got on very well with one another and you could say we were like one big family; our relations with British soldiers were generally very good - with one exception. That was when I was stationed at Marsaxlokk and I used to take my men to see the occasional film at a cinema or to a dance often rounding off the evening in some drinking hole. On the evening in question, two British sailors attempted to leave before they had paid for their drinks; to add insult to injury they dashed a glass of beer into the bar owner's face. We could not just stand and look, of course, and soon there was a battle royal in the place. Fights between British and Maltese servicemen were not all that uncommon in those days and I am afraid fights also occasionally broke out among Maltese soldiers.

GEJTU GRECH

When the war broke out I was a youngster of seventeen apprenticed to a barber who plied his trade at Cospicua. On the first day of the war I reported for duty as usual but as soon as I heard the sound of gunfire I got scared and made my way back as fast as I could to my home at Paola, resolved never to set foot again in Cospicua. I quickly found a job with another barber at Paola.

My family remained at Paola for the first few months of the war, but after the *Illustrious* blitz we decided to move up to Rabat where we found accommodation with a baker who rented one of the rooms in his house to us. It so happened that in the same house there were three teenage girls and my brothers and I were young men and my mother thought that the situation was a bit like placing a box of matches next to a barrel of gunpowder, if you know what I mean, and she decided that things would be safer if we went back to Paola. So back we went to Paola to take up residence again in our house which was situated in the vicinity of Villa Blye on Corradino Hill; incidentally Villa Blye was serving as a field hospital at the time.

A few days after my eighteenth birthday the local police sergeant called at our house and told my mother that I was to consider myself under arrest. He explained to my terrified mother that though I had been repeatedly instructed by post to report at the drafting office, I had failed to turn up and in war time such behaviour was a very serious matter. My mother immediately confessed that as she did not like the idea that I would be called up for military service she used to tear up the draft papers without telling me. Luckily for me the sergeant was a regular customer at the barber shop where I worked and he knew me quite well and was prepared to bend the regulations somewhat for my sake. He told me he would take no further action provided I reported at the office on the morrow. Early next morning I repaired to the office and found several other young men queuing up outside. After going through the formalities and the medical test we were told to board an Army truck which was to take us to Gozo.

A British sergeant and a Maltese lance-corporal were waiting for us at Marfa. We boarded the boat, crossed over to Mġarr and marched up to Rabat where we were shown into a large hall furnished with a large number of Army beds. We were issued with the full kit - shorts, battle dress, boots and rifle - and in next to no time we were going through the usual marching drill at the Jubilee football ground. A few of us did not have the slightest idea of what "left" or "right" meant; the problem, however, was soon solved. These men were given a pebble in their left hand and told to turn to that side when they heard the word "left". During one such drill session, the performance of some half-dozen of the company, including myself, did not quite satisfy the RSM (Regimental Sergeant Major) and we were made to start running along the touch lines and to keep on running until we were given the signal to stop. Three of us were not up to it and they collapsed, exhausted, and had to be conveyed to hospital. As for myself, I could take such punishment quite well because I used to play football and was in very good physical condition.

After three months of that sort of routine, our regiment, the 3 KOMR, returned to Malta and was stationed at Birżebbuġa. One day I was called up before our Commanding Officer, a Dunkirk veteran, whose opening words were, "I am told that you are a barber by trade; is that so?"

"Yes, sir, that is correct."

"Then, as from to-morrow, you are appointed regimental barber."

"Thank you, sir", I replied, "if that means that I'll be excused from parades and watches."

"Shut up! You're a soldier now!" retorted the CO before I was dismissed.

Some four hours later, however, I was called up again and I was told that my request to be excused from some routines was granted.

For several weeks we remained at Birżebbuġa, but then we began to move from one billet to another. Although my work was strictly that of a barber, I had to undergo training like everybody else. Route marches with full kit were quite frequent. Some of these marches were quite long and could be spread over two days. One march I remember, just to give an example, started from Gudia where we were stationed and ended up at Mosta where we spent the night; the following morning, at dawn, we resumed our march to St Paul's Bay, then to Mellieha Bay and Armier and then back through Rabat and Buskett. I remember my feet were covered with blisters and sores after that ordeal. Apparently these marches were meant to prepare us for an imminent invasion.

Among the many incidents of Army life - and there were plenty - I remember the day I had to answer to a charge of dereliction of duty. The incident arose when I decided to take French leave and pay a flying visit to the family. It was not one of my lucky days because as I was returning to my post, the sergeant caught sight of me, the result being that my leave was stopped for a week and I had to report at the guard room every hour. But there was more to come!

"...you have also to clean the toilets..." continued the sergeant.

"That I refuse to do," said I.

"You're asking for another charge! This time it will be the colonel you'll have to answer to."

In those days I was pretty hard-headed and I kept my ground. The sergeant was as good as his word and before the day was out I was standing to attention before the Commanding Officer.

"Can you explain to me how you refuse to obey an order given by your sergeant?"

"The explanation is simple, sir. Since I have to shave you every morning, I think I should be careful not to let my hands come into contact with any dirty material."

"Case dismissed!"

To be fair, I think I should admit that the Army helped to make a man out of me, but at the same time I cannot forget the hard times that I occasionally went through. Sometimes I felt so depressed that I felt like weeping and banging my head against the wall, but that was only in the first few months because as time passed I started getting used to Army life and even to enjoy the comradeship and the practical jokes. Discipline was very strict: you had to shave every day, buttons and bayonet had to be shining, hair to be cut once a week, or else....It was a life that was new to me and it helped me mature. When I was demobilised, I was given a suit, a hat, a pair of shoes and forty-nine pounds in cash.

JOE HOCKEY

I joined the Navy when I was twenty four and after undergoing basic training I was posted on HMS *Devonshire* a heavy cruiser armed with eight 4-inch guns. There were several other Maltese on the *Devonshire*, most of them serving as stewards. Shortly after my joining the Senior Service we were dispatched to Alexandria and when, on the 3rd of September 1939, war was declared the captain summoned the crew on deck and explained the situation. Some time later we proceeded to Malta for some minor repairs and then sailed to Devonport and eventually to Greenock in Scotland. From there we were ordered to proceed to the North Sea on patrol duties. On one occasion we sailed into Norwegian waters to embark the King and the Royal Family who were fleeing the country to seek refuge in Scotland. On the day that the Royal Family was on board there was a massive attack on British units in which the aircraft carrier HMS *Glorious* and two destroyers were sunk; we were not involved in that action however.

On another occasion we were on patrol duties together with two units, the *Afride* and the *Bison*, the latter being a French man-of-war. During a mid-morning attack the *Bison* was sunk and the survivors were picked up by the *Afride* which later on in the afternoon shared the same fate so that those who were saved in the morning were destined to drown in the afternoon. We were repeatedly attacked during the same action but we managed to get away with only one near miss which caused no damage at all. Incidentally during an action we had to wear our gas masks just in case. We had strict instructions not to take to the lifeboats before the captain gave the order to abandon ship. I think all of us were terrified whenever we found ourselves under attack, some more than others. I remember the day when a writer became hysterical and one of the officers dealt him a rabbit punch so that we others would not panic. Generally speaking each tour of duty involved us in two weeks at sea followed by a flying visit to Greenock to take on stores and ammunition and then back to the North Sea.

Letters to my family were few and far between. The family had moved from Senglea to the safer Żebbuġ and their letters, which were always censored, used to reach me after long intervals. My only source of information about the events that were taking place in Malta was the BBC, and I could only tune in to that when we were ashore. I witnessed two very ferocious bombing raids when our ship was in harbour, once in Liverpool and the second time in Glasgow. Our ship was in dry-dock in Liverpool when a large raiding force of bombers attacked that city; we came through unscathed but the destruction which they left behind was unbelievable. I remember *Lewis Store*, the huge supermarket, in flames. During the other raid in Glasgow, where the Clyde works seemed to be the chosen target, there was heavy loss of life.

Life on board was not too bad except of course when our ship was attacked. When I was not on duty I used to spend most of my time in the mess where you could have practically anything except alcoholic drinks. Food was plentiful and I remember the only time we ran out of potatoes and had to do with rice instead.

During the war I saw a lot of places. I was on active service in the North Sea, the Atlantic and the Indian Ocean. In 1943 I crossed over to Malta from Algiers in a merchantman. We arrived at Malta in the middle of the night and we had to heave to off the Grand Harbour until morning when we were given the go-ahead to go through the boom defence. I was billeted at St Angelo and when I walked around the harbour area I was deeply impressed with the destruction which I could see wherever I turned my eyes. I had seen the havoc left behind by the German bombers in Liverpool and Glasgow but that was nothing compared to the destruction I saw in Malta, particularly in Senglea.

CHARLES A MICALLEF

I spent the first two or three months of the war serving as an Air Raid Warden. When conscription came into effect I was among the first to be called up and soon found myself going through the routines of the raw recruit with the Buffs Regiment which had just landed in Malta after the Dunkirk evacuation. After three months of training I was transferred to the 1/KOMR quarters in Mellieha.

The first time I saw the ugly face of war was when I was on telephone duties in the Red Tower and caught sight of one of my officers, Lt Gaffiero and our sergeant major walking down towards Mellieha Bay to remove some explosives which were stored in a beach-post. A little later a tremendous explosion shook the ground and we saw a cloud of smoke and dust rising from where the beach-post had been standing moments before. We rushed down to the spot but there was little we could do. Our sergeant major was dead, his body mutilated beyond recognition and Lt Gaffiero so badly injured that he died soon after.

For some eight months I served as a private but then I was selected to join the Officer Cadets Training Unit (OCTU) and in January 1942 I was commissioned. My duties were mainly in the coastal defence of the Northern part of the Island as well as in the intensive training of personnel. In addition to that I often had to transport my platoon to Luqa airfield to help build pens for aircraft. Travelling to and from Luqa had to be done during the night so that we would avoid becoming targets for the German fighters. The airfield was under almost constant attack from the air and on the occasions when we were caught in one of those raids we would throw ourselves flat on the ground and say our prayers. On our return to barracks, exhausted and hungry, we would still have to do our guard duties.

Among the many memories of the war years one that I will

never forget is when I decided to take my girl friend, now my wife, to see *The Canadian Mounted Police* at the Regent Cinema in Valletta. I had just stepped into the Valletta bus when I received orders to take a few of my men by boat to Fomm-ir-Rih Bay to recover the body of a German pilot which had re-surfaced at Ghadira Bay after being buried at sea about a month before. The body had obviously been floating around for a considerable time and made a gruesome sight; I will spare you the details and will only say that we re-buried the remains. On returning to base I had a phone call from my girl friend who told me that the Regent Cinema had received a direct hit leaving more than forty dead and many more seriously injured, mostly servicemen.

Possibly my worst experience was when in April 1942 several bombs fell in the Blata l-Bajda area, reducing to a pile of rubble our home and the two shops which belonged to us. Fortunately my father had been dead for some three months because otherwise he would without doubt have lost his reason at such a calamity. Mercifully this air-raid did not leave any fatalities and the only person who was injured was the deputy parish priest who was on his way to bless some houses and who as a result walked with a limp for the rest of his life. For a time we went to live at St Paul's Bay until Mr Emmanuel De Marco, father of Professor Guido De Marco, kindly offered us his apartment where we lived until we eventually could go back to Blata l-Bajda.

On the eighth of September 1943 when the Maltese were celebrating the traditional feast commemorating the lifting of the Great Siege of 1565, news broke of the surrender of Italy and as stipulated in the articles of the armistice the Italian Navy laid anchor under the guns of Malta. The Italian men-of-war hove to in St Paul's Bay, at Marsaxlokk and off the Grand Harbour. On that memorable occasion I was stationed in Selmun Tower and together with captain Podesta` and other officers, I used to walk down below the tower as the Italian officers and men came ashore in groups to stretch their legs after long spells on board. Three months later to the day, that is on the 8th December, the President of the United States, Franklin D Roosevelt, stopped at

Malta for a brief visit and I had the privilege of being in the guard of honour mounted for the occasion. On alighting from the plane, the President was given the Presidential salute while the RMA band struck up the *Star Spangled Banner*. With Lord Gort on his flank, the President in a jeep inspected the guard of honour and after halting in the centre read the citation presented in the name of the people of the United States. The words of the citation can be seen carved on a marble tablet fixed to the wall of the Presidential palace in Valletta. Whenever I pass by that tablet, I cannot help recalling that occasion.

US President Franklin D. Roosevelt during his visit to Malta on 8 December 1943.
(Courtesy CA Micallef)

In July 1944 I flew to Benevento in Italy to undergo a military course. On returning to Malta, I learnt that together with a few other Maltese nationals (among whom was Father, now Bishop, Emanuel Gerada), I had been awarded a British Council

Officers of the 1/K.O.M.R. Charles Micallef is seen in top row second from left.
(Courtesy C.A. Micallef).

Scholarship. Before departure, I was asked to go to the Governor's Palace where I was given instructions to look after the six children who had been nominated to take up a Lord Mayor's Scholarship awarded as a mark of appreciation for the bravery shown by Maltese youngsters during hostilities. One of the six children was John Spiteri, destined in due course to become the Commanding Officer of the Armed Forces of Malta.

The trip to England took two weeks. Our ship formed part of an enormous convoy, a precaution taken because of the risks of attacks by German U-boats. When at last we made harbour in Liverpool we were put on a train to London which at the time was the target of the German flying bombs. These bombs were in reality pilotless planes crammed with explosives, flown with nerve wracking regularity from bases on the coast of France, and causing heavy loss of life among the civilian population. After the bombing in Malta I was to experience the bombing and burning in London.

KARMENU PACE

I joined the Navy in June 1939 when I was a young man of twenty two living at Valletta. My first trip was to Alexandria where I was involved in an incident which nearly cost me my life. We were loading torpedoes on to the *Mainstream*, a submarine ship. A launch was towing a lighter loaded with torpedoes and on reaching the ship tied up alongside. We started hauling up the torpedoes one at a time when one of the hooks gave way. The torpedo fell with a splash into the sea and a few seconds later the launch blew up in a tremendous explosion. Six seamen were killed. I was lucky to be ashore at the time, instead of on the launch.

Halfway through 1940 we steamed out of Alexandria harbour and got back to Malta where the crew was stationed in Fort St Angelo. For a time I worked on board the minesweepers which were assigned the task of keeping the harbours and the approaches clear of enemy mines. What we feared most was to be caught in an air-raid when steaming outside the harbours. In such instances there was nothing we could do except put our trust in God and hope for the best. We had only one light anti-aircraft gun mounted on the deck and we felt very vulnerable. When we were in Fort St Angelo, air-raids did not worry us in the least because there were several rock-cut shelters around. On the cavalier where the bell-cot stands there used to be an anti-aircraft gun which one day got a direct hit killing six men.

When the *Illustrious* sailed into the Grand Harbour, she had on board the bodies of more than two hundred men killed in action and having been a tailor's apprentice before joining the navy I was given the task of sewing canvas bags for the bodies to prepare them for burial at sea.

Perhaps my most terrifying experience was when, as we were sailing out of Marsamxett Harbour I saw a string of bombs dropping in the vicinity of the Carmelite Church in Valletta and clouds of dust and smoke rising from the spot. My mother and my brothers and sisters were living within a stone's throw of the church, I was very worried about their safety. When I talked about this with the officer in charge, I was told that as soon as we were back into harbour I could go ashore to see whether I could be of some help. When I stepped ashore I hurried to my mother's house and saw that it was still standing although the buildings across the street were a mass of rubble. I could not see any one of the family and I hurried to the public shelter in St Lucy Street where to my great relief I found them all safe and sound.

During the war I was going steady with a girl; we had become engaged a few months before the war started. She was from Valletta, like me and whenever I had any leave I used to go up to her place to take her out for a walk. Usually we would stroll from the old railway tunnel (then an air-raid shelter), where she used to spend much of her time, to St Publius Church in Floriana or to the Argotti Gardens. I did not like walking about in my sailor's outfit but I could not do otherwise as regulations were very strict about this matter. When her parents' house was destroyed, the family moved to Gzira where some relatives lived.

It was thus that our marriage took place in Gzira on the 25th July 1943. Like every other commodity petrol was in very short supply and people had to make do without regular transport; if you wanted to go anywhere you had either to walk or to hire a horse-drawn cab. For our wedding ceremony I hired a coach-and-pair. Of course we did not have any proper reception after the ceremony, but being a navy man I managed to get hold of a few bottles of whisky while the ship's cooks had between them baked a couple of cakes and a few loaves for sandwiches. The only wedding guests were the members of my family and the bride's family. Food was so scarce at the time that the Admiralty had introduced a procedure whereby we worked seven days on and seven days off so that we would not have to be fed when off duty; instead we were given some money as ration allowance.

After my marriage I went to live at Gzira where I still live to this day.

JOSEPH SCHEMBRI

Before the war I was a student at Flores College in Valletta, but on the outbreak of hostilities the college closed down like most schools. I was then a young lad of sixteen preparing for admission to the University.

Captain E.J.F. Price with a group of King's Scouts at Fra Diego Square Hamrun.
(Courtesy J. Schembri)

I remember well the very first air-raid over the Island. We used to live at Marsa and on hearing the firing of guns in the vicinity my brother and I rushed up to the rooftop to see what was going on. In the neighbourhood of Ta' Ċejlu there was a large oil storage tank which was hit and was soon blazing away in a mass of flames and smoke. When shells started whizzing above our heads we got terrified and ran down to find shelter. Soon after this incident I joined the Boy Scout Spotter Group having for a long time past been a member of the Boy Scout movement. Our main task as spotters was to carry messages from one military post to another. I then joined the NAAFI staff at the St Venera establishment with a weekly wage of three shillings and sixpence (17c5) for which, as a rule, I had to work from half past seven in the morning to half past eight in the evening.

On my eighteenth birthday I was conscripted into the army, assigned to the Royal Army Service Corps (RASC). During the first few months we were under very strict military discipline. We were billeted at the Lintorn Barracks at Floriana and had to undergo several route marches with full kit. Usually these marches would take us up to Mtarfa and after a rest of some ten minutes we would march back to Floriana. When the Allies invaded Sicily we were attached to the Expeditionary Force; our adven-

Feeding the pigeons in St. Mark's Square, Venice.
(Courtesy J. Schembri).

ture started when we set off from Ta' Xbiex on three corvettes of the British Navy and landed at Augusta in December 1943. After a few months' stay there we advanced with the Allied armies into northern Italy as far as Venice and eventually entered Austria. We were entitled to a few days' leave every six months which we could spend in Malta. On one such occasion, on arriving at Malta I was not allowed to go and see my parents as there was an outbreak of the bubonic plague and I had to spend the night in one of the Services' clubs before flying back to my unit at four o'clock in the morning.

I remember once the *Dakota* on which I was flying from the north of Italy to Malta being attacked by a flight of *Messerschmitts*. As a cargo carrier the plane was not equipped to offer any resistance and the South African pilot gave the order to fasten seat belts and dived into a bank of cloud to elude the German fighters, eventually landing on an air-strip somewhere in Sicily. You can imagine my relief as we touched down!

In Italy the most serious risk we ran was that of having our belongings stolen by the local people especially in the area around Naples. It was commonly believed that those people would as likely as not murder you for the sake of getting your boots. This constant fear gave us many sleepless nights and we used to take all sorts of precautions before turning in. I recall one incident in Naples. As I was walking along Via Roma with a Maltese friend who later on married an Italian girl we were stopped by the military police who told us to return to barracks as fighting had broken out between the Fascists and the Partisans. I returned to Malta in June 1947 well after the war was over.

Before I joined the Army and when I was still living with my parents, I always refused to go down into a shelter as I had an inordinate fear of being buried alive; I used to stay in the house and content myself with saying a prayer.

In my case it was a long time before the psychological scars of war healed up. In fact for quite some time after my return to Malta I remember waking up in terror at the slightest noise.

ANGELO VELLA

As a young man I used to help my father run the *OK Bar*, a coffee shop in Birkirkara. At that time Malta was full of servicemen and whenever I happened to see soldiers marching past I used to get into a frenzy of joy, especially if there was a military band playing. I had always been fascinated by everything that was military and I followed the Abyssinian war with great attention. On the 3rd of September 1939 I went down to the recruiting office at Fort St Elmo and joined the Royal Malta Artillery (RMA) and was immediately attached to the Royal Army (RA) to undergo my training at Fort Ricasoli. When I completed my training I was stationed with a British regiment at the Fortina near Vittoriosa. Our armament consisted of 18-pounders and 6-inch howitzers, some still on their old mountings with wooden wheels; these were meant to be used against enemy tanks in the event of an invasion.

On the first day of the war I happened to be on duty at St Thomas Bay together with a company of ten British soldiers. With only four hours leave I could not find the time to go home in my off duty intervals and I usually spent the time under canvas. My father and mother were extremely worried when I did not return home for long periods and I remember once my mother coming all the way in a *karozzin* to St Thomas Bay to look for me. Before that she had not seen me for the best part of three months and you can imagine the fuss she made. I was so much in love with army life that I used to prefer it to life at home, even though I had the disadvantage of having a very limited knowledge of the English language.

When, on the 10th June, Mussolini declared war against Britain our sergeant gave the order for us to put on our steel helmets and have our gas masks at the ready. The guns were prepared for action. We spent the whole of that night waiting for the enemy to show up; none of us seemed to have any clear idea as to what to expect. Our next order was to have by our side two cans filled with water, five days' battle rations (bully beef and biscuits) and a change of underwear. These orders convinced us that on the morrow we would see an invasion force coming into the bay. Throughout the night we were on the alert and at a few minutes to seven in the morning we caught a glimpse of an Italian bomber flying in from the east and dropping a stick of bombs into the sea some five miles off the coast before turning tail and disappearing over the horizon.

Some time later we were transferred to a battery at Spinola where to-day the Hilton Hotel stands; our armament now consisted of four 4.5 inch guns which were new to Malta. Once at about half past four in the afternoon seven *Junkers* came flying in and we were given orders to be at the ready for setting up a harbour barrage. This involved a number of batteries firing all their guns to make a sort of curtain of fire through which the planes were expected to dive. As we were laying the guns in the direction of the harbour we saw the bombers getting into a dive directly overhead and dropping their bomb load over our position. I can still see one of the bombers dropping three bombs which landed and exploded in the middle of our battery. All the guns were put out of action and thirteen of my comrades were killed. The blast from the explosion hurled me against a concrete wall and I lost consciousness. When I came to I felt a burning sensation in my leg; as I tried to get up on my feet I saw a deep gash in my thigh. In a few minutes ambulances were on the scene and took me and the other wounded to hospital. I had to have twenty-one stitches and the scars from them can still be seen to this day. The thirteen gunners who died were all British and came from the 11th Regiment, 3rd Battery AA.

I recall another occasion when we felt convinced that the expected invasion was about to take place. We were posted somewhere near Bahar ic-Caghaq when the message *Asia* came through; *Asia* was the code-word for maximum readiness. Soon after, the complete message was received: "The Italian fleet escorted by an invasion armada is moving south-west of Gozo". I was at the moment in the company of three other Maltese comrades and one of them, obviously scared to death, told us to recite the rosary. I turned on him and said, "You can say the rosary on your own if you like but you know how jittery everybody is; calling for prayers at this moment will only serve to increase the tension". The invasion did not materialise but it was reassuring to see that the soldiers did not panic at the threat of an imminent invasion.

For me the war was not an unpleasant experience; I liked army life too much for that. I was young at the time and the war years were among the happiest of my life. I stayed on in the Army until 1951. I finished my army career as a first class sergeant even though I was nearly illiterate. It was a sad moment when the time came for me to return to civilian life. My father and mother emigrated to Australia soon after that and I took over the running of the *OK Bar.*

Thirteen soldiers were killed when Spinola Battery was attacked by seven JU bombers in April 1942.

NICHOLAS VELLA

I was a sixteen year old student at the Seminary when war broke out. On the very first day of the war I made my way to the Roman Villa, then housing the office of Captain Cassar Torreggiani, and enrolled in the Malta Volunteer Defence Force. Unlike most of the other volunteers, I had a good standard of education and was soon promoted to sergeant. Our main task was to defend a particular area against paratroops and during air-raids, and during the night, we had to take turns keeping a watch for any possible landing of airborne troops. As volunteers we did not receive any pay although we were entitled to receive the same treatment as regular soldiers in case of injury incurred in the course of duty. Although I was still under eighteen I had my own shotgun given to me by my grandfather.

In February 1942, with some three months to go for my eighteenth birthday, I was drafted into the regular army and ordered

Members of the Malta Volunteer Defence Force.

to report for duty at the RAF Seaplane Base at Kalafrana to undergo a crash course. Not many days were to pass before we had our first taste of war. During the night at about nine a flight of *Messerschmitt 109's* attacked the *Sunderland* sea-planes. There were no shelters as yet and we threw ourselves in the water to avoid being hit.

After completing the crash course I was ordered to go to the radar station at Burmarrad, one of the two radar stations operating in those days. I was the only Maltese in the company and I was detailed to undergo a training course in operating radar equipment. Some distance away from the station was a heavy anti-aircraft battery, known as Sally Battery, manned by Maltese soldiers. One day, in April 1942, the battery was the target of a bombing attack by *Junkers 87* which resulted in heavy damage and, if my memory serves me right, the death of a Maltese gunner and the wounding of several others. Our radar equipment gave us ample advance notice of enemy movements and we could tell when aircraft had taken off from one of the airfields in Sicily such as the ones at Fontana Rossa or Comiso. We used to relay such information immediately to Fortress Headquarters situated in the Lascaris Bastion and from there the alert would be relayed to every part of the Island. As a rule, *Messerschmitts* used to take about half an hour to cross over to Malta while the slower *Junkers* took slightly longer.

After a short spell at the Air HQ in Valletta, I was transferred to the Ta' Qali base, probably the worst place to be in during the war. Ta' Qali served as the base for *Blenheims* which were involved in photo reconnaissance duties. An interesting, but little known, fact is that these *Blenheims* used to carry homing pigeons in special crates on reconnaissance flights; the homers were released carrying messages giving indications about enemy movements. The pigeons were used so as not to break the radio silence imposed as a precaution. There was an English corporal in charge of the pigeon loft which was situated on a low hill in the vicinity of Rabat. Eggs laid by these special pigeons were regularly stolen by local pigeon fanciers and I think one would be correct in assuming that many of to-day's racing pigeons are direct descendants of the Air Force homers.

Pigeons' eggs were not the only things to be stolen, of course. Parachutes sometimes disappeared from stores in suspicious circumstances. Probably the culprits were British servicemen who used to go to a certain bar in Mosta and barter the parachutes for bottles of spirits. The owner of the bar would then sell the silk from the parachutes to prospective brides for their trousseaus.

To put a stop to such abuses the Station Commander, Wing Commander Gracie, posted a warning on all notice boards saying "A scaffold has been erected on Mensija Hill not far from the pigeon loft and it will be used against those caught stealing or spying". The Commander apparently was quite serious about the whole matter and he went as far as actually setting up a scaffold on the hill so that it could be seen by all and sundry. It was commonly believed that the Commander was not fully responsible for his actions and that he had probably broken down under the

Ta' Qali airfield in April 1942. The area is covered with bomb craters.

stresses and strains of continual air bombardment. There were also rumours that the bishop had reported the matter to the Governor and after about a week both the scaffold and Commander Gracie disappeared from Ta' Qali. Gracie was replaced by a likeable Scotsman, Group Captain Satchell, who had brought the first Spitfires to Malta and who had a long record of getting on well with Maltese personnel.

Ta' Qali was primarily a fighter station and as such it was to be expected that it would be a constant target for German bombers. Deep shelters were cut into the living rock for protection and some units were located away from the airfield. For instance the Airmen's Mess was moved to Villa Messina opposite St Dominic's Church in Rabat, the Sick Quarters were transferred to Villa Micallef situated just behind the premises now occupied by the L'Isle Adam Band Club, the Pay and Equipment Section to Mdina together with the Officers' Mess, and part of the Sergeants' Mess was housed in the Point de Vue Hotel at Rabat; the Main Sergeants' Mess was re-located in Naxxar.

One night I was on guard duty in the grounds of Torre Cumbo which had been turned into a petrol dump; with me was a Scotsman called Tommy. We had walked for about ten minutes in pitch darkness when suddenly I heard a loud explosion. It was my companion who had stepped on one of the large number of butterfly bombs which had been showered all over the Island. Tommy who was a few paces ahead fell back on me and I could feel the blood flowing over me. I rushed to the guard-room for help and he was soon on his way to the military hospital at Mtarfa. I am not sure as to how he ended up but as far as I was concerned I was lucky to get away with superficial injuries on my forehead and in my left leg; the scars in my leg are still visible after all these years.

I have very happy memories of life in the Air Force. I once expressed a wish to Group Captain Satchell to train as a pilot. He took me at my word and at the first opportunity that presented itself I was put on board a *Beaufighter* which was about to take off on an anti-submarine mission. We flew as far as the coast of Tunisia. We were spotted and we were soon on the receiving end of a stream of anti-aircraft shells but as we were flying at a considerable height we were not hit. That was a memorable experience for me because it was the first time that I had flown in a plane. When my parents came to know of my experience they really made a scene and I had reluctantly to tell Captain Satchell that I had changed my mind and was no longer interested in taking up flying as a career.

Some time later I was promoted to Leading Aircraftman (LAC) and transferred to Luqa. There was no shortage of foodstuffs because Luqa was a transit post for transport aircraft laden with all sorts of food. One may mention here that it was extremely rare in the Air Force for a Maltese serviceman to get a promotion. The policy was that Maltese personnel could not be promoted beyond the rank of sergeant and as far as I can tell there were only ten Maltese sergeants including myself. In addition there were some forty-five Maltese corporals during the war.

As the war receded from the shores of Malta the invasion of Sicily, code-named *Operation Husky*, was launched by the Allies. I found myself involved in an extremely hazardous action connected with *Operation Husky*. In July of 1943, with eleven others, all British, I boarded a *Wellington* which flew us to a point behind German lines in the vicinity of Catania. Our mission was to get in touch with an Italian secret agent, a *Macchi* pilot, who was working for the British. Unfortunately we landed in a minefield and the officer who was in command of the operation stepped on a mine and was badly injured. As the second in command I had to take over responsibility for the mission. My first order was to detail one of the company to look after the injured officer until, hopefully, we returned. Within a short time we made contact with the secret agent who was accompanied by another man. The agent was to deliver some information which had been requested by British intelligence. We started off, with the two Italians leading the way and the rest of us following. We carried side-arms, sten guns and maps of the area. On stepping out of the airfield boundary, we came to a fork where according to our instructions we were supposed to take the road to the right but the two Italians took the left turn. I had overheard, before

Landing craft at Ta' Xbiex prior to the invasion of Sicily.

that, snippets of their conversation which, unknown to them, I could understand and which roused my suspicions. I therefore lost no time in grabbing the agent and relieving him of his gun while my men tied him up. In the brief scuffle, I broke my wrist and nose and tore my hand on some barbed wire; I still carry a few scars to remind me of that enterprise. To this day I have no clear idea as to what happened to the agent's companion, but I can say that Scotsmen are not to be trifled with. We eventually made our way back to the *Wellington,* which had in the meantime been concealed in a derelict hangar, so that I could send a message to base requesting further instructions. I was told to bring the agent back alive. Our little secret mission was now complete and we could now return to Malta with our double agent. As for details about the aftermath my lips are sealed.

INDEX